SOCIAL
PERCEPTION

MAPPING SOCIAL PSYCHOLOGY

Series Editor: Tony Manstead

Current titles:

Icek Ajzen: Attitudes, Personality and Behavior
Steve Duck: Relating to Others
Russell G. Geen: Human Aggression
Leslie A. Zebrowitz: Social Perception

Forthcoming titles include:

Robert S. Baron, Norman Miller and Norbert L. Kerr:
   Group Processes
Marilyn B. Brewer and Norman Miller: Intergroup Relations
J. Richard Eiser: Social Judgement
Howard Giles: Language in Social Interaction
Richard Petty and John Cacioppo: Attitude Change
Dean G. Pruitt and Peter J. Carnevale: Conflict and Bargaining
Wolfgang Stroebe and Margaret Stroebe: Social Psychology
   and Health
John Turner: Social Influence

SOCIAL PERCEPTION

Leslie A. Zebrowitz

OPEN UNIVERSITY PRESS
MILTON KEYNES

Open University Press
Celtic Court
22 Ballmoor
Buckingham MK18 1XT

First Published 1990

British Library Cataloguing in Publication Data

Zebrowitz, Leslie A.
  Social perception.—(Mapping social psychology)
  1. Man. Social Perception
  I. Title   II. Series
  302.1'2

  ISBN 0-335-09861-4
  ISBN 0-335-09860-6 (pbk)

Typeset by Rowland Phototypesetting Limited
Bury St Edmunds, Suffolk
Printed and bound in Great Britain by
Woolnough Bookbinding Limited, Irthlingborough, Northamptonshire

To Caleb and Loren

CONTENTS

LIST OF TABLES
AND FIGURES

Tables

Figures

FOREWORD

There has long been a need for a carefully tailored series of reasonably short and inexpensive books on major topics in social psychology, written primarily for students by authors who enjoy a reputation for the excellence of their research and their ability to communicate clearly and comprehensibly their knowledge of, and enthusiasm for, the discipline. My hope is that the *Mapping Social Psychology* series will meet that need.

The rationale for the series is twofold. First, conventional textbooks are too low-level and uninformative for use with senior undergraduates or graduate students. Books in this series address this problem partly by dealing with topics at book length, rather than chapter length, and partly by the excellence of the scholarship and the clarity of the writing. Each volume is written by an acknowledged authority on the topic in question, and offers the reader a concise and up-to-date overview of the principal concepts, theories, methods and findings relating to that topic. Although the intention has been to produce books that will be used by senior level undergraduates and graduate students, the fact that the books are written in a straightforward style should make them accessible to students who have relatively little previous experience of social psychology. At the same time, the books should be sufficiently informative to win the respect of researchers and instructors.

A second problem with traditional textbooks is that they are typically very dependent on research conducted in or examples drawn from North American society. This fosters the mistaken impression that social psychology is an exclusively North American discipline and can also be baffling for readers who are unfamiliar with North American culture. To combat this problem, authors of books in this series have been encouraged to adopt a broader perspective, giving examples or citing research from outside North America wherever this helps to make a point. Our aim has been to produce books for a world market, introducing readers to an international discipline.

In this volume on *Social Perception*, Leslie Zebrowitz succeeds in striking just the right balance between lively, accessible writing and doing full justice to the complexity of the subject-matter. Her approach to the topic of social perception is one that those who are knowledgeable about this field will recognize as original. First, the range of research considered is broader than is usual; those who have come to regard social perception as synonymous with causal attribution should be pleasantly surprised by the breadth of topics embraced by this book. Second, the contributions of developmental and cross-cultural research to our understanding of social perception are consistent themes in this book and they often afford refreshing insights. Third, the main chapters of the book are consistently subdivided into sections on the *contents* of social perception, the *research methods* commonly used, the principal *theoretical perspectives*, and the contributions to social perception made by characteristics of the *perceiver* and the *target person*; this structural consistency brings coherence and clarity to a field that can seem to be bafflingly complex.

For all these reasons, this volume makes a fine introduction to the topic of social perception for students. It is highly informative without being conventional; the coverage is international in scope and very up to date. However, the book is much more than a mere introduction; Professor Zebrowitz also introduces readers to the ecological approach to social perception with which her name is closely associated, and does so in a way that challenges common theoretical assumptions. Thus, the book should be of great interest to researchers and teachers, as well as students.

Tony Manstead
Series Editor

PREFACE

Social perception is central to social psychology. The traits, roles, emotions, and intentions that we perceive in others not only are interesting in their own right but also serve as mediating variables for other social psychological phenomena, such as social influence, aggression, social interaction, and group processes. The "mainstream" approach to social perception is a cognitive one, focusing primarily on the *processes* of perceiving and judging persons, with scant attention paid to the *content* of these perceptions, to the *stimulus information* on which they are based, or to the *functions* which they serve. While providing coverage of mainstream issues, this book also gives considerable emphasis to the other, neglected concerns.

The entire second chapter is devoted to the contents of social perception, and sections of the chapters on emotion perception and causal attribution also consider this topic. This coverage is rooted in the belief that an adequate theory of process requires attention to content. An emphasis on the stimulus information for social perceptions is reflected in the inclusion of target person determinants of perception within each chapter as well as the devotion of an entire chapter to emotion perception. Emotion perception research has traditionally focused on the stimulus information – for example, facial and vocal qualities – that inform perceptions, and it is often excluded from texts that cover other "mainstream" social perception topics. A concern with the functions served by social perceptions is reflected in the effort to incorporate cross-cultural and developmental research. Discovering cultural similarities and differences sheds light on the origins and functions of social perceptions, as does tracking their development in the life of the perceiver.

Whereas there is a substantial body of cross-cultural and developmental data for some topics, such as emotion perception, these perspectives have rarely been brought to bear on other topics, such as impression formation. I hope that this book will encourage researchers to fill these and other gaps in our knowledge of social perception, and an ecological theory of social perception is offered in the final chapter as a vehicle for achieving this goal. The suggestions for further reading are also designed to acquaint readers with developmental and cross-cultural perspectives on social perception. In sum, a major purpose of this book has been to consider important "what" and "why" questions that have been neglected in the mainstream focus on the "how" of person perception: What attributes do we perceive in people and why? What stimulus information communicates these attributes and why?

I want to express my appreciation to friends and colleagues who in one way or another have contributed greatly to the creation of this book. Reuben Baron has shared and nurtured my commitment to the ecological approach to social perception. Michael Bond forged my nascent interest in cross-cultural research into a conviction that such research is essential for an adequate social psychology, and he provided both encouragement and wisdom as I struggled to incorporate a cross-cultural perspective into this book. My colleagues in the Social/Developmental program at Brandeis – Teresa Amabile, Michael Berbaum, Joseph Cunningham, Margie Lachman, and Mick Watson – have shown me the value of a developmental perspective in social psychology. I am also grateful to other colleagues who generously gave their time to critique one or more chapter drafts: Danny Bar Tal, Diane Berry, Michael Bond, Joe Cunningham, Bella DePaulo, Bill DeJong, Susan Fiske, Garth Fletcher, Judith Hall, Dave Kenny, Joann Montepare, Roger Phillips, and Michael Ross. Also, I must thank the graduate students who tested this book and sharpened my thinking: Sheila Brownlow, Gila Diamond, Heidi Friedman, Kathy Kendall-Tackett, Susan McDonald, Sandra Teare, Liz Tighe, and Peng Ying. My utmost appreciation goes to Judy Woodman for her unfailing editorial help and typing, as well as to Verna Regan for her secretarial and moral support. Finally, the support of Esther and Harry Zebrowitz has meant much to me, and I have been delighted to discover that Caleb and Loren McArthur encourage my scholarship as much as I encourage theirs.

1 / INTRODUCTION

When I was in college, my friend and I fantasized writing a book about the people in our residence hall. The personalities and behaviors of the girls in "Victoria House" were as fascinating to us as the exploits of characters in the "soaps" that so many American college students follow these days.

I'll never forget the day I arrived at the small residence hall that was to be my home while I attended a large Midwestern state university. I was greeted at the door by the "housemother", a buxom, silver-haired woman with a nervous, whiny voice and a dour expression. I shuddered to think what rules and regulations would emanate from this embodiment of *in loco parentis*. (These were the days when the morals of college women were carefully guarded by the school.) The housemother told me my roommate's name, and directed me to my room.

It was tiny – barely enough room for the requisite two beds, two dressers, and two desks, with absolutely no floorspace left over. My roommate had already moved in, and she had left me the choice bed next to the window. Why didn't she take it? In contrast to the room, the closet was huge – and it was practically filled with my roommate's clothes – more sweaters than I had ever imagined owning! Oh great – was my roommate going to be one of those stuck-up rich kids that I had hoped to leave behind in the affluent New York suburb where I grew up? Then she walked in – dashed in, I should say. She gave me a breathless hello, asked if the housemother had told me that we had the same birthday and apologized that she had to run to see her mother off at the airport. And then she was gone – but not from my thoughts. What was it going to be like living with this tall, gorgeous, blonde woman? (We called each other "girls" in those pre-feminist days, but somehow that label didn't seem right for Jayne.) Would we have *anything* in common? Maybe so. After all we did at least have the same birthday.

As I pondered my future relationship with this roommate, the highschool friend I had traveled with to college rushed frantically into my room. Her room was terrible, Diane pronounced, and she had to change roommates! Hers was just too weird. I walked down the hall, finding it hard to believe that her room could be worse than mine or her roommate any more worrisome. But they were. Her room was so small that they had bunkbeds. And then there was her roommate, Sarah. Sarah dressed and acted a part that we would later find commonplace. But at that time we found this "hippie" very strange, with her black clothes, bare feet, waist-length straight hair, and her somber, glazed expression as she stared at the candles that were burning on her dresser. Was she on drugs?

As life in the residence hall unfolded, I was exposed to many more new people whose behavior created strong impressions and raised puzzling questions. There was "Lady Godiva", who pranced between her bedroom and the bathroom down the hall wearing nothing but her long black hair. Did this disregard for modesty represent the behavior of a "loose woman"? And there was por-celain-skinned, forlorn-faced Norri – so neat, so controlled. What caused her terrible headaches? Was she dangerously depressed? And why did her roommate, Nina, so hate men? Could the behavior of Nina's father in a recent divorce be, as she proclaimed, sufficient cause for such generalized animosity? Then there was Lesill (so nicknamed to differentiate her from me), whose room at the top of the stairs was always filled with people. Much as I liked her myself, I wondered at her enormous popularity.

Some of my questions were answered as I learned more about these people. Some were not. And new questions continually arose, as when my roommate later confided that her first impression of me was that I would be easygoing and happy to do her bidding, and we both wondered how she had acquired this most erroneous impression! Or, when the residence hall counselor expressed her grave concern that I wouldn't make it through my first year of college if I kept up my partying, and I knew that her perception of my scholarship was far off the mark. These errors in perceptions of my own character jarred my confidence in my perceptions of others. Were any of them accurate? What were they based on?

What is social perception?

Theory and research in the field of social perception is concerned with explaining the various perceptions I had of the women in my residence hall. What qualities do we perceive in other people? What governs our first impressions? How do we explain other people's behavior? How do we read their moods? Are our perceptions accurate? Sometimes this field is called the study of "naive" psychology, because it represents the scientific study of the layman's "psychologizing". As such, the goal of research in social perception is not to explain why Lady Godiva ran around in the buff, why Norri was depressed, or why Nina hated men. Rather, the goal is to explain why my housemates and I perceived Lady Godiva as "loose", why we perceived Norri as depressed, and why we perceived Nina's man-hating to have multiple causes.

Aside from being interesting in its own right, the study of social perception has important implications for understanding and predicting our own and others' social behavior. Effective action in interpersonal relationships requires a sensitive understanding of the covert psychological processes that underlie people's overt behavior. It also requires awareness of people's emotional states and the environmental circumstances to which they are responding. The importance of understanding social perception is further underscored by the fact that our perceptions of others, whether accurate or not, may exert a significant impact on their behavior.

General theoretical approaches to the study of social perception

Parallels between object and person perception have been noted by theorists in both fields (e.g., Gibson 1979; Heider 1944) as have important differences, including the fact that persons, but not objects, are perceived to have intentions, persons may try to hide their true nature, and the accuracy of person perception is more difficult to assess (Fiske and Taylor 1984). Despite these differences, theoretical explanations for the phenomena of social perception have their roots in theories of object perception, where three major epistemological approaches can be identified: the structuralist approach; the constructivist approach; and the ecological approach. Although "pure" structuralist and constructivist approaches are described below for illustrative purposes, it should be noted that modern theories of object and person perception incorporate elements of both approaches (Brewer 1988; Fiske and Neuberg 1990; Garner 1986).

The structuralist approach to perception

The basic assumption in this approach is that perceptions derive from elementary sensations. The perception of an object is thus assumed to be "data-driven". It is built up from individual sensory elements, each of which bears some relation to the object. For example, an object will be perceived as an old woman if stimulus cues of size, shape, color, and/or sound "add up" to "old woman", as they do in Figure 1.1(a). In the same manner, perceptions of more psychological properties, such as depression or kindness, are assumed to result from the coordination of observable "proximal" appearance and behavior cues to "distal" traits or intentions.

The constructivist approach to perception

The assumption that observable stimulus cues can specify a person's psychological properties or even her age has been criticized by adherents of the constructivist approach to perception. This approach maintains that the way in which we perceive an object

Figure 1.1   The young woman and the old hag

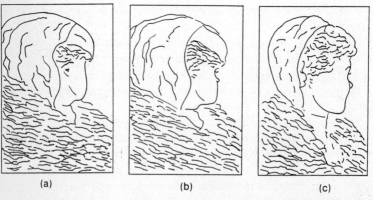

(a)   (b)   (c)

Source: Leeper (1935), p. 62. Adapted by permission of the Helen Dwight Reid Educational Foundation.

cannot be predicted simply by adding up our sensations of the parts. Rather, perceptions are "holistic" and "theory-driven". They are organized and constructed by the mind. Thus, in this approach, the perception of an "old woman" does not reflect simply the sum of various stimulus cues registered by a passive perceiver. Rather, this percept reflects the constructive processes of a perceiver, who actively imposes a holistic structure on the observable cues.

Consider Figure 1.1(b). Having perceived the old woman in Figure 1.1(a), you will probably see the same old woman in this figure. But this perception is not given by the stimulus cues themselves. When Figure 1.1(b) is the first picture that perceivers are shown, some see a young woman whereas others see an old woman. Because perceptions of the same object can vary in this manner, the constructivist approach emphasizes *subjective* perceptions – the object or person as perceived by an individual – rather than an *objective* analysis of the stimulus. And, rather than investigating properties of external stimuli, this approach investigates the perceivers' internal, mental structures, often called "schemas".

The ecological approach to perception

This is an interactive approach to perception, which incorporates aspects of both structuralist and constructivist theories. Like the constructivist approach, it focuses on perceptions of holistic structures – configurations of stimulus information that are not reducible to individual sensory elements. Like the structuralist approach, it assumes that perceptions are grounded in external stimuli rather than being constructions of the mind. The way that the ecological approach can incorporate both of these assumptions is to assume further that the information in the external stimulus is itself *structured* rather than composed of individual elements; and that this structure is *detected* by the perceiver rather than being created by the perceiver.

How, then, does the ecological approach account for the "reversible" woman? Like the constructivist approach, it does emphasize the role of the perceiver. However, rather than asserting that perceivers may differ in the reality that they construct, the ecological approach asserts that they differ in the reality that they detect. Figure 1.1(b) contains the structure of an old woman *and* the structure of a young woman. The mind does not create one or the other. Rather perceivers *detect* one or the other, depending upon the particular stimulus information to which they attend. According to the ecological approach, the perceiver's attention – or "attunement" – will depend upon a number of factors, one of which is perceptual experience. Perceptual experience with the old woman attunes the perceiver to the old woman structure within the ambiguous drawing. On the other hand, experience with the young woman attunes the perceiver to the structure of a young woman – perceivers who begin by looking at Figure 1.1(c), which depicts a young woman, perceive that same young woman in Figure 1.1(b).

Although the social perception topics that we will consider in subsequent chapters are typically much more complex than the perception of age, the three general approaches to perception are none the less represented – albeit with differential frequency. A constructivist approach is represented in research on *perceiver determinants* of social perceptions, sometimes called *theory-driven* perceptions because of the emphasis on the perceiver's theories and concepts. This approach has tended to predominate in research on impression formation. A structuralist approach is represented in research on *target person* determinants of social perceptions, sometimes called *data-driven perceptions* because of the emphasis on the stimulus information provided by the target person. This approach is most prevalent in research on emotion perception. The ecological approach, which emphasizes joint *perceiver–target determinants* of social perceptions, is a relatively recent position that has been explicitly brought to bear on only a few phenomena.

It should be noted that the constructivist and the ecological approaches are not necessarily antagonistic. There is undoubtedly structure in the external environment *and* in people's heads. When social perceptions are formulated in the absence of external structure – i.e., when we think about someone as opposed to watching that person behave – or when the external structure is ambiguous, then the internal constructions of the perceiver will be a significant factor in predicting perceptions. At the same time, one must consider how the internal structures originate. Although some may be innate, it seems reasonable to suppose that many derive from perceptual experiences with structures in the external world. And, once formed, the internal structures become attunements that may guide the detection of external structures. In short, it is likely that there is a congruent relationship between the structure of the mind and the structure of the environment.

Summary and implications

The study of social perception is the study of "naive psychology". The goal of such inquiry is to understand our impressions of other people's traits, our perceptions of their emotions, and our explanations for their behavior. An understanding of these social perceptions not only is of interest in its own right but also has important implications for adaptive social interactions.

Three general approaches to research on object perception are represented in social perception research: a structuralist approach, which emphasizes the impact of external stimulus elements upon perceptions; a constructivist approach, which emphasizes the impact of internal cognitive structures and processes upon perceptions; and an ecological approach, which emphasizes the impact on perceptions of perceivers' attunements to structured information in the external stimulus.

The following chapters will consider four fundamental aspects of social perception. Chapter 2 examines the *contents* of social perception. Chapter 3 considers the factors that influence the evaluative and descriptive *impressions* that we form of others. Chapter 4 considers the perception of *emotion*, and Chapter 5 examines the factors that influence people's *causal explanations* for the behavior of others. In Chapter 6, an ecological theory will be applied to all four aspects of social perception. The length of this book has necessitated two limitations in the literature reviewed in these chapters. First, perceiver personality traits will not be included among the perceiver influences that are examined. Second, although self-perceptions are an important subset of social perceptions, all chapters will focus on perceptions of others.

Several questions are pertinent to the literature reviewed in Chapters 2–5. Although some of these have been more thoroughly addressed by existing research than others have, it is suggested that the reader keep all of them in mind to facilitate an assessment of the current state of our knowledge. They include the following: What are the contents of social perceptions? What are the perceiver determinants? What are the target person determinants? What are the joint perceiver–target determinants? Are social perceptions accurate? Finally, what are the origins and functions of social perceptions?

Further reading

Heider, F. (1958). *The psychology of interpersonal relations*. New York: John Wiley. This seminal work has inspired current theories concerned with social perception contents, causal attribution, impression formation and interpersonal attraction, and it provides insights into emotion perception as well.

Nisbett, R. E. and Ross, L. (1980). *Human inference: Strategies and shortcomings of social judgment*. Englewood Cliffs, NJ: Prentice-Hall. An analogy is drawn between the social judgments of the layperson and those of the scientific psychologist, and social perception errors are explained by the misapplication of simplistic, but often adaptive, inferential strategies.

Tagiuri, R. and Petrullo, L. (eds) (1958). *Person perception and interpersonal behavior*. Stanford, CA: Stanford University Press. This is a collection of classic essays on social perception, representing both structuralist and constructivist approaches, and bearing on social perception contents, impression formation, and causal attribution.

Zajonc, R. B. (1980). Feeling and thinking: Preferences need no inferences. *American Psychologist*, 35, 151–75. Affective reactions, such as like/dislike, are contrasted with perceptual and cognitive judgments, and it is argued that affective reactions typically precede and are independent of cognitive ones. Various differences between affective and cognitive judgments are discussed.

2 / THE CONTENTS OF SOCIAL PERCEPTION

What kinds of qualities do we perceive in other people? Although this question is fundamental to our understanding of social perception, it has received surprisingly little attention from social psychologists. This neglect reflects a greater concern with the *processes* of perceiving and judging persons than with the *contents* of these perceptions. Developmental and cross-cultural psychologists, on the other hand, have been concerned with describing the contents of social perception, perhaps because the "foreignness" of their subjects sensitizes them to the possibility that they do not know what these contents are. Even if social psychologists are interested primarily in social perception processes, social perception contents should not be ignored. The conceptualization and description of these contents is essential to an adequate theory of process, be it a theory of impression formation, emotion perception, or causal attribution.

There is a hierarchy to questions concerning the contents of social perception. At the most general level is the question of what kinds of descriptive categories are reflected in social perceptions. The anecdotes from my college residence hall in Chapter 1 reveal some of the categories that are used: social roles (the "housemother"), appearance characteristics ("buxom", "silver-haired"), personality traits ("dour"), and emotions ("nervous"). We also perceive intentions (was my roommate trying to be nice when she left me the window bed?), causes (were drugs the cause of Sarah's weird behavior?), and affordances, which are the behavioral opportunities that others offer us (my roommate perceived that I would do her bidding). At the next level of analysis is the question of what specific qualities are perceived within each general category. What specific social roles, traits, or physical qualities are people perceived to have? Finally, there is the question of how specific qualities are perceived to interrelate. What specific social roles, traits, and/or physical qualities are perceived to go together?

Social perception categories

Methods for investigating social perception categories

Linguistic analysis

One method for investigating the categories of social perception is a linguistic analysis. Heider (1958, p. 7), in his seminal book on social perception, noted that "the fact that we are able to describe ourselves and other people in everyday language means that it embodies much of what we have called naive psychology", and he argued that a careful analysis of language expressions would clarify psychological phenomena. From such analyses, Heider derived a set of basic person perception concepts that he viewed as important in interpersonal relations. These included the perception that people *belong* with certain persons or objects, that they have positive or negative *sentiments* toward persons and objects, that they *want* certain things, that they *ought* to do certain things, that they *may* do certain things, that they may be *induced* to do certain things by requests or commands, that they *try* to do certain things, that they *can* do certain things, that they have stable *dispositions*, that they *cause* events, and that they may *benefit or harm* other people.

Role construct repertory test

A second approach that has been employed to describe the categories of social perception is Kelly's (1955) role construct repertory test. This method has been used largely to identify individual differences in the categories of person perception. Although it consequently has not provided descriptions of the categories used by people in general, it could be used for this purpose. In this method, individuals are given triads of *elements*, representing roles of importance to them, such as "father", "admired person", and "disliked teacher". Their task is to identify the two that are alike but different from the third and to give a reason for this grouping. The reason given is coded as one of that person's *constructs*. Statistical analyses may then be performed to elucidate the structure of the individual's construct or category system.

Free-response person descriptions

The third, most common, method employed to identify the categories of social perception is to ask subjects to describe a person in their own words. These free-response descriptions are then coded into categories derived from the content of the descriptions as well as the researcher's conceptual scheme. Categories that have been generated include what the people look like, where they come from, what they do, what one does with them, where one finds them, and what they are like internally – i.e., psychologically (Fiske and Cox 1979). Some of the subdivisions in this category of "internal attributes" can be related to Heider's conceptual scheme: abilities ("can"); aspirations ("want"); attitudes ("sentiments"); and traits ("dispositions"). One important internal category that has not emerged in free-response descriptions is emotions. This probably reflects the nature of the instructions given to subjects, which seem to call for information about more enduring and more individuating attributes. As we shall see in Chapter 4, people certainly can employ a complex array of emotion categories in their descriptions of others.

Research findings regarding social perception categories

Perceiver effects

It seems reasonable to propose that the way in which people describe others will depend in part upon what qualities are interesting or important to them as well as upon their own cognitive sophistication. Indeed, a classic study by Dornbusch et al. (1965) found that the descriptive categories children used to describe their friends depended more on the perceiver than on the person being described. Additional evidence for perceiver effects is provided by research revealing that perceivers' age and cultural background exert a significant influence on the categories of person perception that they employ.

The most frequent categories in adult US samples are abstract dispositions – i.e., personality traits and abilities – as well as behaviors. Contextual characteristics, such as social roles, specific social interactions, and social origins also appear in these person descriptions, albeit with much lower frequencies (Korten 1974; Park 1986; Fiske and Cox 1979). Interestingly, the relative frequency of various descriptors is quite different in some non-Western cultures. In Ethiopia, India, and Japan, people tend to emphasize the social context, describing people more often in terms of their social roles and their concrete interpersonal interactions – e.g., he likes to talk with his roommates – than in terms of their abstract dispositions – e.g., he is talkative (Bond and Cheung 1983; Korten 1974; Miller 1984; Shweder and Bourne 1982).

There is an intriguing parallel between the foregoing cultural differences and age differences that have been documented in the US Developmental theorists, such as Piaget (1926), have argued that development proceeds from concrete to abstract modes of conceptualization. Consistent with this thesis, young children's descriptions of their peers tend to focus on concrete, overt behavior and other readily observable attributes, emphasizing the target person's environmental context. With increasing age, peer descriptions become increasingly abstract and context-free, reflecting an ability to make trait inferences on the basis of consistencies in people's concrete behaviors (Beach and Wertheimer 1961; Peevers and Secord 1973; Scarlett *et al.* 1971; Yarrow and Campbell 1963).

The parallel between the person descriptions favored by children and non-Western adults suggested to some early researchers that adults from "traditional" societies may have a less well-developed capacity to make abstract trait inferences (e.g., Korten 1974). However, the research evidence does not support this interpretation, and Miller (1984) proposed that the cultural differences result from more individualistic conceptions of the person in the West. Whereas Western conceptions of the person operate on the premise that enduring traits regulate behavior across contexts, non-Western cultures emphasize the interdependence of the person and the social context.

Miller also collected data pertinent to the assumption that developmental changes in person description reflect a developmental increase in the ability to abstract general traits from behavioral regularities. She found that while US children used more trait descriptors with increasing age, there was no such trend for Hindus. On the contrary, Hindu children used more concrete, contextual descriptions with increasing age, a trend that did not obtain for Americans. Thus, increased cognitive sophistication does not necessarily yield an increase in the use of abstract traits.

The developmental trend in some non-Western cultures toward increasingly concrete, contextual person descriptors should not be regarded as a trend toward less sophisticated descriptions. Rather, these descriptions may be *more* sophisticated than those of adult

Westerners along a dimension that Peevers and Secord (1973) labeled the "depth dimension". This dimension of variation in person descriptors reflects the degree to which behavior is recognized as conditional upon certain situational, temporal, or internal states. The developmental increase in the use of contextual factors for non-Westerners would seem to reflect an increase in the "depth" of person descriptions. On the other hand, the dimension along which US perceivers show development is called "descriptiveness" by Peevers and Secord, and it reflects the degree to which concrete behaviors are recognized as reflecting abstract, global traits.

What is the explanation for these cultural differences in the development of person descriptions? If one makes the reasonable assumption that children become more socially adept with increasing age, it would appear that perceiving persons in terms of abstract dispositions fosters adaptive behavior in the USA, while perceiving persons in a more contextual fashion fosters adaptive action in certain non-Western cultures. This makes sense when one considers cultural differences in the extent to which abstract traits may be manifested in behavior. In the United States and other cultures where people are relatively unconstrained by social roles, their behavior will vary significantly with their traits, making such descriptive categories very useful for adaptive action. In cultures where people are severely constrained by social roles, traits may be less diagnostic of behavior, rendering contextual descriptors more adaptively relevant. Indeed, descriptions of the behavior of various people in various situations reveal that, in England, extraverted behaviors show more variability across persons than across situations, whereas the reverse is true in Japan (Argyle *et al.* 1978).

In addition to reflecting cognitive capacities, age differences in person perception categories may also reflect functional adaptations, just as cultural differences do. The behavioral variations to which young children in any culture are exposed may be due more to variations in the social context and the actors' roles than to variations in their abstract traits. And, as noted above, culturally divergent developmental trends in the categories of person description may reflect increasing sophistication in "descriptiveness" for some cultures and in "depth" for others.

An additional perceiver variable that may influence person description categories is the perceivers' purpose. Although most research has not given perceivers any specific purpose for the descriptions they are asked to provide, purpose does make a difference.

For example, more appearance terms were used when subjects were asked to "write a description so that someone else could pick the person out in a crowd at Grand Central Station" than when asked to "write a description so that someone else would know what it's like to be around the person," which elicited more personality trait and interpersonal relationship descriptors (Fiske and Cox 1979).

The effects of the perceivers' purpose on their person descriptions has implications for our understanding of the effects of perceiver age and culture. Different groups of perceivers may interpret differently the assignment to describe a person, some taking this to be a request for abstract personality traits and others taking it to be a request for more concrete information. Perceivers from different age or cultural groups may also differ in their own goals when describing a person. Although such differences in purpose would in and of themselves be interesting, since they suggest group differences in the *salience* of various descriptive categories, they do not imply differences in the *ability* to use these categories. Indeed, there is evidence to indicate that young children can make trait inferences when they have a reason for doing so. When US children expect to interact with a target child viewed on videotape, they generate more trait descriptors than when they expect no interaction, presumably because they are more motivated to identify the target's general response tendencies (Feldman and Ruble 1981).

Target effects

Any interpretation of group differences in the categories of person description must consider the possibility that such differences reflect variations in the targets being described rather than variations in the perceivers themselves. For example, the tendency for adults in certain non-Western cultures to make less use of abstract traits than US adults could derive from the fact that each group was describing persons from their own culture. As noted earlier, it could be that concrete, contextual descriptors are more useful for predicting the behavior of targets from some non-Western cultures, while abstract traits are more useful for predicting the behaviors of targets from the West. If so, then regardless of their own cultural background, people who live in a bicultural context may describe Western targets in terms of their abstract traits, while describing non-Western targets in terms of their social roles and context.

Like cultural differences in person descriptions, age differences could conceivably reflect variations in the targets being described. Perhaps the tendency in the USA for children to make less use of abstract traits than adults derives from the fact that children were asked to describe other children, whereas adults were asked to describe other adults. However, researchers have found no support for this hypothesis. In fact, children's descriptors are less abstract – i.e., less "adultlike" – when they describe adults than when they describe children (Livesley and Bromley 1973). This may reflect a tendency for adults' behaviors toward children to depend more upon their roles and the situational context than upon their abstract traits.

Quite aside from the question of whether the target of description can explain the effects of perceiver age and culture, target effects are interesting in their own right. Do we employ the same categories of social perception to describe lovers, friends, and family members? With the exception of research on stereotypes, which will be discussed below, there is little evidence concerning variations across targets in the general categories of social perception or in specific trait descriptors. One of the few target effects that has been investigated is familiarity. US adults' descriptions of friends focus relatively more on personality traits, whereas descriptions of strangers focus on context (Fiske and Cox 1979). Moreover, as US strangers became more familiar with one another over a seven-week time span, their descriptions of each other became more abstract (Park 1986).

Specific qualities perceived in people

As noted above, a full understanding of the contents of social perception requires not only an elucidation of the *general categories* of descriptors that people use but also of the *specific descriptors* within those categories. What are the specific personality traits, behaviors, social roles, goals, physical and demographic qualities that people employ as descriptors? Pertinent research is confined largely to the domain of personality traits. This exclusive focus on traits leaves an unfortunate gap in our understanding of the contents of social perception. Indeed, the studies discussed above reveal that personality traits make up only a little more than 40 per cent of Western adults' open-ended person descriptors, and even a smaller fraction of the person descriptors in other cultures.

Linguistic analyses

Researchers employing a linguistic analysis of trait descriptors typically begin with a search for trait names in a dictionary. Since many of the trait names generated in this fashion are similar in meaning, researchers have reduced the raw list by grouping synonyms together on the basis of their own semantic judgments. The assumption underlying linguistic analyses is that those traits "that are of the most significance in the daily transactions of persons with each other will eventually become encoded into their language" (Goldberg 1981a, p. 142). This process is illustrated in the classic example of Eskimos and snow. The Eskimo has many more terms to represent snow than do English-speaking peoples, presumably because the different varieties of snow have more significance for the Eskimo's actions. It is assumed that the same process occurs for words that are used to describe persons. Thus, not only should the specific contents of person perception be reflected in the natural language, but also cultural differences in the traits that are of the most significance for social interactions should be reflected in the number and types of trait terms in the different languages.

Allport and Odbert (1936) conducted an exhaustive search for English trait names in *Webster's New International Dictionary* (1924) and came up with approximately 18,000 terms that appeared "to distinguish the behavior of one human being from that of another" (p. 24). Of these, Allport (1937) later designated a subset of 4,504 terms as "real" traits, describing generalized and stable qualities rather than specific or temporary behaviors. Cattell (1957) further reduced this trait list to 171 synonym groups. Although Cattell's trait groups became the basis of much later research, they were not representative of the most common trait terms in English, and other researchers sought to attain better representativeness.

Norman (1963) added words from Webster's third (1961) unabridged dictionary to Allport and Odbert's list, excluding all physical appearance descriptors and purely evaluative terms. The 7,300 terms that remained were sorted into three major categories: stable traits (approximately 2,800 terms); temporary states (approximately 3,000 terms); and social roles (approximately 1,500 terms). While Norman's list of 2,800 trait terms may be more representative than Cattell's shorter list, it is far too extensive to be used by person perception researchers. One can hardly ask subjects to rate other persons on 2,800 trait scales! For this reason, other researchers have attempted to cull a smaller, but still representative sample of trait terms from Norman's list.

Goldberg (1982) reduced the list to 731 by restricting it to adjectives and eliminating all terms that were not listed as entries in the 1973 *American Heritage* dictionary or were slangy, sex-linked, peripheral to personality, redundant, or unclear to university undergraduates. These terms were then classified into 42 trait categories. In addition to this trait taxonomy, Goldberg (1982) also developed a preliminary taxonomy of terms for describing people's temporary states and their social roles.

Goldberg (1982) found that some trait categories were represented by more adjectives than others. For example, the category of "pessimism–optimism" had 64 different adjectives, whereas the category of "undependability–reliability" had only five. This fact led Peabody (1987) to go beyond the categorization of trait terms to create a set of scales that would be representative in the sense that the number of scales for a given category of adjectives is proportional to the total number of adjectives in that category. To this end, Peabody grouped 571 adjectives taken from earlier classifications according to evaluative and descriptive similarity. Thus, for example, "modest" (a positive trait) and "unassured" (a descriptively similar, but negative trait) would not be grouped together and neither would "self-confident" (a positive trait) and "conceited" (a descriptively similar, negative trait). As shown in Table 2.1, Peabody's analysis yielded ten major categories of trait adjectives, and the adjectives within these categories were paired with their descriptive *and* evaluative opposites to form 53 scales.

A more circumscribed analysis of the lexicon is found in Asch's (1958) research on metaphor, which investigated cross-cultural similarities in the tendency to describe people with terms that also describe properties of the physical world. Examining languages that belonged to different families and were widely separated in time and space, Asch reported that all possessed terms that simultaneously describe both physical and psychological qualities in the same manner as English. For example, the word for "straight" universally designates "honesty", "righteousness", and "correct understanding", while the word for "crooked" means "dishonesty" and "guile".

Similarities between trait terms and physical properties are also found in an ancient Greek theory of temperaments. According to Galen, a second-century physician, the "melancholic" temperament

Table 2.1 Peabody's (1987) representative trait scales

Category	Number of adjectives
1 ASSERTIVENESS	56
independent–conforming	
forceful–submissive	
bold–timid	
self-confident-unassured	
frank–secretive	
talkative–silent	
2 UNASSERTIVENESS	48
cooperative–uncooperative	
polite–rude	
cautious–rash	
modest–conceited	
discreet–indiscreet	
3 AFFILIATION	83
generous–stingy	
unselfish–selfish	
kind–unkind	
lenient–harsh	
warm–cold	
friendly–unfriendly	
sociable–unsociable	
good-natured–irritable	
peaceful–quarrelsome	
4 IMPULSE EXPRESSION	47
trustful–distrustful	
spontaneous–inhibited	
light-hearted–grim	
cheerful–gloomy	
enthusiastic–unenthusiastic	
5 IMPULSE CONTROL	23
thrifty–extravagant	
self-controlled–impulsive	
serious–frivolous	
6 CONSCIENTIOUSNESS	70
active–inactive	
ambitious–unambitious	
persistent–non-persistent	
thorough–careless	
orderly–disorderly	
organized–disorganized	

Category	Number of adjectives
responsible–irresponsible	
practical–impractical	
7 VALUES	38
moral–immoral	
fair–unfair	
broad-minded–narrow-minded	
honest–dishonest	
8 EMOTIONAL STABILITY	27
stable–unstable	
relaxed–tense	
calm–temperamental	
9 INTELLIGENCE AND ABILITY	63
capable–incompetent	
reflective–unreflective	
perceptive–imperceptive	
logical–illogical	
intelligent–unintelligent	
imaginative–unimaginative	
curious–uninquisitive	
10 CULTURE	20
refined–unrefined	
natural–affected	

Note: Peabody's 53rd scale, flexible–inflexible did not fall into any of the ten major classes of traits.
Source: Peabody (1987, p. 61). Reproduced by permission of the American Psychological Association.

(e.g., pessimistic and conservative) is related to black bile, which is formed of earth; the "sanguinic" temperament (e.g., optimistic and irresponsible) is related to yellow bile, which is formed of air; the "choleric" temperament (e.g., active and impetuous) is related to blood, which is formed of fire; and the "phlegmatic" temperament (e.g., apathetic and controlled) is related to phlegm, which is formed of water. These associations are also found among modern-day perceivers. When subjects sorted English words denoting physical objects and trait terms with the instruction to place at least one object and one trait into the same category, they created categories that paralleled Galen's theory. For example, earth terms, such as dirt, stone, and mineral were placed into the same category as

melancholic terms, such as heavy-hearted, worried and pessimistic (Martindale and Martindale 1988).

Asch argues that metaphorical person descriptors reflect similarities in the functional properties of persons and things. For example,
to call a physical object "hard" is to describe a mode of interaction
with it – the object resists physical change when it is physically
pushed or pressed. To call a person "hard" describes a similar
interaction – the person will resist psychological change when
pushed or pressed with psychological force. The metaphors implicit
in Galen's theory may also be interpreted in terms of functional
parallels. For example, earth can weigh us down physically,
and interacting with "melancholic" people can weigh us down
psychologically. Fire is volatile and unpredictable, as are active and
impetuous "choleric" people.

Descriptor analyses

The analysis of free-response person descriptions that typifies research on the categories of person perception has also been employed, albeit less frequently, to identify specific trait descriptors.
Although the researcher's data base is descriptive protocols rather
than the lexicon, the task of coding free-response descriptions
involves the same judgments and decisions as a linguistic analysis.

Rosenberg and Sedlak (1972) asked US university students to
describe people they knew well by generating a list of traits and to do
the same for people whom they knew mainly by reputation. They
were instructed to pick some people whom they liked, some whom
they disliked, and some about whom they were ambivalent, and to
provide at least five adjectives for each person, excluding physical
descriptions. The results yielded a total of 110 trait categories with a
frequency of usage of at least ten. "Intelligent" was by far the most
frequent descriptor employed by these college students, followed by
"friendly". Indeed, these were so common, that the descriptors "very
intelligent" and "very friendly" were treated as separate categories
(see Table 2.2).

It is interesting to compare the trait categories generated in
free-response person descriptions with those derived from a linguistic analysis. "Intelligent", "friendly", and "hard worker" are the top
three categories in Rosenberg and Sedlak's free-response data, and
"intelligence", "affiliation", and "conscientiousness" are the top

Table 2.2   Free-response trait descriptors

Trait	Frequency	Trait	Frequency
Intelligent	143	Easy to get along with	18
Friendly	80	Idealistic	18
Hard worker	54	Nervous	18
Helpful	51	Sarcastic	18
Honest	50	Trustworthy	18
Kind	47	Dedicated	17
Self-centered	37	Extrovert	17
Sense of humor	36	Happy	17
Sincere	36	Liar	17
Generous	34	Warm	17
Sensitive	34	Bigot	16
Conceited	31	Brilliant	16
Ambitious	30	Confident	16
Very intelligent	30	Conscientious	15
Stubborn	29	Fun-loving	15
Understanding	29	Independent	15
Athletic	28	Individualistic	15
Outgoing	27	Loving	15
Considerate	26	Loyal	15
Quiet	26	Insecure	14
Shy	26	Active	14
Easy-going	25	Aggressive	14
Selfish	25	Concerned	14
Conservative	24	Inconsiderate	14
Thoughtful	24	Dependable	14
Emotional	23	Very friendly	14
Interesting	23	Snobbish	14
Moody	23	Narrow-minded	13
Religious	23	Open-minded	13
Talkative	23	Outspoken	13
Determined	22	Pleasant	13
Humorous	22	Polite	13
Immature	22	Affectionate	12
Smart	22	Cold	12
Lazy	21	Considerate	12
Egotistical	20	Cool	12
Liberal	20	Courageous	12
Witty	20	Cynical	12
Proud	19	Good-natured	12
Domineering	18		

Table 2.2 continued

Trait	Frequency	Trait	Frequency
Introvert	12	Popular	10
Responsible	12	Reliable	10
Sweet	12	Irresponsible	10
Arrogant	11	Self-sacrificing	10
Calm	11	Sloppy	10
Cheerful	11	Sympathetic	10
Demanding	11	Quick-tempered	10
Drinker	11	Carefree	10
Hypocritical	11	Concerned about others	10
Unintelligent	11	Forceful	10
Naive	11	Interested in others	10
Phony	11	Likeable	10
Unselfish	11	Nice	10
Sophisticated	11	Optimistic	10
Talented	11		
Untrustworthy	11		
Two-faced	11		

Source: Rosenberg and Sedlak (1972). Reprinted by permission.

three in Peabody's representative linguistic data (see Tables 2.1 and 2.2). Despite these similarities in the overall pattern of results, there are also some notable differences. Whereas "intelligent" is the most frequent trait in the free-response descriptions reported in Table 2.2, not to mention the related traits of "very intelligent", "smart" and "brilliant", Peabody's linguistically based category "intelligence and ability" is only the third highest in adjective frequency (see Tables 2.1 and 2.2). Also, adjectives in the category of "assertiveness" are relatively frequent in Peabody's linguistic analysis, whereas assertive traits such as "determined", "domineering", and "outspoken" have relatively low frequency in the free-response descriptions.

Discrepancies between the results of linguistic analyses and free-response descriptor analyses throw into question the assumption that there will be more words in the lexicon to describe those traits that are the most significant in people's daily lives. Although a lexical analysis may be representative of the universe of possible person descriptors, it is not necessarily representative of the universe of descriptors that people actually employ. A better index of the significance of a particular trait may be the frequency of its mention in free-response descriptions. Indeed, the high frequency of the trait "intelligent" in Rosenberg and Sedlak's (1972) study may reflect its significance to college students. Other traits may be more relevant to other populations, with concomitantly higher usage. Thus, children frequently mention aggressive qualities in their descriptions of peers at summer camp, but rarely mention intelligence (Yarrow and Campbell 1963).

The advantages of deriving trait categories from free-response descriptions rather than from a linguistic analysis go beyond their greater representativeness. Categories based on free-response descriptions also allow one to address theoretically important questions concerning the development of person perception as well as individual and group differences in person perception. More specifically, one can investigate cognitive and social determinants of the kinds of traits that are perceived in others by comparing the number and types of traits that people of different ages and backgrounds employ in their spontaneous person descriptions.

Perceiver effects

Age

Livesley and Bromley (1973) investigated the development of trait taxonomies, finding that the number of different trait terms used in English children's descriptions of a variety of known others increased throughout the 7–15 year age range. With increasing age, trait terms not only increased in numbers but also in precision. Those used by seven-year-olds were vague and global as well as strongly evaluative – e.g., nice, yukky. With increasing age, these nonspecific terms differentiated into generous, friendly, greedy, conceited, etc.

The conceptual categories into which specific trait terms could be placed also varied with age. In particular, there were age differences in the kinds of interpersonal relationships that were most frequently described. Dominance – e.g., "bossy versus not bossy" – was prominent in the younger children's descriptions, and it showed a linear decrease with age. Pro-social traits – e.g., helpful, considerate, understanding – were used infrequently by the younger children, and showed a strong linear increase with age. Traits pertaining to aggressiveness – e.g., bully, rough, cruel – were moderately frequent across the entire age range studied.

Age-related variations in the frequency of different trait descriptors may reflect variations in the interpersonal relationships experienced by perceivers of different ages. Younger children may be particularly attuned to a target person's dominance because they are so vulnerable to it. Older children, less readily dominated, may become more sensitive to pro-social traits which have a relatively greater impact on their social outcomes. An investigation of the relative frequencies of specific trait descriptors across the entire lifespan might provide additional insights regarding the qualities that are most central to social relationships at different ages.

Gender

Perceiver gender, like age, has been shown to influence the salience of various traits. Males more often describe others in terms of their abilities – e.g., "he's a good artist" – while females describe them in terms of their self-concepts – e.g., "he thinks he's a good artist" (Korten 1974; Beach and Wertheimer 1961). In addition to these sex differences in trait descriptors, there are some interesting differences within the category of concrete behaviors. Males' behavioral descriptions include more non-social activities – e.g., "he likes to ski" – whereas females' include more interpersonal interactions – e.g., "he likes to talk with his friends". Like age differences in the utilization of various traits, these sex differences may reflect a focus on qualities that are adaptively relevant. Since studies indicate that male friendships are characterized by shared activities while female friendships are more likely to involve shared feelings (Caldwell and Peplau 1982; Rubin 1980), it makes sense that men are more attuned to people's abilities and activity preferences whereas women are more attuned to their social interactions and feelings about themselves.

Implicit personality theories

The perceiver effects that become apparent when trait terms are organized into conceptual categories illustrate the advantages of going beyond a simple listing of trait descriptors to create a more structured taxonomy. Although grouping traits into categories provides some structure, additional information may also be derived by considering the relations that a person perceives among specific traits. For example, if one knows that people generally perceive the traits of industriousness and intelligence to co-occur, this will help to predict impressions of a person whose industry is known but whose intelligence is not. Perceived relationships among traits are frequently referred to as a person's *implicit personality theory*. More formally, an implicit personality theory can be defined as "hypothetical cognitive structure, often held nonconsciously, that comprises the attributes of personality that an individual believes others to possess and the set of expected relations (i.e., inferential relations) between these attributes" (Ashmore 1981, p. 38). This organized knowledge about personality may be called a *self-schema* when it pertains to the self, a *person type* when it pertains to a particular psychological grouping of people (e.g., extraverts), and a *stereotype* when it pertains to a particular social group (e.g., Americans). The latter structures may include attributes in addition to personality traits.

Methods for studying implicit personality theories

Multidimensional scaling

One method that has been employed to investigate the perceived relationships among traits is multidimensional scaling analysis. The basic datum required for this method is a number which reflects how closely two traits are related psychologically. This may be accomplished by asking subjects to judge the similarity of the traits or to judge their co-occurrences in target persons. Trait-sorting is another method used to get at perceived co-occurrences. Subjects are asked to describe several persons by sorting personality trait names into different groups, each group representing a different person. The assumption is that traits assigned to the same person are more psychologically similar than those which are not.

What multidimensional scaling does with the basic data is to provide a geometric representation of the set of traits in which greater physical distances between traits correspond to greater differences in their psychological relatedness. This is accomplished by a computer program which reveals the number of dimensions required to capture the relationships among the traits, and which plots the traits according to the psychological distances among them. Consider for example, the depiction of traits in Figure 2.1. Those that are physically closer to one another have been judged to be more psychologically similar than those that are further apart.

Figure 2.1   Two dimensional configuration of 60 traits showing the best-fitting dimensions

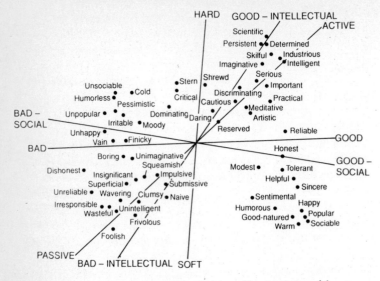

Source: Rosenberg *et al.* (1968, pp. 289–90). Adapted by permission of the American Psychological Association.

The next question in a multidimensional scaling analysis is what conceptual dimensions can describe these inter-trait relationships. To answer this question requires that the traits be independently rated on a set of potential dimensions and that statistical analyses be performed to locate dimensions in the trait space that correspond to the rated properties of the traits. For example, the relationships among the traits depicted in Figure 2.1 can be understood in terms of their positions on conceptual dimensions such as "good" versus "bad", and "active" versus "passive", etc. Obviously, the choice of dimensions on which the traits are rated is a crucial decision in this method. Moreover, statistical analyses can reveal more than one set of dimensions that provide a good fit to the data, and these analyses provide no basis for choosing among them.

Factor analysis

Factor analysis is a second method that has been employed to investigate implicit personality theories. The basic datum required for this method is a matrix of trait-by-trait correlations.[1] Such a

Table 2.3   Hypothetical correlations among traits

	Talk-ative	Soci-able	Open	Respon-sible	Persever-ing	Scrupu-lous
Talkative	—	0.85	0.75	0.25	0.35	0.20
Sociable		—	0.80	0.30	0.10	0.15
Open			—	0.25	0.20	0.35
Responsible				—	0.80	0.85
Persevering					—	0.70
Scrupulous						—

matrix may be generated in a number of ways. For example, subjects may be asked to indicate the probability of two traits being attributes of the same person, or inter-trait correlations may be computed from a subject's ratings or rankings of a number of other people on a number of traits. What the factor analysis does is to identify the dimensions which underlie the inter-trait relationships.

Table 2.3 provides a hypothetical example in which the dimensions underlying the trait correlations are obvious without the benefit of factor-analytic methods. In particular, the correlations reveal two distinct clusters of traits. The traits "talkative", "sociable", and "open" are more highly intercorrelated with each other than any of them are with the traits "responsible", "persevering", and "scrupulous", and vice versa. What factor analysis does is to identify statistically the minimum number of dimensions that can summarize a set of trait correlations such as these even when the dimensions are not so evident to the naked eye. The researcher's task is then to name each dimension, based on a consideration of the traits that belong to it. In the example given, one dimension might be named "extraversion" and the other might be named "conscientiousness". As we shall see below, these are actually two important dimensions of trait perception.

An assumption underlying multidimensional scaling and factor analysis is that perceivers think about other persons in terms of a set of basic traits, along which they may be graded. An alternative assumption is that perceivers conceive of people in terms of more or less distinct personality types, placing them into categories that are defined by a constellation of a few traits and other attributes (e.g., the "cynic" is very distrustful, misanthropic, pessimistic, and dour-looking; the "fool" is very naive, silly, gullible, and happy-looking). These categories or types may be hierarchically organized or

relatively unrelated. This possibility is taken into account by hierarchical cluster analysis, a third method for investigating implicit
personality theories.

Cluster analysis

Cluster analyses can accept the same data as multidimensional
scaling. A computer program partitions the traits into a set of
non-overlapping clusters, such as those depicted in Figure 2.2. The
clustering is hierarchical in that each new clustering consists of the
union of two clusters from the preceding clustering. For example, the
clusters of traits labeled "politician", "clown", and "bully" are
joined to form a cluster labeled "extraverts". The clusters lower in
the hierarchy are produced when an increasingly larger distance
between traits is taken as the criterion for putting traits into the same
cluster. As is true for the naming of trait dimensions in multidimensional scaling and factor analysis, the labeling of trait clusters
is a subjective process. However, researchers need not rely on their
own subjective judgments. Rather, they can establish a consensually
agreed-upon label by asking subjects to name the clusters that they
have created in the initial sorting of trait terms.

Research findings regarding implicit personality theories

The "big five"

The early work of Cattell employed factor-analytic methods to
determine the interrelationships among the trait groups that he had
identified and the basic dimensions underlying them. Whereas
Cattell found 12 personality factors, Norman (1963) and other
researchers employing Cattell's original behavioral ratings have
repeatedly identified five relatively independent dimensions of perceived traits – often dubbed the "big five": extraversion; agreeableness; conscientiousness; emotional stability; and culture. Table 2.4
shows the traits that fall on each of the five factors.

   If two traits belong to the same factor, that indicates that a person
who is perceived to have one of the traits tends to be perceived as also
having the other one. For example, a person who is perceived to be
talkative also tends to be perceived an adventurous, because both
traits fall on the same pole of the extraversion dimension. On the
other hand, if two traits belong to different factors, then a person
who is perceived to have one of the traits may or may not be
perceived to have the other one – it could go either way. For example,

Figure 2.2 Cluster analysis of person types

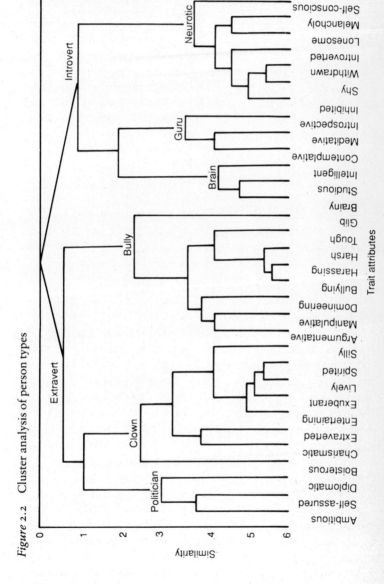

Source: Andersen and Klatzky (1987, p. 238). Adapted by permission of the American Psychological Association.

Table 2.4 Trait scales for the "big five" trait dimensions

Factor name	Number	Abbreviated scale labels Pole A–Pole B
I Extraversion or surgency	1	Talkative–Silent
	2	Frank, open–Secretive
	3	Adventurous–Cautious
	4	Sociable–Reclusive
II Agreeable-ness	5	Good natured–Irritable
	6	Not jealous–Jealous
	7	Mild, gentle–Headstrong
	8	Cooperative–Negativistic
III Conscien-tiousness	9	Fussy, tidy–Careless
	10	Responsible–Undependable
	11	Scrupulous–Unscrupulous
	12	Persevering–Quitting, fickle
IV Emotional stability	13	Poised–Nervous, tense
	14	Calm–Anxious
	15	Composed–Excitable
	16	Not hypochondriacal–Hypochondriacal
V Culture	17	Artistically sensitive–Artistically insensitive
	18	Intellectual–Unreflective, narrow
	19	Polished, refined–Crude, boorish
	20	Imaginative–Simple, direct

Source: Norman (1963). Reprinted by permission of the American Psychological Association.

a person who is perceived to be talkative may or may not be perceived as good-natured. This is because the factor analysis has shown that the extraversion dimension, on which talkativeness falls, is relatively independent of the agreeableness dimension, on which good-natured falls.

Cross-cultural investigations have revealed that at least some of the "big five" factors may be culturally universal. The factors of agreeableness, extraversion, and conscientiousness are practically the same for Filipino, Japanese, and Hong Kong Chinese perceivers as they are for US perceivers when all are asked to describe people with the same set of trait terms (Bond 1979; Guthrie and Bennett 1971). Moreover, Yang and Bond (1985) found three factors very similar to these when students from Taiwan and the Republic of China were asked to describe people with indigenous Chinese trait adjectives. These findings provide impressive evidence for the cul-tural universality of some dimensions of trait perception. They may also reflect universals in human thought, since Bond (1979) has noted that the factors of agreeableness, extraversion, and conscientiousness are similar in meaning to the semantic differential factors of evaluation, activity, and potency, which are the basic dimensions of human judgment about a wide range of stimuli (Osgood et al. 1975).[2]

In addition to the foregoing cross-cultural commonalities in implicit personality theories, there are some noteworthy differences. Research using indigenous traits has revealed some dimensions that are culturally specific, and even those dimensions that appear to be culturally universal do show some differences. For example, for all groups but Americans, "intellectual" was part of the conscientiousness factor, along with "responsible" and "persevering". For Americans, it fell on the culture factor, along with "artistically sensitive" and "polished".

Cultural differences raise the interesting question of what experiences influence one's implicit personality theory. Bond (1979) suggested that when educated people have strong social obligations due to their relatively small numbers, as they do in Japan, China, and the Philippines, then intellectual behavior will be more strongly associated with behaviors indicative of conscientiousness than it will be when higher education is more widely available, as in the USA. It should be noted that this explanation assumes that implicit personality theories are based upon the actual co-occurrences of traits in people known to the perceiver. As discussed below in the section on the validity of implicit personality theories, this assumption is actually quite controversial.

Social/intellectual goodness

The "big five" is not the only organization of perceived trait relationships that researchers have uncovered. Multidimensional scaling analyses conducted by Rosenberg et al. (1968) revealed that traits provided by researchers to US raters could be plotted in a three-dimensional space along the semantic differential factors evaluation (good–bad), activity (active–passive), and potency (hard–soft). The evaluative dimension accounted for the most variability in inter-trait relationships, an effect which replicates judgments about relationships among a wide range of stimuli. Accordingly, an equally good description of the inter-trait relationships was provided by a second set of dimensions each of which had an evaluative component: social good–bad and intellectual good–bad. These two dimensions are similar to the factors of agreeableness and conscientiousness from the "big five", suggesting that the methods of factor analysis and multidimensional scaling yield somewhat similar trait relationships (see Figure 2.1).

Although the perceived trait relationships revealed by the two methodologies are similar, they are not identical. Differences between the two may reflect in part differences in the specific traits that were employed. Interestingly, the multidimensional scaling results were not as clear-cut when subjects generated their own trait descriptors rather than rating people in terms of traits supplied by the investigator (Rosenberg and Sedlak 1972). Thus, the semantic differential dimensions revealed in factor analyses and in multidimensional scaling may represent, at least in part, biases entering into the investigator's selection of traits rather than the basic organization of people's implicit personality theories.

A circumplex model

Additional efforts to derive a taxonomy of trait descriptors include that of Wiggins (1979), who distinguished six kinds of stable traits: what people do to each other (*interpersonal* traits, such as "aggressive"); what people give to each other (*material interpersonal* traits, such as "miserly"); people's styles of emotional reactivity (*temperament* traits, such as "lively"); people's *social roles* (such as "businesslike"); people's adherence to proper behavior (*character* traits, such as "dishonest"); and people's qualities of mind (*mental* traits, such as "analytical"). Wiggins (1979) classified 1,710 adjectives from an earlier analysis of the lexicon into one or the other of these six categories plus a miscellaneous category.

The 800 *interpersonal* traits that emerged in this classification were then distributed across conceptual categories represented in a circumplex model (see Figure 2.3). This is a two-dimensional circular ordering of interpersonal traits in which, theoretically, traits opposite to each other are negatively correlated; those perpendicular are uncorrelated; and those in adjacent quadrants are positively correlated. The principal theoretical axes in Wiggins circumplex model are shown in Figure 2.3. Three of the orthogonal axes in this model are similar in meaning to the semantic differential factors of evaluation (warm-agreeable versus cold-quarrelsome), activity (gregarious-extraverted versus aloof-introverted), and potency (ambitious-dominant versus lazy-submissive) (DeJong 1988). Thus the trait organization identified by the circumplex model shows some

Figure 2.3   Circumplex model of interpersonal traits

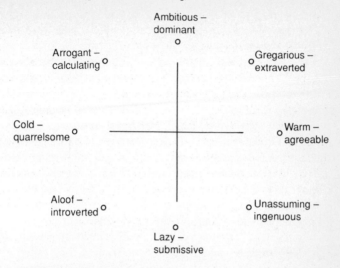

Source: Wiggins (1979, p. 399). Reprinted by permission of the American Psychological Association.

overlap with that identified by multidimensional scaling and factor analysis.

The advantage of the circumplex model is that it provides an explicit conceptual definition of the universe of interpersonal traits. Any behavior that meets the definition of a meaningful interpersonal event can be represented as a vector originating from the center of the circle. A second advantage is that it alerts the investigator to noticeable gaps in a set of person descriptors. Of course, the set of person descriptors that is theoretically possible may not correspond to the set that is commonly used. Wiggins did find, however, that the circumplex model provided a good fit to people's descriptions of their own personality traits when they were given a large set of adjectives to choose among.

Person types
Factor analysis, multidimensional scaling, and the circumplex model all place the targets of perception on a graded set of trait scales. However, one could argue that people do not really perceive others in terms of the complete set of traits. Rather, the factors that have been labeled "extraversion", "conscientiousness", etc., may reflect

the personality traits of particular types of persons. For example, Guthrie and Bennett (1971) noted that the behaviors indicative of low conscientiousness for Filipinos were characteristic of a rural, unsophisticated type of person. Research on person types is consistent with this view, placing the targets of perception into discrete categories that reflect distinct personality traits, appearance qualities, and social and demographic roles.

Person categories such as "nerds", "jocks", and "yuppies" provide anecdotal evidence that person types figure importantly in social perceptions.[3] However, there is little systematic research investigating the set of person types that perceivers have in their repertoire or the contents of these types. Cantor and Mischel (1979) did study the hierarchical structure of person types – that is, the nested relationships among them. Drawing on the "big five" dimensions of person perception, they studied the types "extraverted" person, "cultured" person, "committed" (i.e., conscientious) person, and "emotionally unstable" person. More specifically, they asked subjects to sort 32 social and occupational roles – e.g., phobic, claustrophobic, social activist, antiwar protestor – into the foregoing major person types and then to subdivide each as seemed appropriate. Using a hierarchical clustering analysis, they found strong consensus in the resultant taxonomic structures, which tended to have three levels (see example of "emotionally unstable person" in Figure 2.4).

Cantor and Mischel also investigated the traits and other attributes that perceivers associated with each person type. They found that types at the middle level were the richest, most vivid and most distinctive. For example, there are many, concrete attributes that characterize a "phobic" and these attributes are not completely

Figure 2.4   A tentative taxonomy of persons

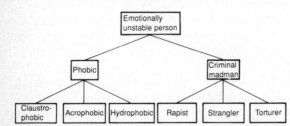

Source: Cantor and Mischel (1979, p. 16). Reprinted by permission.

identical to those associated with the other middle-level type – "criminal madman". These findings led the authors to suggest that the middle-level types may be the ones that are used most frequently in everyday person perception, since they seem optimal for describing what a person is like in general, for distinguishing how two people differ from each other, and for fleshing out the description of a particular person. It is interesting to note that categorization at the middle level puts together people who are perceived to look alike and to provide similar social interactions. This parallels research on the categorization of objects conducted by Rosch and her associates (see, for example, Rosch 1978).

With the exception of a few examples, Cantor and Mischel do not report exactly what attributes are contained in the person types they investigated. However, Andersen and Klatzky (1987) have identified traits associated with two general person types – extraverts and introverts – and three more specific types within each of these (see Figure 2.2).

Considerable research on person types has also been conducted by Brewer and her associates (see, for example, Brewer 1988), who argue that person types are not defined by verbal trait lists, but rather by hierarchically organized *picture-like representations*. This proposition is consistent with research indicating that physical appearance is a frequent element in free-response person descriptions. It is also supported by research demonstrating that subjects who are shown photographs of males and females of various ages tend to agree on which photos go together as a category. This work has further revealed that subjects' verbal descriptions of these "person types" incorporate roles, traits, and behaviors.

Although Brewer's research convincingly demonstrates the existence of picture-like representations of various person types, it has not specified what appearance qualities, roles, traits, and behaviors characterize each type. For example, the categorization of a set of photographs of elderly persons revealed a variety of types that the researchers labeled "grandmotherly", "elder statesman" and "senior citizen". What remains for future research is to analyze systematically subjects' category descriptions as well as the physical features of the photographed persons so that the defining characteristics of these various "person types" can be determined.

Stereotypes
The constellation of physical characteristics that define a person's

gender, age, and ethnicity may serve as a basis for the person types that we commonly call "stereotypes".[4] A classic study in the 1930s (Katz and Braly 1933) revealed a clear consensus among Princeton University students regarding the traits of various national and ethnic groups. More recent research indicates that although US college students' stereotypes of black Americans are more favorable than they were 50 years ago, certain traits remain more frequently associated with blacks than with whites – e.g., musical, very religious, happy-go-lucky, lazy, and ignorant (Dovidio and Gaertner 1986).

Gender stereotypes are also well documented. "Communal" traits, reflecting warmth and expressiveness (e.g., affectionate, emotional, softhearted), are more strongly associated with women than men, whereas "agentic" traits, reflecting competence and rationality (e.g., independent, self-confident, objective), are more strongly associated with men (see Broverman *et al.* 1972; Spence *et al.* 1975). Moreover, research has revealed that these stereotypes are manifested by age five in 25 very diverse cultures (Williams and Best 1982). Research by Ashmore (1981) indicates that the traits associated with males versus females reflect differences along the semantic differential dimension of potency (hard–soft) more than the dimension of evaluation. Other research has shown that, in addition to being characterized by trait associations, gender stereotypes also contain role behaviors and physical appearance characteristics (Deaux and Lewis 1984). Indeed, cultural universality in the roles and appearance of males versus females may contribute significantly to the universality in the traits associated with each gender (Eagly 1987).

Although age stereotypes have been documented in a number of studies, there is less consensus on the traits associated with "old people" than there is on gender stereotypes (see Kite and Johnson 1988). The mixed evidence regarding the traits associated with the elderly in Western cultures is paralleled by inconsistency across cultures. This inconsistency reflects in part cultural differences in the valuation of ageing (see Kimmel 1988). It also reflects the fact that some people reckon age by function rather than by chronology. Interestingly, Braithwaite (1986) found that a 71-year-old who was described as high in physical or mental functioning was not perceived any differently from a similarly functioning 26-year-old, whereas 70-year-olds in general were perceived as more concerned for others, more responsible, less active, and less sociable than 25-year-olds.

Thus, stereotypes of the elderly are more apt to be manifested when information about their functioning is not available. This is consistent with the observation that cultures which define old age chronologically are more likely to associate negative traits with people over 65 than those which define old age by the functions people perform (Keith 1985).

The validity of implicit personality theories

As noted above, there is considerable controversy concerning the origin of implicit personality theories. According to the *accurate reflection* hypothesis, our intuitions about personality structure are derived from observations of co-occurrences among behaviors and traits in the real world (Passini and Norman 1966; Block *et al.* 1979). An alternative explanation, called the *systematic distortion* hypothesis, argues that implicit personality theories tend to be inaccurate with respect to how behaviors actually covary, confusing "what is like what" with "what goes with what" (Shweder and D'Andrade 1980). Specifically, this position holds that the pattern of correlations among retrospective trait ratings can be explained by the semantic similarity of the trait terms. Thus a person may be described as intelligent and industrious not because intelligence and industry actually co-occur (behavior-based associations), but rather because the words "intelligent" and "industrious" are semantically similar (semantic associations).

Two kinds of evidence have been offered in support of the systematic distortion hypothesis. First, the inter-trait correlations derived from ratings of actual target persons are very similar to those derived from judgments of the semantic similarity between the trait terms. Second, the inter-trait correlations that appear in implicit personality theories do not always correspond to the actual correlations among behaviors. For example, Shweder and D'Andrade (1980) asked subjects to rate the behaviors of four family members in a documentary videotape. The behavioral associations that subjects recalled after viewing the tape were similar to semantic associations among the behaviors, but different from the actual associations among the behaviors revealed in "online" ratings made by observers as they watched the tape. Since implicit personality theory research has been based on retrospective rather than "online" ratings, these results are consistent with the argument that implicit personality theories may reflect the degree to which the traits are similar in meaning rather than reflecting the relationships actually observed in behavior.

In contrast to Shweder and D'Andrade's evidence for the systematic distortion hypothesis, Mayer and Bower (1986) provided evidence supporting the accurate reflection hypothesis. Subjects were exposed to 60 hypothetical persons who were described in a written format similar to the case-report summaries that clinical psychologists use. The subject's task was to learn to identify the people who belonged to a certain "personality type" which was arbitrarily invented by the researchers so that it would not correspond to personality categories that subjects might have known earlier. As in real life, the people were described by a multiplicity of information that bore only a probabilistic relation to their category membership. After reading each description, subjects were informed whether or not that person was the type they were looking for.

Despite the task's complexity, subjects were able to distinguish accurately among category members and non-members. They were also able to rank accurately eight new people in order of their likelihood of belonging to the personality type, and they could identify the attributes that occurred more often in those who exemplified the personality type. It thus appears that people can indeed learn about trait co-occurrences through observation.

The fact that Mayer and Bower's research supported the accurate reflection hypothesis, while Shweder and D'Andrade found evidence of systematic distortion, may reflect methodological differences between the two studies. Most notably, subjects in the Mayer and Bower study were exposed to arbitrary behavioral correlations that did not map onto any existing implicit personality theories, whereas the behavioral correlations in the Shweder and D'Andrade research were naturally occurring ones. Thus, the behaviors to which Shweder and D'Andrade's subjects were exposed may have been assimilated in memory to existing conceptual structures, while, for Mayer and Bower's subjects, this distortion was prevented by the arbitrariness of the relationships as well as by the trial by trial error feedback.

A different test of the systematic distortion hypothesis was provided by Weiss and Mendelsohn (1986) who employed a methodology in which the correlations among perceived traits could not be influenced by pre-existing semantic structures because each rater made only one trait rating for each of several well-known targets – e.g., Jane Fonda, Idi Amin. Inter-trait correlations were then computed from ratings made by different subjects. The results using this

method were compared to those obtained with the standard procedure of having each rater make multiple ratings of each target, a
method which is vulnerable to the influence of semantic associations
among the trait terms. The results revealed that the inter-trait correlations were highly similar for the two methods, although they were
lower when raters gave only one rating of a target person than when
they gave multiple ratings. These results indicate that although
semantic associations do not *create* the inter-trait correlations manifested in implicit personality theories, they may exaggerate them.

The foregoing evidence suggests that although people can acquire
their implicit personality theories from observing actual behavioral
co-occurrences, those theories, once acquired, may operate as conceptual structures that can systematically distort *recalled* relationships among subsequently observed behaviors. Thus, although
sociable behavior may indeed co-occur with talkative and adventurous behavior in "extraverted" persons, perceivers may come to
expect and recall a stronger degree of concordance than actually
exists. Research conducted by Berman and Kenny (1976) has demonstrated that is what actually occurs. When subjects were asked
to recall traits that had been attributed to various target persons, the
resultant inter-trait correlations were an additive function of the true
correlation plus a constant influence of the assumed relationship
between the traits.

Two important questions concerning the "accuracy" versus "distortion" controversy remain. One is why the intercorrelations generated by semantic similarity judgments so closely resemble those
generated by trait ratings. One possibility that should not be ignored
is that observed intercorrelations among traits influence the structure
of semantic similarity, rather than vice versa. A second question is
whether or not perceivers actually do acquire their implicit personality theories by observing behavior. A necessary condition for this to
occur is that traits actually be manifested in behavior. Although this
assumption has been disputed in recent years on the grounds that
people show little cross-situational consistency in behavior (see
Mischel and Peake 1982) [the current evidence indicates that traits
do have an important influence on behavior] (see Ajzen 1988;
Kenrick and Funder 1988). Moreover, research suggests that the
pattern of relationships perceived among people's traits has an
objective referent in their actual behaviors. More specifically,
Gifford and O'Connor (1987) found that actual interpersonal behaviors could be mapped onto the circumplex model of trait relations

that emerged in subjects' self-reported personality traits. For example, the frequency of initiating acts in a free-ranging conversation was positively correlated with self-ratings on the gregarious-extraverted dimension, negatively correlated with self-ratings on the opposing aloof-introverted dimension, and uncorrelated with self-ratings on the perpendicular unassuming-ingenuous and arrogant-calculating dimensions. Whether or not behaviors would show the same pattern of correlations with *observer* ratings remains to be determined.

The question of whether cognitive structures, such as implicit personality theories, accurately reflect the structure of behavior is an issue of external validity. Another, equally important, question concerns construct validity. Which of the several trait organizations that have been identified best captures the phenomenology of the perceiver? One approach to this issue is to see which proves the most useful in predicting social perceptions such as impression formation. Although it will be seen in Chapter 3 that researchers do assume that cognitive structures influence impressions, they have not systematically investigated the predictive utility of one particular organization of traits versus another.

Another approach to the question of construct validity is to assess the perceivers' phenomenology. Some research suggests that typologies may capture perceivers' phenomenology better than a matrix of traits (Andersen and Klatzky 1987). Other research further suggests that the use of traits depends upon the perceivers' observational purpose. For example, Hoffman *et al.* (1981) found that perceivers organized a target's behavior in terms of her traits when their purpose was to form an impression of her or to predict her future behavior, while they organized the same behavior in terms of the target's goals when their purpose was to empathize with her or to remember her behavior.

Perceivers may organize behavior in still another way if they are actually interacting with a target person, a situation that has rarely been studied. In particular, when interacting with someone, which is typical in naturalistic social perception, perceivers may organize the target person's behavior in terms of what it affords them – that is what consequences it has for them (e.g., benefit, harm) and what responses it calls for. Given the variety of alternatives to organized trait representations, much may be learned about the contents of social perception from research on the structure of other categories, such as goals, roles, affordances, and types.

Summary and implications

In this chapter we have considered the kinds of qualities that we perceive in other people. Linguistic analyses and free-response person descriptions have revealed that the categories of social perception include demographic attributes, social roles, non-social behaviors, interpersonal interactions, traits and abilities, intentions, motives, sentiments, and physical appearance. This research has further shown that the perceiver's cultural background and age exert a significant impact on the frequency with which the various categories of description are employed. The origins of these differences have not been systematically investigated. However, it is suggested that they may reflect perceiver differences in the qualities that are adaptively relevant as well as in the ability to discern that behavior is conditional upon certain situational, temporal, or internal states and/or that it reflects abstract, global traits.

In addition to identifying various categories of social perception and establishing their relative frequency of usage, considerable research has investigated the specific contents of one particular category – personality traits. Free-response descriptions of people yield somewhat different results from lexical analyses, and they may be more representative of the working contents of social perception. An interesting question for future research concerns the origins and consequences of age and cultural differences in the frequency of usage of different traits. Other questions that remain to be addressed concern the specific contents of social perception categories other than traits – e.g., social roles, interpersonal interactions, goals.

A notable gap in the research on the contents of social perception is the lack of evidence concerning variations across targets in the general categories of perception or specific trait descriptors. Those that are most apt to be employed may depend not only on the target of perception – e.g., children versus adults – but also on the joint effects of the perceiver and the target. For example, US perceivers describe their friends in terms of traits and strangers in terms of context. A clearer understanding of target and perceiver–target interaction effects is needed if the contents of social perception are to inform predictions regarding various social perception processes, such as impression formation and causal attribution.

The interrelationships that are perceived among traits have also been considered in this chapter. Considerable research indicates that people from a variety of cultures share similar "implicit personality theories" regarding what traits go together – at least when they have been given a predetermined set of traits on which to rate other people. Moreover, research using a variety of methods has consistently organized these traits along a small number of dimensions which, though not identical from method to method, do show some convergent validity.

Although the external validity of implicit personality theories has been a matter of some dispute, the evidence seems to indicate that they may accurately reflect actual trait co-occurrences, not merely the semantic associations of the perceiver. Whether or not they reflect the way perceivers typically think about people is another matter. Research suggests that typological structures, which include information about physical appearance, social roles, and concrete behaviors, in addition to traits, may capture the contents of social perception better than trait relationships alone. A crucial basis for evaluating the various structures lies in their usefulness for predicting and explaining various processes of social perception, such as impression formation and causal attribution. Unfortunately, however, although researchers have investigated the effects on impressions and attributions of cognitive structures such as implicit personality theories and stereotypes, they have rarely compared the predictive utility of one type of structure with that of another.

Further reading

Holland, D. and Skinner, D. (1987). Prestige and intimacy: The cultural models behind Americans' talk about gender types. In D. Holland and N. Quinn (eds), *Cultural models in language and thought*. Cambridge: Cambridge University Press. An investigation of American gender types reveals that various types are associated with prototypical male/female relationships and interactions rather than simply with a set of attributes.

Livesley, W. J. and Bromley, D. B. (1973). *Person perception in childhood and adolescence*. London: John Wiley. This book presents an in-depth analysis of age and gender differences in the contents of social perception based on 'free response' person descriptions generated by children aged 7–15. Target effects on perceptions (age, gender, and likeability) are considered in addition to perceiver effects.

Shweder, R. A. and Bourne, E. J. (1982). Does the concept of the person vary cross-culturally? In A. J. Marsella and G. M. White (eds), *Cultural conceptions of mental health and therapy*. London: D. Reidel, pp. 97–137. Three ways of interpreting cultural differences are described and evaluated – universalist, evolutionist, and relativist – and each is applied to cultural differences in the contents of person descriptors.

Williams, J. E. and Best, D. L. (1982). *Measuring sex stereotypes: A thirty-nation study*. Beverly Hills, CA: Sage. This book documents pancultural similarities in adult-defined sex stereotypes and in the development of these stereotypes among children. The universality of sex stereotypes is explained in terms of biologically based sex differences in social roles.

Notes

1 The following brief explanation is intended for students who are unfamiliar with statistical theory. Given two variables which appear to vary with each other, the correlation describes the degree of *linear* relationship between them (that is, how closely this relationship can be represented by a straight-line graph); it can take any value between −1 and +1. If an increase in one variable is associated with an increase in the other, the correlation will be positive; if an increase in one is associated with a decrease in the other, it will be negative. If the straight-line graph captures this relationship perfectly, then the correlation will be +1 if an increase in one variable is associated with an increase in the other, and −1 if it is associated with a decrease. If there is no linear relationship at all between the variables, the correlation will be zero. It should be noted that no account is taken here of the possibility of an non-linear (for example, quadratic or cubic) relationship between the variables.

2 The *semantic differential* (Osgood *et al.* 1957) measures the meaning of various concepts by determining what dimensions can account for intercorrelations among ratings of those concepts on various scales such as pleasant–unpleasant, harmful–beneficial, weak–strong. The factors of evaluation, activity, and potency have emerged in analyses of ratings of many different concepts.

3 For the reader unfamiliar with US slang, "nerds" may be roughly translated as "brainy individuals with few social skills"; "jocks" as "athletic individuals with little intelligence"; and "yuppies" as "successful professionals with materialistic values".

4 Although the term "stereotype" may theoretically be applied to assumptions about the attributes of any group of people, it is commonly used to describe assumptions about known social groups. Gender, age, and ethnic groups are used here for illustrative purposes because stereotypes of these groups have been extensively studied.

3 / IMPRESSION FORMATION

In many situations we form first impressions of others based on rather limited information. When you talk to a stranger on the telephone, the person's voice may create a distinct impression, even if the content of the conversation is relatively uninformative. When you enter a room filled with strangers, be it a meeting, a classroom, or a party, the physical appearance of each person may create a distinct impression even before you converse. Another source of first impressions is verbal descriptions, as when a friend tells you what someone is like or when you read a personal ad in the newspaper. Finally, regardless of what type of information you have, the first impressions that you form may depend upon your own characteristics, such as your stereotypes, your mood, what information you are seeking, or your cultural background.

First impressions are important because they influence the likelihood of pursuing a relationship with someone. My college friend wanted to change roommates because the "hippie" who had been assigned to her looked and acted so weird. Similarly, if your friend's description of a potential date or the self-description in a personal ad mentions qualities that you dislike, you will probably pass up the opportunity for an introduction. First impressions not only influence our willingness to interact with a person, but they also influence our inferences about unspecified traits that we associate with the known qualities. My roommate's large sweater collection led me to infer that she would be stuck-up and rich, although the truth of the matter was that her father was in the sweater business. Such effects represent the functioning of implicit personality theories that were discussed in the last chapter.

Research on impression formation has addressed several questions. A constructivist approach, which emphasizes "theory-driven" perceptions, is reflected in questions concerning the impact on impressions of a perceiver's cognitive and affective processes. A structuralist approach, which emphasizes "data-driven" perceptions, is reflected in questions concerning the impact of a target person's physical and behavioral characteristics. Both approaches have been brought to bear on evidence concerning how impressions are influenced by the behavioral context in which trait or behavioral information occurs. In all of this research, the emphasis is on perceptions of a person's traits. Perceptions of more contextual qualities, such as social roles and relationships, will not be considered in this chapter because these have rarely been studied. The substantial literature regarding perceptions of a person's emotions will be considered in Chapter 4.

Methods for studying impression formation

A common method for studying impression formation is to present subjects with a list of trait adjectives that describe a target person and to assess their impressions of the person on rating scales that assess liking for the person and/or inferences about other traits. Less frequently, open-ended descriptions of persons and predictions of their behavior may be assessed. Recall of the descriptive information is also a frequent dependent measure, and "person memory" is a research topic in its own right. This literature will not be reviewed in the present chapter, both because of space limitations and because recall of descriptive information bears no clear-cut relation to impressions when they are most typically formed, namely "on-line" at the time that we encounter a target person (Hastie and Park 1986).

The emphasis on trait adjective descriptors as stimuli in impression-formation research fails to capture many of the essential elements of the typical impression-formation situation. Despite the fad of individuating T-shirts, people don't usually walk around wearing trait labels on their sleeves. Rather, our first impressions of others more frequently rely on the information provided by their appearance, voice, and behavior. To investigate the impact of such information, researchers assess impressions of target persons based on photographs, audiotapes, videotapes, or brief interactions.

Theories of impression formation

Although there is no grand theory of impression formation, there are several smaller-scale models that bear on the general approaches to the study of social perception discussed in Chapter 1. A structuralist or "data-driven" approach is manifested in Anderson's linear combination models (Anderson 1981); a constructivist or "theory-driven" approach is manifested in Asch's Gestalt model (Asch 1946) as well as more recent schema models. Aspects of both structuralism and constructivism are integrated into Brewer's (1988) dual-process model, Fiske and Neuberg's (1990) continuum model, as well as McArthur and Baron's (1983) ecological model.

Linear combination models

Linear combination models assume that the individual elements in the information we have about a person will be summed or averaged to "build up" an overall impression such as the person's likeability. These models thus take a structuralist approach to impression formation. An *additive* model holds that each element of information makes the same contribution to the final overall impression regardless of other available information. Assume, for example, that you are trying to decide which of three personal ads to answer. Loren's self-description includes three trait adjectives: "intelligent", "energetic", and "warm". Terry's includes the same three adjectives plus "honest". And, Chris's includes the same four as Terry's plus "punctual". Suppose you believe that all of these traits are positive ones, and that being intelligent is worth 7 points on a 10-point scale of evaluative positivity, being energetic is worth 5 positivity points, being warm is worth 9 points, being honest is worth 7 points, and being punctual is worth 4 points. Applying the additive model gives Loren a total of 21 points, Terry 28 points, and Chris 32 points. Thus, according to this model you should mention as many positive traits as you can in a personal ad, since each one will boost the favorability of the reader's overall impression.

The *averaging* model predicts a different outcome. According to this model, the contribution of a particular trait to the overall impression depends upon how favorable it is compared with the other traits. Specifically, adding moderately positive information to a set of highly positive traits is predicted to *lower* the overall impression because the average value of the traits will be lowered. Consider the personal ads once again. According to the averaging model, your impression of Loren will be a "7", which is the average positivity of your evaluation of the three traits that Loren mentioned. Your impression of Terry will be no higher. Even though the positive trait of honesty has been added, the average positivity of the four traits is still 7. Finally, your impression of Chris will be *lower* than that of Loren or Terry because the extra trait of "punctual" was not as positive as the other three, and it pulls the average value of Chris' traits down to 6.4.

So, how should you write a personal ad? Research testing these two models has produced mixed results and led to the formulation of a *weighted average* model (Anderson 1981). According to this model, an overall impression of someone reflects the average *scale value* of the individual traits – i.e., how positively each trait is evaluated – weighted according to the trait's importance to the perceiver. The *weighted average* model further holds that the overall impression will depend upon the perceiver's initial impression, which can be considered as a kind of general perceiver bias. For example, if the perceiver is skeptical of anyone who advertises in the personals, then the initial impression may be negative.

Research comparing impressions of people as a function of the number, quality and mix of the trait adjectives with which they are described has generally supported the weighted average model. Although this model does provide a good fit to the data, it is difficult to use it to make *a priori* predictions regarding impressions. While perceivers from a common culture may agree as to the positivity of various traits, it is very difficult to predict how different traits will be weighted, since this may vary from perceiver to perceiver as well as from context to context.

Gestalt and schema models

In contrast to the linear combination models of impression formation, Asch (1946) holds that traits are organized to form a *Gestalt*, a whole which is not simply the sum or average of the individual trait elements. Rather, each trait affects the *meaning* of each of the others such that the final impression is not easily predicted from the individual traits. For example, when coupled with the trait "warm", "industrious" may convey a tendency to work hard helping others, a connotation which could increase the likelihood of perceiving the person as generous. On the other hand, when "industrious" is coupled with "cold", it may conjure up a "do not disturb" sign, which could increase the likelihood of perceiving the person as "irritable". Thus for Asch, the perceiver constructs a holistic impression from a set of traits and this impression can, in turn, generate inferences about other qualities the person might have.

Schema theories represent a more extreme constructivist approach to impression formation. Whereas Asch's theory is concerned with the construction of an impression from a target person's traits, thereby acknowledging that impressions are in part "data-driven", schema theories are concerned with the construction of an impression from the perceiver's *self-schemas* or *group stereotypes*. Self-schemas and stereotypes are trait structures like those discussed in Chapter 2. They represent organized knowledge about the self or various types of people, and they contain both the attributes of the person and the relationships among these attributes. Schema researchers focus on how perceivers' prior concepts and theories about the self or some category of people influence their impressions of a specific target person. For example, if the perceivers' schema for a female is activated, the target person may be perceived as warm and dependent regardless of her actual behavior. As such, schema theories espouse the view that impressions are constructions of the mind – i.e., "theory-driven" rather than "data-driven".

Mixed models

Brewer's (1988) dual-process model of impression formation incorporates theory-driven, constructivist processes as well as data-driven, structuralist processes. According to this model, the same social information can be processed either way, depending on decisions made by the perceiver. After an initial, "automatic" perception of a target person's demographic characteristics (e.g., gender, age, race), impressions will be determined by other target attributes – i.e., "data-driven" – if the perceiver feels interdependent with the target or ego-involved in the judgment task. In the absence of such involvement, impressions will be determined by stereotypes of the category into which the target person is placed – i.e., "theory-driven". According to Brewer's model, these category-based impressions differ from person-based impressions both in their organizational structure and in their format: category-based impressions are less complex and differentiated and they are represented in a visual rather than a verbal format.

Whereas Brewer's model proposes two different types of impressions – category-based *or* person-based – Fiske and Neuberg (1990) have proposed a continuum model of impression formation which proceeds from constructivist processes, in which impressions derive from pre-existing concepts and theories about a particular category of people, to structuralist processes, in which impressions derive from some linear combination of the target person's actual attributes. According to this model, constructivist processes are the most commonplace, with structuralist processes engaged only when the target is interesting or personally relevant to the perceiver and the perceiver is unable to fit the target's attributes to an initial categorization. Thus, perceiver motivation *and* target attributes influence the process of impression formation in the Fiske and Neuberg model. Finally, whereas Brewer's model posits differences in the format of category-based and person-based impressions, Fiske and Neuberg propose a common type of representation that simply becomes more elaborated as one moves along the continuum.

McArthur and Baron's (1983) ecological model of impression formation emphasizes the joint effect on impressions of processes in the perceiver and attributes in the target person. According to this model what we perceive in others are their *affordances*, which are defined as the opportunities for acting or being acted upon that a particular target provides. The detection of certain affordances is postulated to depend not only on the structured stimulus information provided by a target but also on the perceiver's *attunements* – that is the particular stimulus information to which he or she attends. Attunements, in turn, depend upon the perceiver's social goals, perceptual learning, and actions. Thus, according to the ecological model, impressions emerge from the affordances of the target person for a particular perceiver.

Perceiver determinants of impressions

Various perceiver characteristics influence impressions of a target person, including cognitive, affective, and demographic factors. Cognitive factors include short-term mental states, such as expectations and trait descriptor accessibility; stable mental structures, such as personal constructs, stereotypes, and self-schemas; and various information-processing strategies, called cognitive heuristics. Affective factors include the perceiver's goals and emotional states. Demographic factors include the perceiver's gender, age, and cultural background. Each of these perceiver characteristics may impact impressions by influencing what information about others is registered, what is recalled, how it is weighted, and/or what meaning it has for the perceiver.

Cognitive factors

Priming effects

Priming is a phenomenon whereby perceivers' impressions of a person reflect those descriptive terms that are most accessible because they have been recently and/or frequently activated or "primed". For example, Higgins *et al.* (1977) primed perceivers by exposing them to positive or negative trait descriptors (e.g., adventurous versus reckless). Then, in a supposedly unrelated study, the same perceivers read about Donald, who shot rapids, drove in a demolition derby, and planned to learn skydiving. People primed with the relevant positive trait *adventurous* evaluated Donald more positively than those who had primed with *reckless*. This effect did not occur when people were primed with a positive or negative trait irrelevant to Donald's behavior. Thus, priming effects require some match between a target's behavior and the perceiver's most accessible descriptors. Even so, these results suggest that what you read before glancing through the personals may have an impact on how you evaluate the people described in the ads.

Expectancy effects

Considerable research has shown that perceivers' impressions of a person may move in the direction of their expectations. Kelley (1950) found that students' impressions of a teacher were much more favorable when they expected him to be "warm" than when they expected him to be "cold". Langer and Abelson (1974) found a similar effect upon clinician's impressions of a person. Traditional therapists who were expecting to interview a "patient" evaluated the person as more disturbed than those who were expecting to interview a "job applicant".

Although impressions of a person are often assimilated to the perceiver's prior expectations, there is also evidence for a reverse, contrast effect. When behaviors are not too discrepant from expectations, perceivers show an assimilation effect. But, when a target person manifests behaviors that clearly fall outside of this range of assimilation, the result is a "contrast" effect in which impressions move in a direction opposite to expectations (Manis *et al.* 1988). Thus, if a person who is expected to be warm shows distinctly chilly behavior, that person may be perceived as even colder than someone for whom there was no expectation.

The ultimate influence of an unexpected behavior on impressions may be influenced by a variety of factors in addition to its degree of discrepancy. If discrepant behaviors are viewed as induced by situational forces, they are likely to be discounted and to have less influence on impressions than expected behaviors (Crocker *et al.* 1983). The source of the expectancy is also important. Perceivers' impressions are influenced less by unexpected behaviors when their expectations derive from the target's own self-descriptions than when they derive from the descriptions of a third party (Jones *et al.* 1984). The perceiver's goals also influence the impact of unexpected information. Assimilation effects are less likely to occur when the perceiver's dependence on a target person requires accurate impressions (Neuberg and Fiske 1987). Finally, the influence of an unexpected behavior on impressions will depend upon the relative strengths of the expectancy and the contradictory behavioral data (Higgins and Bargh 1987). It should be noted that perceivers' expectations can influence not only their impressions, but also the target's behavior. Such effects are discussed below in the subsection on "Accuracy versus bias" (pp. 82–5).

Group stereotypes

As noted in Chapter 2, people's group membership exerts a strong impact on our implicit personality theories – or stereotypes – regarding their traits. Like expectations about a person provided to us by informants, these stereotypes can influence our impressions of a specific person's observed behaviors. In a study by Duncan (1976), perceivers watched a videotape of two people engaged in a heated discussion which culminated in one person shoving the other. When the "shover" was black, white perceivers were much more likely to perceive him as violent than when he was white, in which case he was viewed as "playing around". This effect, which is consistent with the cultural stereotype that blacks are more aggressive than whites, held true regardless of the race of the person who was shoved.

An interesting question is whether Duncan's findings reflect the impact of a target person's *race per se* on impressions or the impact of the perceiver's *racial similarity* to the target. Sagar and Schofield (1980) argued for the former interpretation, reporting that both black and white perceivers rated ambiguously aggressive behaviors as more mean and threatening and less playful and friendly when the perpetrator was black than when he was white. On the other hand, Jones (1983) has noted that Sagar and Schofield's data reveal that black and white perceivers do not differ in their impressions of the aggressiveness of a perpetrator who is the same race as they are — blacks' impressions of a black perpetrator are identical to whites' impressions of a white perpetrator. The difference is in impressions of a racially dissimilar perpetrator: whites perceive a black perpetrator as more aggressive than blacks perceive a white perpetrator to be. This suggests that perceivers are fairly objective in their impressions of "ingroup" targets, but assimilate the behavior of "outgroup" targets to ethnic stereotypes.

Gender stereotypes have also been shown to influence impressions. In particular, the behavior of male and female targets is assimilated to the stereotype that males are more competent than females. Targets engaged in a taperecorded getting-acquainted conversation were perceived as less nervous, less emotional, and more logical when their voice was male than when it was converted by computer to a female voice of the same intonation and intensity (Robinson and McArthur 1982). Impressions of the works of males and females, like impressions of their verbalizations, are also assimilated to gender stereotypes. In Goldberg's (1968) classic study, female college students' perceived the author of a journal article in a traditionally masculine field as more competent when the article bore a male rather than a female name. Although subsequent work has revealed that such effects are elusive and relatively small, when biased evaluations do occur, they regularly favor males (Swim *et al.* 1989).

Additional research has revealed that the more favorable impression of men's work reflects the assimilation of ambiguous information to perceivers' expectancies regarding the likely competence of men and women. The impression of lesser competence in females is mitigated when some clear recognition of achievement has been given to the works of targets of both sexes (Pheterson *et al.* 1971). Other evidence that the effect of target gender on impressions requires behavioral ambiguity is provided by the finding that a man

was seen as more assertive than a woman when only non-relevant
behaviors were known (e.g., getting a haircut and arriving in class on
time), whereas impressions of their assertiveness were virtually
identical when relevant behaviors were available (e.g., abruptly
interrupting another student in class) (Locksley *et al.* 1980). However, relevant target behaviors are able to override gender
stereotypes only when those behaviors show temporal consistency. A
single relevant behavior does not offset the impact of stereotypes on
impressions (Krueger and Rothbart 1988).

Contrast as well as assimilation effects may be manifested in
impressions of people from various demographic groups if their
behavior strongly violates our expectations. Thus, in contrast to the
stereotype of male competence, incompetent male scholarship applicants are rated *lower* than females of equally low competence by men
and women alike (Deaux and Taynor 1973). And, in contrast to the
stereotype of male emotional strength, passive-dependent men are
perceived as *less* well adjusted than equally passive women (Costrich
et al. 1975).

In addition to assimilating or contrasting impressions of a person
to group stereotypes, perceivers' impressions support an *ingroup
favoritism hypothesis*: we see more positive qualities in the behavior
of people in our "ingroup" than those in an "outgroup". For
example, after a particularly rough football game between Dart-
mouth and Princeton, students from both schools perceived their
rival's team as playing a much dirtier game than their own team, even
when they were shown a replay of the entire game (Hastorf and
Cantril 1954). Such differences in impressions of ingroup versus
outgroup members are expressed more clearly in favoritism toward
ingroup members than in hostility toward outgroup members
(Brewer 1979).

Interestingly, the ingroup–outgroup effects on impressions can be
produced by the mere act of categorization, and do not require a
long-standing identification with the ingroup. Studies utilizing the
"minimal group paradigm" have revealed that when subjects are
assigned to groups on the basis of some arbitrary criterion, they
typically rate the ingroup and the outgroup very differently on a
variety of personal characteristics (Tajfel 1970; Tajfel *et al.* 1971;
Turner 1978). The effects of membership in some arbitrary group are
sufficiently strong that crossing arbitrary categories with socially
relevant ones can offset ingroup favoritism toward the latter. Thus,
the performance of same-sex persons was rated higher than that of

different-sex persons when targets could only be categorized on the basis of gender, whereas this same-sex favoritism was eliminated when targets were categorized on the basis of gender *and* a cross-cutting category "team color" (Deschamps and Doise 1978). This neutralizing effect presumably occurs because some targets who are ingroup members in terms of gender are outgroup members in terms of team color and vice versa. It has also been suggested that it may reflect a loss of category salience due to greater judgmental complexity for crossed categorizations, although the evidence for this is mixed (Brown and Turner 1979; Arcuri 1982).

Another hypothesis regarding impressions of ingroup versus outgroup members is the *outgroup homogeneity hypothesis*: people perceive outgroup members as being more homogeneous in their traits and behavior than ingroup members (Park and Rothbart 1982). For instance, undergraduates' impressions of the personality traits of people in their own club showed a much wider range than did their impressions of people who belonged to other clubs.

Still another postulate is the *evaluative extremity hypothesis*: the more homogeneous conceptions of outgroup members yield more extreme evaluations of them. Specifically, it is argued that conceptions of ingroup members involve many more dimensions than conceptions of outgroup members, which dampens the impact on ingroup evaluations of any single positive or negative behavior. The result is more mixed judgments about ingroup members and more evaluative moderation. Consistent with this hypothesis, young men evaluated an "outgroup" old man more positively than an "ingroup" young man when given favorable information and more negatively than a young one when given unfavorable information. Similarly, whites gave higher ratings to a strong black law school applicant than to a comparable white applicant, whereas they rated a weak black applicant lower than a comparable white one (Linville and Jones 1980). Gender "outgroup" had a parallel effect, with male and female subjects forming more extreme impressions of strong and weak law school applicants of the opposite sex than of the same sex.

There are several factors that may contribute to the effects of a target person's group membership on impressions. Divergent impressions of people from various social groups, despite identical behaviors, may reflect the assimilation or contrasting of a target's behaviors to group stereotypes; the impact of the simplicity of outgroup representation on evaluative extremity; the impact of affective ambivalence toward outgroup members on evaluative extremity (Katz 1981); the illusory correlation of salient behaviors and salient targets (see subsection on "Target and behavioral salience", pp. 66–9); and/or the influence of positive versus negative affect on attention to or labeling of the target person's behaviors (see subsection on "Affective factors", pp. 59–62). Research which has simultaneously investigated several of these influences on impressions of ingroup versus outgroup members reveals that a model integrating multiple influences is superior in explanatory power to one which posits a single influence (Jussim *et al.* 1987).

Personal constructs and self-schemas

Personal constructs are those descriptors that an individual most frequently uses to describe others (Kelly 1955). These stable constructs influence impressions of others in much the same way that temporarily primed constructs do. Constructs affect the information that is emphasized in impressions when there is a range of information available. Thus, if you read about someone who is warm and intelligent and witty, your resultant impressions will contain more information related to his intelligence if intelligence is a central construct for you and more information related to his warmth if warmth is a central construct (see Higgins *et al.* 1982). Constructs also influence how you process ambiguous information about others. If someone's behavior just hints at being shy, you will perceive more shyness if that is a central construct for you than if it is not (Bargh *et al.* 1986).

A self-schema has been defined as "a cognitive generalization about the self, derived from past experience, that organizes and guides the processing of self-related information contained in the individual's social experiences" (Markus 1977, p. 64). It has been proposed that self-schemas may influence our impressions of others by virtue of focusing attention on schema-relevant behavioral information. Consistent with this notion, perceivers weight information relevant to their self-schemas more heavily when forming evaluative impressions – i.e., judging a target's likability (Carpenter 1988). They also seek out information about others that is related to their own self-schemas. People who think of themselves in terms of masculine or feminine gender stereotypes are more apt to comment on the sex of a target person than are those who are not strongly sex-typed (Frable 1987). People who think of themselves as extraverts seek information about others' extraversion, while those with an introversion self-schema seek information about others' introversion

(Fong and Markus 1982). Furthermore, perceivers are quicker to judge whether or not someone has traits that are extremely like or unlike their own than to make this judgment for traits which are only moderately self-descriptive (Kuiper 1981). This finding suggests that self-schemas are bipolar, containing generalizations about what one is not as well as what one is.

The desirability of traits in the self-schema also affects their influence on impression formation. Perceivers' highly desirable traits are more central to impressions of others than their less desirable ones. For example, if a person views herself as very intelligent but not very warm, then the perceived intelligence of others is more strongly related to additional impressions of them than is their perceived warmth (Lewicki 1983). Perceivers are also more quick to notice their own desirable traits in liked others and slower to decide that these traits are absent, whereas the reverse is true for impressions of disliked individuals (Lewicki 1984).

Although the foregoing evidence indicates that self-schemas influence the process of impression formation, there is no consistent tendency for them to influence the content of impressions. Sometimes people do project their own traits onto others, but they may also project complementary traits, depending upon which type of projection enhances their self-esteem (Holmes 1968). For example, a person who thinks of himself as generous may perceive liked others as similarly disposed, while perceiving disliked others as stingy. Target characteristics not only influence the direction of self-schema effects, but also their very existence. For example, perceivers' impressions of various targets reflect the actual gender and sex-typedness of the target rather than the perceivers' own gender-related schemas (Park and Hahn 1988). Thus, those with a masculine self-schema do not perceive more masculine qualities in targets of either sex than those with a feminine self-schema, and those with a highly sex-typed gender schema do not perceive more sex-stereotypic qualities in targets than those who are less sex-typed.

Although self-schemas do not reliably affect judgments about the target person that can be informed by the objective information available to perceivers, they do affect more conjectural judgments. A schema-relevant trait seems to be embedded within an implicit personality theory which causes the perceiver to go beyond the information given in forming impressions of a target person (Catrambone and Markus 1987). Thus, if a person's behavior unambiguously reveals him to be "independent", then perceivers form the same impression of his independence regardless of their own self-schemas. However, if dependency is relevant to the perceivers' self-schemas, then they do make more inferences about an independent person's *other traits* than do perceivers for whom dependency is schema-irrelevant – i.e., those who do not think of themselves as particularly independent or dependent.

Cognitive heuristics

Complex problems can often be solved by means of shortcuts which reduce them to a sequence of simpler operations. Such shortcuts, called *heuristics* (Kahneman and Tversky 1973; Tversky and Kahneman 1974) may be used in forming impressions of others. One shortcut is called the *availability* heuristic. It is manifested in a tendency to judge the probability or frequency of an event according to the ease with which you can think of examples. For example, your impression of how irritable your best friend is may be influenced by how easily you can think of instances of her losing her temper.

Since the actual frequency of an event influences the ease with which you can think of examples, the availability heuristic often yields accurate perceptions. That is, the more often your friend has lost her temper, the more easily you will recall instances of this event, and the more irritable you will correctly perceive her to be. However, other factors, such as recent exposure to certain events or their perceptual salience may also influence their availability in recall. Thus, if your best friend has very recently lost her temper or if she threw a tantrum the single time that she lost her temper, then this infrequent event will be highly available in recall, causing you to overestimate its actual frequency and to thereby overestimate your friend's irritability. Behavioral salience need not be as drastic as a temper tantrum to yield biased impressions via the availability heuristic. Some behaviors are by their very nature more apt to be publicly displayed than others and the former may exert an undue impact on trait impressions.

A second shortcut to impressions is called the *representativeness heuristic*. It is manifested in a tendency to judge the category membership of people according to the extent to which they are similar to or "representative" of the average person in that category. Suppose you read the following personal ad: "Single white male, loves good pizza, wild parties, bowling, and country and western music." Contrast your guess about his occupation with your guess about the following person: "Single white male, loves fine French food, foreign movies, bicycling, and Beethoven." If you are an American, chances are you would guess a blue-collar occupation for the first man and a professional occupation for the second because these two men resemble common conceptions of the average blue-collar worker and professional, respectively.

Like the availability heuristic, the representativeness heuristic often serves the perceiver well, since similarity to people in a given category is often an accurate indicator of category membership. For example, the telephone operator who irately insisted that I put Professor Zebrowitz on the phone, when I was deliberating whether or not to accept a collect call, would usually be correct to assume that my female voice was representative of a secretary rather than a professor. However, the focus on representativeness may sometimes blind perceivers to other determinants of category membership, causing erroneous judgments.

One factor that representativeness may cause perceivers to ignore is the actual incidence of people in the category that a target person resembles. What if the two personal ads described earlier were published in the *New York Review of Books*? Your judgment that the first man is a blue-collar worker should be tempered by the fact that the personal ads published by professionals in this particular magazine far outnumber those published by blue-collar workers. Nevertheless, people often ignore such *base rate* information (i.e., information about the population the ad came from), forming their impressions solely on the basis of the representativeness of the behavioral information. This inappropriate reliance on the representativeness heuristic is corrected in certain situations including the following: those in which the behavioral information suggests several categories equally or comes from an unreliable source; those in which attention is drawn to the base rates (Bar-Hillel and Fischhoff 1981); and those in which the task is framed as a statistics problem, which implicitly requires base rate information, rather than as a psychology problem, which implicitly requires behavioral information (Schwarz *et al.* 1988).

Although the impact of cognitive heuristics on impressions may be seen after the fact, it is a more difficult problem to make *a priori* predictions, because one must have information about the particular perceiver and target. What is most "available" depends in part upon the particular perceiver – e.g., her personal constructs – and the particular target – e.g., his past behavior. What category a target represents also depends upon the perceiver – e.g., what categories she uses and the characteristics of the average member of each category – as well as the category-matching characteristics of the target.

Affective factors

Goals

Do we perceive qualities in others that we want or need to find? Research indicates that this kind of "wishful seeing" can occur, at least when behaviors are somewhat ambiguous, and such effects seem to be mediated by both attentional and interpretive responses to the target (Fiske and Neuberg 1990). An early study by Bruner (1951) revealed that when perceivers were briefly exposed to an ambiguous picture of a man, what they saw depended on their own value orientations. Those with strong religious values tended to see the picture as a man praying, while those with strong values related to the work ethic tended to see the picture as a man working.

Short-term goals as well as stable values can influence impressions. When people like us, we tend to perceive them as having more power over our outcomes than when they dislike us. When people have the power to give us something that we want, we tend to perceive them as liking us more than those who behave the same way toward us, but have no power over our outcomes (Pepitone 1949). These effects could reflect wishful thinking and/or selective attention to those behaviors that would in fact facilitate our goals. We do pay more attention to people on whom our outcomes depend, and we form more positive impressions of their traits. For example, men formed more uniformly positive impressions of a woman when they were committed to taking her out on a date than when they were not (Berscheid et al. 1976).

Seeing what we want to see may induce a complacency that prevents our taking actions necessary to achieve our goals. Thus, it is not too surprising to find that an opposite effect sometimes occurs – people perceive in others the qualities that threaten their goal attainment. For example, Vallone et al. (1985) found that pro-Israeli and pro-Arab students rated the same US TV coverage of the Beirut massacre as biased against their own side. The direction of the impact of goals on impressions may depend upon whether or not we have prior reason to believe that the target may thwart our goal attainment. Thus, if the TV coverage of the Beirut massacre were attributed to an Israeli producer, then perhaps only pro-Arab students would view it as biased against their side.

Sometimes perceivers' goals influence what information they accurately detect rather than creating biased impressions. Dependent perceivers notice how affiliative others are, which is pertinent to their goal of eliciting approval and support in social interactions. On the other hand, dominant perceivers notice how assertive the same people are, information that is more pertinent to their interpersonal goals (Battistich and Aronoff 1985). Finally, when the perceiver's primary goal is to be accurate rather than to find particular goal-fulfilling or goal-threatening qualities in a target, biases in impression formation will decrease. Thus, perceivers who are accountable for their impressions show less stereotyped judgments (Kruglanski and Freund 1983), and those who expect to check their impressions against accurate information form more complex and accurate impressions (Tetlock and Kim 1987).

When we do not distort a target person's ability to fulfill our goals, then our liking for that person will vary as a function of whether or not they can do so. Assor *et al.* (1981) found that perceivers motivated to dominate others gave less favorable evaluations to a high- than to a low-status person, whom they could hope to dominate. On the other hand, perceivers who prefer to be dependent on others evaluated the low-status person less favorably than the high-status person, on whom they could depend.

Emotions
Can our impressions of others be biased by our emotional state? The folk psychology concept of seeing the world "through rose-colored glasses" says "yes", and several studies have documented the influence of transient moods on judgments of the attractiveness of others. People are perceived as more attractive by those whose mood has been elevated and as less attractive by those whose mood has been depressed. Even when a negative mood results from an impersonal event, like hot, humid temperatures or sad movies, it can result in decreased attraction to a person (Forgas and Bower 1988; Griffitt 1970). Interestingly, the negative emotion of fear has been shown to increase attraction under certain circumstances. Men who interacted with an attractive woman on a high, fear-arousing, suspension bridge were more attracted to her than those who interacted on a less frightening bridge (Dutton and Aron 1974).

The finding that fear has a different impact on impressions than sadness may reflect the fact that fear is a high arousal state. Easter-brook (1959) has proposed that an increase in arousal causes us to attend selectively to the most salient cues in a situation. Extrapolating to the realm of person perception, aroused perceivers should attend more to salient target characteristics and rate targets more extremely on pertinent dimensions. Such an attentional focus could account for Dutton and Aron's finding that fearful perceivers found an attractive female more attractive than did unafraid perceivers, since the former group would attend more to her salient, attractive features. Had her salient features been unattractive, fearful perceivers would presumably have found the woman less attractive than those who were unafraid. More direct evidence that arousal focuses perceivers' attention on a target's most salient characteristics has been provided by the finding that sexually aroused men rated attractive breasts and hips more positively than unaroused men did, while they rated unattractive breasts and hips more negatively (Istvan *et al.* 1983).

A selective attention explanation has also been offered to account for the impact of other positive and negative emotions on impressions. This explanation holds that a perceiver's mood makes certain information more salient. Happy people form more positive impressions of others because they pay more attention to positive information (Forgas and Bower 1988).

Misattribution provides another explanation for the impact of fear and other emotional states on attraction. This explanation argues that when perceivers are uncertain about the causes of their own emotional states, they may attribute a happy mood to liking for a target person or a sad mood to disliking for the target. They may also mistakenly attribute a highly aroused state to sexual attraction rather than to its true cause, such as a fear-arousing situation.

Other explanations for the impact of emotions on impressions include classical conditioning and priming. According to the classical conditioning explanation, a negative (positive) judgment of a target person is a conditioned response which results from associating the target with an unpleasant (pleasant) stimulus that elicits the unconditioned response of negative (positive) affect. Thus, a person who is present when you receive bad news may be associated with the negative affect that the bad news elicits. The priming explanation (see Clark and Isen 1982) assumes that when perceivers are experiencing a happy or sad mood, the concepts that are commonly used in these moods are more readily activated. Thus, when we feel happy, mood-consistent descriptive categories, such as pleasant or kind, will be primed and used to label ambiguous behaviors by a target person while the same behaviors may be labeled in a negative way when we feel sad. Level of arousal, rather than a specific mood, may also serve as a prime. Perceivers who feel highly aroused may label ambiguous behaviors with descriptive terms previously associated with that level of arousal (Clark *et al.* 1983). Classical conditioning, priming, misattribution, and selective attention may operate simultaneously or independently to yield the documented effects of emotions on impressions.

Demographic factors

Although there is little research concerning the influence of demographic factors on impressions, it seems reasonable to suggest that a perceiver's age, gender, or cultural background will exert a significant impact on impression formation by virtue of an impact on cognitive or affective factors. The content categories that are primed, perceiver expectancies, stereotypes, and schemas, as well as perceiver goals, may each covary with age, gender, or culture.

Jones (1986) has argued that one central cultural difference which may affect impression formation is temporal perspective. Specifically, he proposed that whites in the United States are more likely than blacks to make character judgments based on time-relevant behaviors. This is because US whites more often have a future-time perspective, which leads them to place greater value on time than US blacks, who more often have a present-time perspective. Thus, white perceivers may judge a person who is late as indifferent, unreliable, or lazy while black perceivers will not form these negative impressions.

Research documenting an effect of culturally linked perceiver goals on impressions has been provided by Bond and Forgas (1984) who argued that information about a person's conscientiousness is more adaptively relevant to Chinese than to Australian perceivers because the Chinese live in a collectivist culture where people are more interdependent. Consistent with this proposal, descriptive information regarding a target person's conscientiousness had more impact on Chinese than on Australian perceivers' impressions of the target's trustworthiness.

Sex stereotypes attributing greater interpersonal sensitivity to women suggest that a woman's impression of how others feel about her or themselves should be more accurate than a man's impression will be. Although there is little research on this matter, Snodgrass (1985) found that the effects of perceiver gender depend upon the sex of the target person as well as the role in which the perceiver is placed. People of either gender are more accurate in forming impressions of how a member of the opposite sex feels about them than how a same-sex person feels. Also, people of either gender are more accurate in forming impressions of how a target person feels about them when they are in a subordinate role than when they are in a leadership role. Thus, any tendency for women's impressions of others' feelings to be more accurate than men's may reflect the fact that women are more often in a subordinate role.

Target person determinants of impressions

Existing evidence affirms the common-sense view that our impressions of others' traits are strongly influenced not only by our cognitive structures and affective states – what we expect or want to perceive – but also by characteristics of the target person, including both behavior and appearance.

Trait and behavioral information

Primacy and recency effects

The folk wisdom that you should always "put your best foot forward" suggests that the first information that we acquire about a person will have a strong impact on our impressions, and considerable research evidence documents such *primacy* effects. A person who is described as "intelligent, industrious, and irritable" creates a more positive impression than one who is described as "irritable, industrious, and intelligent". Similarly, a person who shows successful performance before failure is perceived as more intelligent than one who shows failure before success (Jones *et al.* 1968). Sometimes, however, our impressions of others are influenced more by the information that we acquire last, which is called a *recency* effect. Recency is more apt to occur when the later information supplants early information, when the impression concerns an attribute that is likely to change over time as opposed to a stable trait, and when the perceiver's attention is focused on the later information (Jones and Goethals 1972). Despite instances of recency effects, primacy is probably more frequent in everyday life. As we learned in Chapter 2, perceivers (at least Westerners) tend to think of others as packages of stable traits, which fosters primacy.

Halo effects

Our impressions of others may be heavily influenced not only by early information but also by a single, central trait which is either very positive or very negative. Similarly, our evaluations of a particular trait may be influenced by the context in which it appears – a trait label is evaluated more positively when the person's other traits are positive than when they are negative. These are called *halo* effects. For example, Asch (1946) discovered that a single difference in a list of trait descriptors could make an enormous difference in the overall impression of two people. Impressions of a person described as "intelligent-skillful-industrious-*warm*-determined-practical-cautious" were very different from impressions of someone who was described as "intelligent-skillful-industrious-*cold*-determined-practical-cautious". When the trait "warm" was included in the list, the person was more likely to be seen as generous, wise, happy, and good natured than when it was not included or when it was replaced with the trait "cold".

Dilution effects

The impact of certain behaviors on impressions is weaker when they appear in the context of other uninformative, neutral behaviors than when they appear alone, a phenomenon that is called the *dilution* effect (Nisbett *et al.* 1981). For instance, learning that a person has extremely high college grades typically creates impressions of high ability and predictions of continued high performance. However, when information about high grades is embedded in the context of other behaviors irrelevant to ability, such as "drives a Honda, always wears plaid shirts, and formerly worked part-time as a draftsman", then predictions of continued high performance become much more conservative (Zukier 1982).

Primacy, halo, and dilution effects are often called "context effects", because they are concerned with how the impressions created by specific trait or behavioral information are influenced by the behavioral context in which that information occurs. Two major explanations have been offered for these context effects. In the constructivist tradition, Asch's explanation holds that the *meanings* of a person's various traits are influenced by each other. Thus, if the first information you receive about someone indicates that he is courageous and frank, then when you learn that he is also "undecided" you make take "undecided" to mean "open-minded" rather than "wishy-washy". Similarly, as noted earlier, the meaning of "industrious" may differ when it is coupled with the trait "warm" or "cold", and this may yield different inferences about other, unspecified traits. Thus, for Asch, a set of traits produces an integrated impression – a *Gestalt* – in which the meaning of one trait has been influenced by the others and which can generate inferences about other traits not given in the set.

Implicit personality theories provide a somewhat different constructivist account of context effects. Wishner (1960) found that the impact of the traits warm and cold on inferences about other traits depends upon their prior associations with those traits. Thus, "warm" and "cold" affect inferences of traits like "generous" and "happy" because these traits are all associated in people's implicit personality theories, whereas "warm" and "cold" do not affect inferences of other traits, such as "reliable" and "important". This suggests that the traits "warm" and "cold" need not be incorporated into different *Gestalten* to have the effects on trait inferences that Asch documented. Consistent with this suggestion, Asch found only negligible differences in the traits inferred from the traits "warm" or "cold" alone and those inferred when "warm" and "cold" were embedded in a context of other traits.

Although the trait associations in people's implicit personality theories may account for differing impressions of a cold and a warm person, the meaning of various traits may nevertheless be altered by the context in which they appear, as Asch originally suggested. This hypothesis has been tested by directly measuring the meaning of a target's traits (Hamilton and Zanna 1974; Zanna and Hamilton 1977). For example, if a person were described as "proud", subjects indicated what this pride meant to them on a scale ranging from "confident" to "conceited". The results revealed that the meaning of "proud" is placed closer to "confident" when it appears in the context of positive traits and closer to "conceited" when it appears in the context of negative traits.

In contrast to the constructivist explanations for context effects, Anderson's structuralist explanation argues that later or peripheral traits are *weighted less* than earlier or central traits rather than changed in meaning, and that the context in which a trait occurs influences its *scale value* – how positively it is evaluated – but not its meaning. The trait "proud" may be evaluated more positively when it appears together with the trait "warm", but its essential meaning will remain the same. Empirical efforts to settle this theoretical dispute have resulted in a draw, since neither theory is precise enough to generate data that the other cannot explain (Ostrom 1977). Whatever the theoretical explanation, the fact remains that if you want to write a personal ad that creates a positive impression, you should mention your most favorable attributes first, you should not mention uninformative, neutral attributes, and you might do well to consider how one trait descriptor may change the meaning of another.

Target and behavioral salience

A salient attribute is one which draws attention by virtue of properties such as intensity, color, size, or novelty. Not only do we attend more to salient people and salient behaviors (McArthur and Ginsberg 1981; Fiske 1980), but also our impressions of people are significantly influenced by the salience of their behaviors and/or their appearance. Such effects are more evident when various people or behaviors compete for our attention than when "vivid" or attention-drawing social stimuli and less vivid ones are presented separately (McArthur 1980; Taylor and Thompson 1982).

Salient behaviors

When a friend lets you down, does this outweigh a history of helpful behavior? Research indicates that targets' negative or extreme behaviors draw more attention and are generally weighted more heavily in impressions than their less salient positive or moderate behaviors (Fiske 1980). These effects may reflect not only the greater novelty and intensity of extreme and negative behaviors, but also their greater information value. Consider the moral domain, for example. Respect for others' property may at times be manifested by the thief as well as the honest man, whereas stealing is diagnostic of dishonesty. Accordingly, immoral behaviors should be weighted more heavily in impressions than moral ones. In other domains, such as ability, positive behaviors may be more informative and carry more weight in impressions. Stupid behavior can be manifested by anyone, but clever behavior is diagnostic of intelligence (Reeder and Brewer 1979; Skowronski and Carlston 1987).

Salient people

While it may often make sense for salient behaviors to have more impact on impressions than less salient ones, it is surprising that physically salient people create more polarized impressions when behavior is held constant. Studies investigating impressions of videotaped or live targets show more extreme trait ratings for those who are salient by virtue of having their face rather than their back to the perceiver; being seated in a bright light; exhibiting movement; possessing a physical attribute that is novel within the situation, e.g., minority race or sex; possessing a physical attribute that is novel in the perceiver's cultural context, e.g., wearing a leg brace, having red hair, or being pregnant on a college campus (McArthur 1981; Taylor and Fiske 1978).

Should you try to "stand out" from the crowd? That does depend on your behavior, since more polarized impressions of a salient than of a non-salient person can take the form of more positive or more negative evaluations. The direction depends upon the baseline favorability of the impression that the person creates. A person who is basically friendly and incompetent is perceived as even more friendly and more incompetent when she is salient by virtue of a novel physical attribute than when this attribute is concealed from perceivers (McArthur and Solomon 1978). Similarly, impressions of salient targets are polarized in the direction of their most frequent behaviors and the perceiver's expectations (Sanbonmatsu *et al.* 1987; Strack *et al.* 1982).

The tendency for increased attention to increase the polarization of impressions is consistent with research manipulating the frequency of perceivers' exposure to various people. Increased frequency of exposure to photos of negatively evaluated men – criminals – yields decreases in attraction, reflecting polarization of evaluations in the negative direction, whereas increased frequency of exposure to photos of positively evaluated men – *Who's Who* designates – yields increased attraction (Perlman and Oskamp 1971). Other research has shown that such divergent exposure effects require that positive or negative affective associations accompany the repeated exposures (Zajonc *et al.* 1974). In the absence of such associations, increased attention – that is *mere exposure* – seems to yield *increased* attraction. Interestingly, this effect is not dependent on consciously knowing or perceiving that the person is familiar, and it can be produced by subliminal exposure to photographs of a target person (Bornstein *et al.* 1987; Moreland and Zajonc 1979). Thus, the more we see people who elicit no particular affect to begin with, the more we will like them.

Illusory correlation

The tendency for evaluations of physically salient persons to be polarized in the direction of their most salient behaviors is related to illusory correlation effects in impression formation. Considerable research has demonstrated that when people are exposed to a series of paired events, their perceptions of the correlation between the events are most influenced by those pairs that draw attention (see Chapman 1967). In the realm of social perception, when people observe behaviors by members of two different groups, their perceptions of the correlation between group membership and behavior are most influenced by the actor–behavior pairs that draw the most attention. The result is an illusory correlation between salient people and their salient behaviors.

Hamilton and Gifford (1976) demonstrated the illusory correlation effect in impression formation by showing perceivers a series of slides, each of which attributed a desirable or undesirable behavior to a member of some abstract group of persons, A or B. There was actually no correlation between person group and behavior type, since the proportion of desirable and undesirable behaviors was the same for each group (see Table 3.1). However, perceivers' attention

Table 3.1   Behavior frequencies within minority and majority groups yielding illusory correlation

Behaviors	Group		
	Majority	*Minority*	*Total*
Desirable	18 (69)	9 (69)	27
Undesirable	8 (31)	4 (31)	12
Total	26	13	39

Note: The numbers in parentheses represent the percentage of desirable and undesirable behaviors performed by members of each group. The frequency of desirable and undesirable behaviors was reversed for half of the subjects such that desirable behaviors by minority group members was the least frequent category.
Source: Hamilton and Gifford (1976). Adapted by permission of Academic Press.

was drawn to one type of behavior and to one category of people by making each less frequent within the set of slides. As expected, subjects perceived an illusory correlation between being a member of the minority group and performing behaviors that were infrequent. Impressions of the minority group were more negative than impressions of the majority when negative behaviors were the infrequent ones, whereas the reverse was true when positive behaviors were the infrequent ones.

Other research has revealed that the strength of the illusory correlation between minority group members and infrequent behaviors depends upon factors that influence the salience of the various behaviors apart from their relative frequency of occurrence. The illusory correlation between infrequent behaviors and minority group members does not occur when it is the *frequent* behaviors which are more salient to perceivers either because they render the target similar to themselves (Spears *et al.* 1985) or because they are already associated with the minority group members (McArthur and Friedman 1980).

The phenomenon of illusory correlation is one possible source of negative stereotypes about real minority group members. In most social contexts, the person–behavior pairs that are most salient to perceivers consist of minority group members, who are infrequent, performing negative actions, which are also infrequent. The preferential weighting of these salient pairs in impressions creates the illusion that minority persons and negative behaviors are more correlated than they really are, thus yielding negative impressions of minorities.

Information in the face

Although modern psychologists scoff at the notion that character can be read from the face, facial qualities do play a central role in the layman's judgments of character. Liggett (1974) reported that over 90 per cent of surveyed university students believed there are important facial guides to character. Other research has shown that people who look alike are judged to be alike; when someone's appearance varies a lot, that person is not perceived to have stable traits; and perceivers more readily ascribe personality changes to someone whose appearance also changes (see McArthur 1982, for a review of this literature). Although people's facial appearance clearly influences our impressions of their traits, the question remains as to what facial characteristics communicate what traits and why they do so. Programmatic research is confined to two general facial qualities: attractiveness and babyishness.

Attractiveness

Although we believe that we really should not "judge a book by its cover", the fact is that a person's physical attractiveness has a very strong impact on impressions, and often outweighs other "more important" qualities. A classic illustration of such effects is provided in a study in which college freshmen were matched with a blind date for a big dance. A great deal was known about these freshmen, including their scores on IQ tests, personality tests, and ratings of their physical attractiveness. The only thing that predicted whether or not partners wanted to see their dates again was the date's attractiveness – the date's IQ and social skills made no difference (Walster *et al.* 1966).

The results of the blind date study do not necessarily imply that people do not care about anything but attractiveness when choosing a romantic partner. The fact is that attractiveness influences our impressions of a person's other attributes. More specifically, attractiveness creates a strong halo effect such that perceivers attribute positive qualities and abilities to attractive people and negative ones to unattractive people. Consequently, we may feel that we like a particular person because she has many positive traits, not simply because she is attractive. Impressions of men and women depicted in photographs revealed that those who are more attractive are seen as warmer, kinder, stronger, more sensitive, sexually responsive, interesting, poised, modest, sociable, outgoing, and as having a "better character" (Berscheid and Walster 1974). This strong tendency to perceive that "what is beautiful is good" is tempered a bit by some negative impressions of attractive people. In particular, attractive women are rated as more vain, egotistical, materialistic, snobbish, likely to get a divorce, and likely to have extramarital affairs (Dermer and Thiel 1975).

Whereas laboratory research has revealed a strong preference for more attractive partners, studies of the attractiveness of real-world couples support a *matching hypothesis*, which holds that we prefer those who are similar to ourselves in attractiveness (Feingold 1988). A reconciliation of these discrepant findings has been proposed by Kalick and Hamilton (1986), who constructed a computer simulation which demonstrates that significant matches in attractiveness could actually derive from everyone preferring the most attractive people: the most attractive men and women pair up, followed by the pairing of the most attractive remaining men and women, and so on. While this simulation does predict significant matches in attractiveness solely from a preference for attractive people, the correlations in within-couple attractiveness in the real world are somewhat larger than those that the simulation model would predict, which suggests that factors other than pure attractiveness-seeking are operative (Aron 1988).

More favorable reactions to attractive adults are not limited to situations involving heterosexual attraction. Good-looking people are less likely to be detected committing a crime (Mace, 1972). If they are caught, they are less likely to be convicted (Kulka and Kessler 1978; Stephan and Tully 1977). And, if they are convicted, judges and jurors are more likely to give lenient sentences unless the crime was one that exploited their attractiveness – e.g., a "con artist" (Sigall and Ostrove 1975; Stewart 1980).

More favorable impressions of attractive individuals obtain for targets of all ages. Cute babies are perceived as more likeable, smarter, and easier to care for than less attractive ones (Stephan and Langlois 1984). More attractive elementary school children are perceived by teachers as more popular and having better characters as well as more intelligent and more likely to get advanced degrees, even when the teachers know the children's grades, attitudes toward school, and work habits (Clifford and Walster 1973; Dion 1972). Attractiveness creates a more favorable impression even in old age. Attractive people between the ages of 60 and 95 are perceived to have more socially desirable personality characteristics than their less attractive peers (Johnson and Pittenger 1984).

More favorable reactions to attractive people obtain not only for targets of all ages, but also for perceivers of all ages. Indeed, even infants as young as three months of age show greater preference for looking at slides of attractive adult female faces than at faces rated as unattractive. Infants also prefer infant faces judged as attractive by adults, although they do not seem to show any preference for attractive male faces. Finally, 12-month-old infants show more avoidance of an unattractive stranger as well as more negative affect in her presence (Langlois in press). The foregoing research contradicts the adage "beauty is in the eye of the beholder". Not only is there a strong consensus among adults regarding who is attractive, but also at least some standards of attractiveness are manifest at too early an age to have been learned through cultural norms. Research revealing that faces viewed as attractive in Western cultures are also seen as attractive by non-Westerners provides further evidence that judgments of attractiveness may not reflect arbitrary norms (McArthur and Berry 1987; Thakerar and Iwawaki 1979). Cross cultural research has also revealed that the halo effect in impressions of attractive people is not limited to Western cultures.

While the attractiveness halo is very pervasive, two significant questions remain. First, why does attractiveness elicit such favorable impressions? And second, what qualities constitute attractiveness? Little research has addressed the question of what makes a face attractive. Indeed, many scholars have argued that this is an intractable question (see Hatfield and Sprecher 1986). However, ethologists and evolutionary biologists have proposed that attractiveness may be related to reproductive fitness and health (Eibl-Eibesfelt 1970a; Guthrie 1976). This is certainly likely at one end of the attractiveness continuum, where unattractive physical anomalies often coincide with functional problems that limit fertility or viability. Early in human history, the perception of negative traits in those with serious physical deformities may have been adaptive for species survival. Today such perceptions may be overgeneralized to those whose physical unattractiveness is less marked.[1]

If attractiveness is related to reproductive fitness and health, then it should be greatest for faces that appear healthy, of reproductive age, prototypical for their gender, and receptive. Supporting these predictions, women who are perceived as more attractive are also perceived as healthier and more fertile (Cunningham 1986), and both mate preferences and the perceived attractiveness of men and women across the lifespan correspond to reproductive capacity (Buss 1989; Deutsch et al. 1983). There is also some evidence that faces prototypical for their gender are more attractive than those that are not. Babyish features are perceived as less attractive in adult male faces than in adult female faces, which typically retain more infantile characteristics (Keating 1985; McArthur and Apatow 1983–4). Finally, transient facial characteristics indicative of receptivity are positively related to perceived attractiveness: heightened eyebrows, dilated pupils, and wide smiles increase the attractiveness of female faces (Cunningham 1986).

In addition to the possibility that more favorable impressions of attractive people result from the association of attractiveness with reproductive fitness and health, it is also possible that these favorable impressions are accurate (Goldman and Lewis 1977). In particular, the responses that an attractive person elicits from others may create the very traits that are expected. (See the section on "Accuracy of impressions", pp. 84–5, for a fuller discussion of such self-fulfilling prophecy effects.) Of course, such a process cannot explain why these traits are expected in the first place.

Babyishness

Reproductive fitness and health are not the only attributes whose detection is adaptive for the survival of the species. Detecting the attributes of infants is also adaptive, and considerable research has established that the facial qualities that characterize infants, such as relatively large eyes and cranium, do reveal their dependency and approachability. In addition, perceivers' adaptive reactions to the facial information that identifies infants and their attributes may be overgeneralized to adults who resemble the young. In particular, adults with the infantile features of large, round eyes, a short nose, a large forehead, or a small chin are perceived as physically weaker, more submissive, more naive, warmer, and more honest than those with more mature features (Berry and McArthur 1986). These effects of a babyface are also manifested in impressions formed of pre-schoolers, elementary school children, adolescents and elderly adults (Zebrowitz and Montepare 1990).

Like the halo effect for facial attractiveness, the impact of a babyface on impressions holds true not only for targets of various ages, but also for perceivers of various ages and cultural backgrounds. Infants as young as four months of age show a preference for babyish facial stimuli (McCall and Kennedy 1980), and impressions of weakness and warmth in babyfaced adults obtain for child as well as adult perceivers (Montepare and Zebrowitz-McArthur 1989). Such impressions also obtain for perceivers from a variety of cultures, even when the target is of a different racial background from the perceiver (Keating 1985; McArthur and Berry 1987).

The foregoing data suggest that, like the reaction to facial attractiveness, the reaction to facial babyishness does not reflect arbitrary cultural norms. Rather, it may be prewired or universally learned through exposure to babies. Like impressions of attractive people, perceivers' impressions of the traits of babyfaced people may also be accurate as a consequence of self-fulfilling prophecy effects. Once again, however, such a process cannot explain why these traits are expected in the first place.

The effect of facial babyishness on impressions goes beyond simple trait ratings. Judges in a simulated trial more often recommended the conviction of baby-faced men than mature-faced men for alleged crimes of negligence, which is consistent with the perception of babyfaced men as more naive. On the other hand, babyfaced men were less often perceived as guilty of intentional crimes, which is consistent with the perception of babyfaced men as more honest (Berry and Zebrowitz-McArthur 1988; Zebrowitz and McDonald 1990). Similarly, parents judge the misdeeds of babyfaced children as less intentional than the same behavior by mature-faced children who are equal in age and attractiveness (Zebrowitz, Kendall-Tackett and Fafel 1990). Whereas the impression of babyfaced persons as naive leads perceivers to judge them as more apt to be negligent, the impression that they are warm leads perceivers to judge them as more qualified for a job requiring nurturant qualities (Zebrowitz, Tennenbaum and Goldstein, 1990). The jobs assigned to children are also influenced by their facial maturity. Parents allocate less demanding tasks to babyfaced than to mature-faced children even when they know that all the children are the same age (Zebrowitz, Kendall-Tackett and Fafel 1990).

Information in the voice

A person's voice quickly and clearly reveals important demographic characteristics. Speech accents reveal a speaker's cultural background, and even a very brief voice sample reveals gender and age (Scherer and Giles 1979). In addition to influencing our judgments about people's demographic characteristics, vocal qualities influence our impressions of their traits. It should be noted that research assessing these impressions has separated the effects of voice qualities, such as loudness and pitch, from those of speech content using methods that will be described in more detail in Chapter 4.

A higher-pitched voice increases impressions of extraversion and decreases impressions of dominance (Scherer and Scherer 1981), whereas speakers with loud, fast or highly inflected voices are perceived as both extraverted and dominant. They are also perceived as more competent than those with soft, slow, or monotone voices, at least in Western cultures (Brown 1980; Robinson and McArthur

1982; Rose and Tryon 1979; Scherer and Scherer 1981). Korean men, on the other hand, are perceived by their compatriots as more competent when they speak slowly than rapidly, an effect attributed to the high valuation of silence in Korean culture and the association of fast speech with talkativeness (Lee and Boster in press).

Impressions of positive social qualities, such as friendliness and dependability, are also affected by voice qualities, with speech that is slow or accented yielding more negative impressions than un-accented or faster-paced speech (Giles 1979; Street and Brady 1982). Once again, the effects of speech rate are culturally variable, with Korean men evaluated as less socially attractive and less trustworthy when their speech is rapid (Lee and Boster in press). Finally, the timbre of the voice also influences impressions. A wide variety of socially undesirable characteristics are attributed to speakers with nasal voices, and those with flat voices are perceived as cold, sluggish, and withdrawn (Addington 1968).

Two explanations have been offered for the association of particular traits with particular vocal characteristics. The *accuracy* hypothesis holds that personality traits are externalized in vocal qualities, and that perceivers accurately infer speakers' character from their voices. Support for this hypothesis has been mixed. On the one hand, research has revealed no consistent relationship between impressions of speakers' traits and their actual traits as assessed by various personality measures (Kramer 1963). On the other hand, particular vocal qualities are in fact associated with various personality measures (Scherer and Scherer 1981). However, this evidence suffers from the difficulty of objectively measuring a speaker's personality traits. Often peer-ratings are used, and such trait ratings may actually be influenced by vocal qualities rather than being an independent and accurate assessment of personality.

The strong agreement among perceivers regarding a speaker's traits, together with the failure to find clear evidence for the accuracy of these voice-based impressions, has yielded the alternative hypothesis that the impressions reflect *speech stereotypes*. If so, then the question remains as to where these stereotypes come from. Montepare and Zebrowitz-McArthur (1988a) proposed that perceptions of submissiveness, incompetence, and warmth in people with certain vocal characteristics may reflect the resemblance of their voices to those of children, which do accurately communicate such traits. More specifically, they noted that vocal characteristics, like facial ones, covary with age and that just as "babyfaced" adults are perceived to have childlike traits, so may adults with immature voices. Consistent with this hypothesis, adult speakers reciting the English alphabet are perceived by US listeners as weaker, less competent, and warmer if they have childlike voices than if their voices sound more mature.

If stereotyped impressions of adults with childlike voices derive from the overgeneralization of reactions to children's voices, then perceptions of such adults should be culturally universal inasmuch as immature vocal and psychological qualities are universal. Consistent with this hypothesis, a second study by Montepare and Zebrowitz-McArthur (1988a) found that the impact on trait ratings of a childlike voice was very similar for Korean and US subjects. While this study compared only two cultures, the fact that they differ markedly in both cultural traditions and in linguistic background strongly suggests that the effects will replicate more widely. And what these effects indicate is that speech stereotypes regarding dominance, competence, and warmth may be explained at least in part by reactions to age-related vocal qualities. These data further reveal that, like the reaction to facial attractiveness and facial babyishness, the reaction to certain vocal qualities does not reflect arbitrary cultural norms, although it could be universally learned through exposure to children's voices.

Information in the body and gait

"Stature" refers not only to a person's bodily height, but also to social importance, and this double meaning is echoed in impressions of people who are large or small in physical stature. Subjects viewing a videotaped job applicant who appears taller than the interviewer rate him more positively than an applicant who appears shorter than the interviewer. Outside the lab, there is a positive relationship between height and leadership roles in academic and corporate settings. Height also influences elective leadership – the winners in US presidential campaigns have almost always been taller than the losers (Roberts and Herman 1986). Finally, it has been reported that the privileged status of tall men generalizes across a variety of cultures (Gregor 1979). Whether or not height is equally advantageous for women has not been investigated, although this phenomenon could contribute to the less privileged status of women, who are typically shorter than men.

Although there is evidence to indicate that different body builds are associated with different traits (Sleet 1969), there is little research assessing the impact of body build on impressions of a specific target person. Some evidence for such effects is provided by the finding that overweight individuals are less likely to be admitted to college than their equally qualified and motivated normal-weight peers. Similarly, overweight job applicants who were depicted on videotape performing two job-related tasks received lower recommendations for the job than did normal-weight applicants with identical task performance. These effects may reflect the stereotype that overweight people are less energetic and intelligent than others. (See DeJong and Kleck 1986, for a review of pertinent research.)

Explanations for the varied impressions of people with different body builds parallel explanations for impressions of people with different voices. The *accuracy* hypothesis, manifested in Sheldon's (1954) theory of somatotypes holds that people with different body builds actually have different traits. Although there is some evidence to support this hypothesis (Rees 1968), the correlation between physique and intelligence is too low to account for differential evaluations of overweight and normal weight people. The *stereotype* hypothesis holds that the impact of body build on trait impressions reflects social stereotypes. If so, the origin of these stereotypes still remains to be explained.

Like the effects of a babyface on impressions, the effects of a short stature and a pudgy body may derive from adaptive reactions to age-related variations in height and physique. Indeed, the reported impulse to protect or cuddle a target depicted in schematic drawings decreases as body height or body proportions increase in maturity (Alley 1983). Since children are less intellectually competent and less suited to leadership positions than adults, our perceptions of adults versus children may be overgeneralized to taller versus shorter and thinner versus chubbier adults.

Little research has examined the influence of gait information on impressions, although such information may be very important. Indeed, gait often has the advantage of primacy effects, since it is among the first things we see as a stranger approaches. Research using a "point-light" technique has been employed to study reactions to a person's gait independently of other aspects of appearance, such as face and body build. To create point-light displays, walkers are videotaped with reflective tape affixed to their main limb joints. When these tapes are played with the brightness reduced and the contrast maximized, the pattern of a person walking is represented as small luminous dots moving across a black background, rather like a stick figure made out of dots.

The results of the point-light research indicate that a person's gait reveals important demographic characteristics. Perceivers can recognize their friends from gait information; they can identify the relative, though not the absolute, age of walkers; and they can identify the gender of an adult stranger with better than chance accuracy. The gender of child walkers, on the other hand, cannot be discerned, which is consistent with the fact that gender identification for adult walkers derives from movement qualities associated with sex differences in the ratio of shoulder to hip width (Kozlowski and Cutting 1977; Montepare and Zebrowitz-McArthur 1988b).

A person's gait not only reveals demographic attributes, but also influences impressions of the walker's traits. Children and elderly adult walkers are perceived as less sexy than adolescents and young adults. And younger walkers are perceived as happier and more powerful than older walkers across the age span of 5–70 years. Moreover, impressions of adult walkers are influenced by the extent to which their gait resembles that of a young person. Youthful walking adults are perceived as happier and more powerful than their older walking peers (Montepare and Zebrowitz-McArthur 1988b). Finally, the impact of a youthful gait on impressions may be culturally universal, since Korean and US perceivers form very similar impressions of US walkers, and the impressions of both groups are similarly influenced by a youthful gait (Montepare and Zebrowitz 1990).

Like impressions of people with a babyface or a childlike voice, impressions of those with a youthful gait may reflect *gait stereotypes*, which manifest the overgeneralization of reactions to the young.[2] Alternatively, these impressions may be *accurate reflections* of the traits of adults with youthful versus older gaits. People who feel powerful and happy may walk in a more youthful manner than those who do not.

Accuracy of impressions

Are our first impressions of others accurate? This question was of paramount concern to early researchers in social perception. The fact that standardized intelligence tests could measure individual differences in cognitive skills led researchers to attempt to measure individual differences in social skills, and many studies correlated perceivers' impressions of a target person with measures of the target's traits. However, interest in the accuracy question waned when the research met with methodological and substantive assaults. The methodological issue derived from the difficulty of objectively measuring perceiver accuracy. The substantive issue derived from the growing evidence that the perceivers' cognitive and affective characteristics could have a marked impact on impressions. In the face of such perceiver effects, most researchers concluded that impressions could not be accurate, and attention was focused on the study of perceiver biases (see Nisbett and Ross 1980).

The measurement of accuracy

Two methodological problems arise in assessing accuracy. One is the *criterion problem*. If you perceive your classmate as irritable, we must have some objective measure of her irritability to ascertain the accuracy of your impression. Criteria employed by researchers have included interjudge agreement, the target's self-ratings, friends' ratings, personality test scores, and evaluations of trained clinicians. Each of these criteria is problematic. Your classmate's self-rating may be inaccurate either because she doesn't realize how irritable she is or because she is unwilling to acknowledge a negative trait. Her friends may be inaccurate because they do not see the irritability she manifests around strangers and people she does not like. Personality tests are often poor predictors of behavior (Mischel 1968). And even trained clinicians can disagree or be vulnerable to bias.

Despite the difficulty in finding acceptable criteria for assessing accuracy, some reasonable options exist. For certain accuracy questions, self-ratings are a valid criterion. For example, if perceivers are asked to guess how much a person likes them, then the person's self-reported liking for the perceiver has high validity as an accuracy criterion. Objective measures, such as the person's behaviors, also have high validity, although these are laborious to measure. If you predict your "irritable" classmate's responses to frustrating events, then we can ascertain the accuracy of your impression by seeing how she actually does respond.

A second methodological problem concerns *measurement artifacts*. Cronbach (1955) argued that differences between the perceiver's impressions and the criterion measures may reflect factors

Table 3.2 Elevation accuracy revealed in mean ratings across three traits

Rater	Target person			
	A	B	C	Mean
Criterion	8	7	6	7
Loren	7	8	6	7
David	5	6	7	6
Caleb	5	4	3	4

other than the perceiver's true accuracy. To illustrate these factors, let us assume that three perceivers (Loren, David, and Caleb) have rated three targets (A, B, C) on three trait dimensions (intelligent, warm, honest) and that the researcher's goal is to determine which perceivers are the most accurate according to the criterion of target self-ratings. Although self-ratings are used for illustrative purposes, the same measurement problems obtain for clinician ratings or peer ratings.

One perceiver may appear the most accurate simply because he uses the rating scales in the same way that the targets do. Consider the example illustrated in Table 3.2. Because the targets all give themselves high ratings, David and Loren, who use the high end of the scale when rating others, appear more accurate than Caleb because there is less absolute discrepancy between their ratings and the targets' self-ratings. Cronbach called this source of apparent accuracy *elevation accuracy*, which denotes the degree of correspondence between the mean judgment of a perceiver and the mean self ratings. What it reflects is similarity in the response sets of the perceiver and the criterion judge (in this case, the targets) rather than true accuracy in impressions.

Differential elevation accuracy denotes the perceiver's ability to order the targets accurately on all traits combined. As shown in Table 3.3, if we correct the elevation of each perceiver's score so that it matches the elevation in the self-ratings, then Caleb shows the highest accuracy inasmuch as his rank ordering of the targets is the same as the ordering of their self-ratings.

Stereotype accuracy denotes the perceivers' ability to order the traits accurately, averaging across target persons, as opposed to rank-ordering the targets, averaging across traits. The question is, are perceivers aware that people are highest in honesty, lowest in intelligence, and intermediate in warmth? As the mean ratings in

Table 3.3 Differential elevation accuracy revealed in mean ratings across three traits corrected for elevation

| Rater | Target person | | | Correction |
	A	B	C	
Criterion	8	7	6	—
Loren	7	8	6	0
David	6	7	8	+1
Caleb	8	7	6	+3

Table 3.4 reveal, a perceiver who fails to show differential elevation accuracy may nevertheless show stereotype accuracy. While failing to discern the relative favorability of the three targets on all traits combined, David accurately discerns the relative values of the three traits across these three targets. Stereotype accuracy is often viewed as an artifact, reflecting similar response sets in the perceiver and the criterion judge – i.e., in the example given, both tend to perceive much honesty and little intelligence. However, stereotype accuracy may sometimes be "true" accuracy in that it may reflect sensitivity to the actual traits of a particular sample of people.

Differential accuracy denotes the perceiver's ability to order the targets accurately on each trait after correcting for elevation or stereotype accuracy. This is the accuracy component that researchers regard as "true" accuracy because response sets are eliminated. However, at the time of Cronbach's critique of accuracy research, it was extremely difficult to compute the various components of accuracy, and this was a significant factor in moving researchers away from this area of research. Today, easy access to high-speed computers coupled with a new methodology, the social relations

Table 3.4 Stereotype accuracy revealed in mean ratings across three target persons corrected for elevation

| Rater | Trait | | |
	Smart	Warm	Honest
Criterion	5	7	9
Loren	9	5	7
David	5	7	9
Caleb	7	9	5

model, introduced by Kenny and his associates (Kenny and Albright 1987), have reduced computational difficulties.

The *social relations model* is a statistical model that focuses on when and how people are accurate rather than who is accurate. As such it considers the accuracy of a given trait impression across a set of perceivers and targets rather than accuracy of a given perceiver across targets and traits. The social relations model not only partitions accuracy into components, as advocated by Cronbach, but also uses each person as both perceiver and target so that accuracy can be assessed in ongoing social interactions.

According to the social relations model there are four types of accuracy. The first, called *individual accuracy*, measures how much perceivers' impressions of a target correspond to how the target behaves across interaction partners. The second, called *dyadic accuracy*, measures how much perceivers' impressions of a target correspond to how the target behaves with them. The remaining two types of accuracy reflect response sets. One corresponds to elevation accuracy and the other corresponds to stereotype accuracy.

Accuracy versus bias

This chapter is filled with examples of perceiver biases in impression formation. How can this evidence be reconciled with the thesis that perceivers may have accurate impressions of others? First, as noted by Schneider *et al.* (1979), *bias* refers to a kind of prejudice or prejudgment, and need not necessarily imply error. Second, taking an ecological approach, McArthur and Baron (1983) argue that perceptions should be viewed as erroneous only when they do not permit adaptive action – i.e., when they do not allow one to accomplish behavioral goals. They further suggest that perceptions that are indeed erroneous may reflect inadequate stimulus information, an inactive perceiver, and/or the overgeneralization of highly adaptive perceptual attunements. Funder (1987) likewise notes that perceptions should not be viewed as "mistakes" merely because they are wrong in relation to a laboratory stimulus. Rather, such perceptions may be right in a wider, more broadly defined social context and they may reflect processes that lead to accurate judgments under ordinary circumstances. Finally, Swann (1984) notes that perceivers are often concerned only with *circumscribed accuracy*, which is the accuracy of their impressions of targets' characteristics when they are in the perceiver's presence for a brief time in a limited number of contexts. This is similar to dyadic accuracy in the social relations model.

Defining an accurate impression as one that facilitates adaptive behaviors in circumscribed contexts rather than one that is unbiased and holds true across perceivers, contexts, and time raises the possibility that perceivers are more accurate in real life than they appear to be in laboratory experiments. Several factors can contribute to such accuracy. First, perceivers will form impressions on those trait dimensions that they spontaneously use in judging others rather than those provided by an experimenter, and judgments on the former dimensions are more accurate (Park and Judd 1989). Second, perceivers will be more likely to make trait inferences from behaviors that are seen in situational contexts, and such contextual information increases the accuracy of impressions (Shoda *et al.* 1989). Third, perceivers will be more highly involved in the task of forming impressions in real life, and high involvement and accountability yields more active information-seeking, more complex judgment strategies, and greater accuracy (see Borgida and Howard-Pitney 1983; Harkness *et al.* 1985; Neuberg and Fiske 1987; Tetlock and Kim 1987). Fourth, Funder (1987) notes that perceivers typically choose to interact with targets who are similar to themselves, in which case even simple judgment strategies such as the availability and representativeness heuristics can yield accurate impressions, despite being "biased".

In real-life interactions, the target's behaviors may also enhance accuracy. Indeed, personality judgments by acquaintances who have considerable experience with the target's behaviors show greater accuracy than those of strangers according to the criterion of subjects' self-judgments (Funder and Colvin 1988). Targets may increase accurate impressions by gravitating toward perceivers who view them accurately, by deliberately manifesting certain non-verbal cues (i.e., "looking the part"), or by providing corrective feedback to those with inaccurate impressions. Swann (1984) calls these *self-verification* effects.

Evidence of "self-verification" is provided in a study by Bond (1972; 1987) who found that targets behaved more warmly toward perceivers who expected them to be "cold" than toward perceivers who expected them to be "warm". However, such corrective feedback does not totally correct perceivers' impressions. Although students labeled as "slow" actually outperformed those labeled as "bright", teachers nevertheless rated the so-called "bright" students as higher in ability, even after teaching them (Swann and Snyder 1980). Similarly, perceivers expecting to interact with a warm person rated the target as warmer than those expecting a cold person even after receiving behavioral evidence to the contrary. However, perceivers were not immune to the behavior of the target, since their pre- and post-interaction impressions differed considerably. Moreover, the extent to which perceivers' post-interaction impressions moved away from their initial expectation was significantly correlated with the extent to which the target's behavior actually departed from that expectation (Bond 1987). In short, although perceivers' impressions may remain influenced by initial expectations despite self-verification efforts by the target person, these impressions do respond to disconfirming feedback, and with prolonged disconfirmation of expectancies, impressions may be completely corrected.

When corrective feedback from a target is weak or absent, then a perceiver's expectations may elicit the very behaviors that are anticipated, yielding accuracy via *behavioral confirmation*. Such effects are often called *self-fulfilling prophecies*. Consider, for example, the expectation that attractive people are friendly and warm. Research has shown that if a man has been led to believe that a woman is attractive, then he elicits more outgoing and warm behavior from her in a telephone conversation than if he thinks she is unattractive, thereby confirming his expectations (Snyder *et al.* 1977).

Such self-fulfilling prophecy effects may be mediated by subtle non-verbal behaviors that covary with the perceivers' expectations. When men think a woman is attractive, their telephone conversation is more animated, and this may elicit the warmth and sociability that they expect. When teachers think a student is bright, they smile more at the student, a behavior which has a positive impact on achievement (Harris and Rosenthal 1985). Similarly, negative attitudes of white interviewers toward black job applicants are manifested in more psychologically distant non-verbal behaviors toward the blacks, and such behaviors elicit poorer performance from applicants, regardless of their race (Word *et al.* 1974).

Like non-verbal behaviors, the perceivers' verbal behaviors can also vary with their expectations and elicit behavioral confirmation. If a man wants to find out whether or not the attractive woman with whom he is conversing is indeed sociable and outgoing, he may steer the conversation in the direction of sociable activities, which makes her sound sociable and outgoing even to someone with no prior expectations. Such hypothesis-confirming interrogative strategies have been found to occur even when perceivers are actively attempting to assess the accuracy of their expectations, rather than accepting them as true (Snyder 1981). However, the preference for hypothesis-confirming questions occurs in a relatively narrow range of situations. It is not manifested when an explicit alternative hypothesis is provided or when perceivers are allowed to generate their own questions rather than drawing on a biased pool of questions presented by the experimenter. Furthermore, there is a greater preference for highly diagnostic questions than there is for hypothesis-confirming ones (Higgins and Bargh 1987; Skov and Sherman 1986; Trope and Bassok 1982; Trope *et al.* 1984). Finally, it should be noted that when a hypothesis-confirming strategy does occur, it may serve us well. In particular, this strategy is more likely to be used when relatively extreme traits are expected, in which case the strategy is likely to be highly informative (Klayman and Ha 1987; Trope and Bassok 1983).

The question remains as to when self-verification or behavioral confirmation will occur. Research suggests that behavioral confirmation may occur only when perceivers have very strong expectations *and* targets are uncertain of their self-conceptions. For example, if you definitely expect Margie to be outgoing and sociable and if Margie is not sure how outgoing she is, then you are likely to elicit sociable behavior from her. On the other hand, if you are not confident in your expectation or if Margie is quite confident that she is an introvert, then self-verification prevails or there is a stalemate (Major *et al.* 1988; Swann and Ely 1984). These findings suggest that when a person actually has a particular attribute, then perceivers will detect it despite expectations to the contrary. Such detection is particularly likely when perceivers' interaction goals cause them to probe for the truth of their expectations (Darley *et al.* 1988).

Summary and implications

Consistent with a constructivist or "theory-driven" view of social perception, a number of perceiver characteristics have been found to influence impressions. These include short-term mental states, such as trait descriptor accessibility and expectations; stable mental structures, such as personal constructs, stereotypes, and schemas;

various information processing strategies, called cognitive heuristics; goals; emotional states; and demographic characteristics.

In keeping with a "data-driven" view of social perception, characteristics of the target person also exert a significant effect on impressions. The influence of the target's behavior is reflected in primacy, recency, dilution, and salience effects. The influence of the target's face is reflected in familiarity, attractiveness, and babyface effects. A person's voice, body build and gait also elicit distinct impressions. And the joint effect of salient target qualities and salient behaviors is reflected in illusory correlation effects. It remains for future research to ascertain the combined effects of a target's behavior, face, voice, and other physical attributes, an endeavor that is likely to complicate our predictions regarding impression formation (O'Sullivan *et al.* 1985).

Another significant gap in the impression-formation literature is the paucity of research examining the joint effects of the perceiver and the target. Do the stereotypes or schemas or affective states of the perceiver interact with the attributes of the target person to yield an impression that cannot be predicted from information about the perceiver or the target alone? It has been shown that perceiver effects are most pronounced when target information is weak or ambiguous. But, other, more interesting perceiver–target interactions remain to be discovered. The demonstration that the impact on impressions of attractive versus unattractive secondary sexual characteristics depends upon the perceiver's level of sexual arousal is an example of such emergent effects. More research like this is needed. Not only will it be of interest in its own right, but also it will focus researchers' attention on the rather neglected question of what functions impressions serve.

Another neglected question in the impression-formation literature concerns the origins of the various perceiver and target effects. Developmental and cross-cultural research is needed to answer questions such as where schemas come from, how cognitive heuristics are acquired, and how body build comes to influence impressions.

The vast majority of research on impression formation has focused on trait perceptions. Yet we frequently form impressions of more contextual qualities, such as social roles and relationships. Although some research has investigated these impressions (see Archer and Akert 1977), additional attention to this question is needed. Equally important is a systematic study of what specific *behaviors* and what specific *contexts* elicit what impressions. What actions and situations convey the roles, the relationships, and the myriad traits that we perceive? Although work on gait, vocal qualities, and other non-verbal behaviors (see Ellyson and Dovidio 1985) has begun to address this question, a more comprehensive investigation of such behavioral effects is needed. Similarly, although it has been shown that our impressions are influenced by the context in which an action is observed (Trope *et al.* 1988), a systematic mapping of context effects awaits future research.

The fact that "extrabehavioral" qualities have a profound effect on our impressions of others has thrown into question the accuracy of these impressions. Research on accuracy has been beset by measurement problems, including the difficulty of selecting an appropriate accuracy criterion and various measurement artifacts. However, recent theoretical and methodological developments have revitalized this topic, and we can expect our knowledge to grow significantly in the future.

It has been noted that the influence of extrabehavioral factors on impressions reflects biases which do not necessarily lead to erroneous impressions. For one thing, these biases may give rise to a chain of events that elicits behavioral confirmation by the target, in which case the perceiver's impression is indeed accurate. Moreover, to the extent that a perceiver is concerned primarily with perceiving the qualities of a target that emerge when she is interacting with him, only the circumscribed accuracy of this behavioral confirmation will be of interest. Finally, when a target's actual attributes strongly conflict with those that the perceiver's biases would lead him to perceive, the target's behavior will often refute this false impression.

Further reading

Battistich, V. A. and Aronoff, J. (1985). Perceiver, target, and situational influences on social cognition: An interactional analysis. *Journal of Personality and Social Psychology*, **49**, 788–98. This article tests the hypothesis that the perceiver's impressions of and liking for a target person reflect the interactive effects of the target's behavior, the perceiver's social motives, and the perceiver's expected relationship with the target. These findings are interpreted within the framework of a utilitarian model of social perception.

Bull, R. and Rumsey, N. (1988). *The social psychology of facial appearance.* New York: Springer-Verlag. This book presents a comprehensive review of research investigating the effects of facial appearance on social perceptions in a variety of social contexts, including dating and marriage, employment, the criminal justice system, and the educational system.

Jussim, L., Coleman, L. M. and Lerch, L. (1987). The nature of stereotypes: A comparison and integration of three theories. *Journal of Personality and Social Psychology*, 52, 536–46. This article contrasts predictions regarding the effects of outgroup stereotypes on impressions that are made by three theories – complexity-extremity; assumed characteristics; and expectancy-violation – and these divergent predictions are tested by examining how a job applicant's race, social class, and dialect affect the impressions formed by white, middle-class observers.

Swann, W. B. Jr (1984). Quest for accuracy in person perception: A matter of pragmatics. *Psychological Review*, 91, 457–77. This article argues that perceivers are quite accurate in predicting the behavior of targets in the circumscribed conditions with which they are most concerned – e.g., when the target is in the presence of the perceiver. It is further argued that social interactions between an active perceiver and target facilitate accurate perceptions.

Notes

1 It should be noted that this argument suggests that the attractiveness halo reflects negative impressions of very unattractive people more than it reflects positive impressions of the very attractive. To test this hypothesis, one would need to compare impressions of people who are low, moderate, and high in attractiveness. Unfortunately, most research has not included a moderately attractive comparison group.

2 The fact that a younger gait is perceived as more powerful, whereas a babyface is perceived as less powerful, may reflect the fact that the gait research assessed impressions of adults with a youthful gait rather than an infantile, toddling gait.

4 / PERCEIVING EMOTIONS

In contrast to the warning "don't judge a book by its cover" that is invoked when we form first impressions of people's traits, we speak quite comfortably about "reading" someone's emotions and of fear being "written" on the face. These metaphors suggest that we view emotions as transparent and that we expect our perceptions to be accurate. Given the importance of perceiving others' emotions and people's reluctance to come right out and tell us what they feel, it would be adaptive if this view of emotions were correct.

The assumption that people's expressive behaviors will specify their emotions is consistent with the emphasis on "data-driven" determinants of perceptions found in a structuralist approach to social perception. Although the bulk of the research evidence follows this layman's view of emotion perception, there is also evidence that such perceptions may be colored by the perceiver's cognitive and affective characteristics, as predicted by a constructivist approach.

The first question one must address in investigating emotion perception is what emotions are perceived. Next, we will review the methods for studying emotion perception, followed by theoretical accounts of how we achieve the ability to "read" emotions. We can then investigate what is it that we are "reading". Finally, we will consider whether or not emotion perception is influenced by perceiver characteristics such as culture, age, gender, mood and expectancies.[1]

The contents of emotion perception

People have implicit theories of emotions, analogous to their implicit theories of personality. Understanding this cognitive structure is important to the study of emotion perception because it may reflect and also influence the emotions that are perceived. Just as there are a host of words in the lexicon for describing personality traits, so are there a host of words for describing emotions. Bush (1972) located a total of 2,186 such adjectives in English, and Clore *et al.* (1987) identified 255 English terms that refer to genuine emotions, as opposed to affectively laden cognitive and physical states.

As in the case of trait terms, researchers have attempted to reduce the universe of emotion descriptors to a manageable and representative number. Cluster analyses performed on emotion categories formed by subjects who were asked to sort 135 emotion names according to similarity revealed six basic emotion categories: love, happiness (joy), surprise, anger, sadness, and fear (Shaver *et al.* 1987). Shaver *et al.* also found meaningful subordinate-level categories within each of the five basic emotion clusters. For example, love can take the form of "affection" or "lust"; anger can be, among other things, "irritation" or "rage", and sadness includes "shame" and "embarrassment" (see Figure 4.1).

It is interesting to note that the six basic emotion categories overlap substantially with those mentioned when people are asked to list all the emotions that come readily to mind, with the emotions that children learn to name first, and with the basic emotions identified by researchers who study emotional experience, as opposed to emotion perception (Schwartz and Shaver 1987). Only surprise fails to be included in laymen's spontaneous listing of basic emotions or to be used by many children, which is consistent with the suggestion that surprise is a state that precedes true emotions, becoming transformed into an emotion when the eliciting event is appraised as positive or negative (cf. Izard 1977). The basic emotion categories have also been replicated across diverse cultures as well as across age groups, and some have concluded that the central tendencies named by basic emotional terms are probably universal (Levy 1983).

A cluster analysis of emotion terms used by people living on a small Pacific atoll, Ifaluk, has provided more systematic evidence for cross-cultural universality in emotion categories. This research revealed five emotion clusters, four of which were very similar to the basic emotion categories in the English lexicon. These were labeled "emotions of good fortune", which map onto the Western clusters of love and joy; "emotions of danger", which map onto fear and surprise; "emotions of loss", which parallel sadness; and "emotions

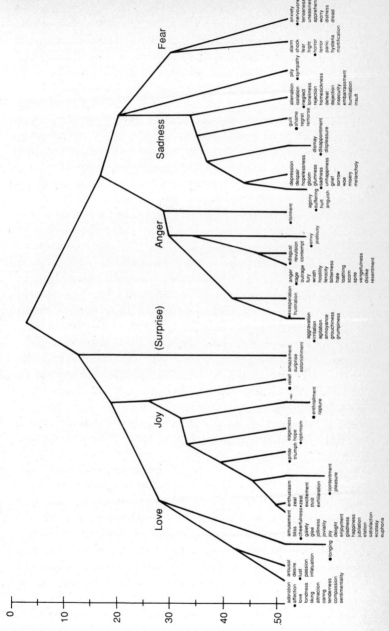

Figure 4.1 Hierarchical cluster analysis of 135 emotion names

Note: Cluster strength can be determined by referring to the numerical scale on the left. ● indicate empirically selected cluster names
Source: Shaver *et al.* (1987, p. 1067). Reprinted by permission of the American Psychological Association.

of human error", which parallel the Western category of anger (Lutz 1982).

Lutz has argued that there is a crucial cultural difference in these apparently similar emotion categories: for the Ifaluk, the clusters are based on the eliciting situation or antecedents, whereas, for Westerners, they are based on internal states. While it is certainly true that Western research on emotion perception has largely ignored the eliciting situation, there is evidence to indicate that such antecedents are in fact incorporated into Westerners' conceptions of emotion. Indeed, open-ended descriptions of various emotions reveal that the prototypical emotion incorporates a set of *antecedents* in addition to a set of physiological, cognitive, expressive, and behavioral *responses*. Moreover, research conducted in 27 countries spanning all five continents has revealed striking similarities in the perceived antecedents of the basic emotions as well as in the emotional responses (Wallbott and Scherer 1986a; Schwartz and Shaver 1987).

Each of the facets included in the representation of an emotion may affect its perception. For example, if a prototypical fear response is displayed (e.g., running and screaming) this may increase the likelihood of perceiving fear. Similarly, if an antecedent condition in the prototypical fear emotion is known to be present (e.g., being in the presence of a grizzly bear) this too may increase the likelihood of perceiving fear. With few exceptions, however, researchers have ignored the influence on emotion perception of information about antecedent conditions, and this chapter will consequently emphasize the influence exerted by expressive and behavioral responses. Table 4.1 lists the responses that subjects mentioned most frequently in their descriptions of five basic emotions.

Some researchers have taken a multidimensional approach to the representation of emotions, arguing that emotions are better conceptualized as points located on a small set of continuous dimensions than as separate, distinct, entities. Multidimensional scaling analyses have revealed that emotion terms can indeed be represented along two dimensions – evaluation (pleasure–displeasure) and a combination of potency and activity (arousal–sleep). Moreover, the relationship among the emotions in this two-dimensional space fits a circumplex model just as the relationship among traits has been shown to (Russell 1980) (see Figure 4.2). This circumplex model of emotion concepts fits the structure of the same emotion terms when

Table 4.1 Descriptions of responses in five basic emotions

	Face	*Voice*	*Body*	*Movement*
Fear	eyes darting	shaky screaming speechless crying	shaking sweating	hurried walk hiding not moving
Sadness	frowning	slow quiet monotone talking little crying	slumped	slow shuffling
Anger	frowning showing/ gritting teeth flushed	loud screaming crying	fists clenched	stomping throwing things walking out
Joy	smiling glowing	excited laughing talking a lot	energetic	bouncy jumping
Love	eye contact smiling			kissing touching hugging

Source: Shaver *et al.* (1987).

they are translated into several languages besides English – Chinese, Japanese, Gujarati and Croatian (Russell 1983). It also fits the organizational structure of children's emotion concepts (Russell and Ridgeway 1983).

For emotion theorists, the choice between a dimensional approach and a categorical approach depends upon how actual affective experience is conceptualized.[2] For those who study emotion *perception*, the question is which representation best captures the phenomenology of the perceiver. Although there are some advocates of the dimensional approach, emotion perception researchers have more often treated emotions as separate categories. Accordingly, most of the research reviewed in this chapter will consider the influence of target and perceiver characteristics on the perception of discrete emotion categories.

Figure 4.2   Two-dimensional scaling solution for 28 English
emotion-related words

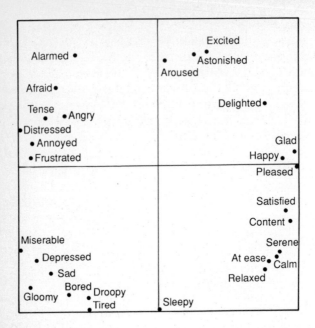

Source: Russell (1980). Reprinted by permission of the American Psychological
Association

Methods for studying emotion perception

Research on emotion perception includes studies designed to address
the following questions: Do perceivers agree about a target person's
emotion? Are perceivers accurate in judging emotion? What expressive information communicates an emotion? To conduct this
research requires emotion-perception measures, accuracy criteria,
and measures of the expressive information provided by the target.

Emotion-perception measures

The emotions that we perceive in others have been assessed with
measures that reflect various views regarding the contents of emotion
perception. Following a multidimensional approach, some investi-

gators have subjects rate various emotional expressions on scales such as "pleasantness" and "arousal". Others use categorical measures. One variant is the open-ended labeling of emotions by perceivers. A problem with this method is that there are many different words for the same emotion, and it is difficult to ascertain whether or not various subjects are perceiving the same emotion. For example, should the label "irritated" be treated as equivalent to the label "angry"? A common solution to this problem is to require subjects to choose among a fixed set of labels. Another measurement technique is related to the finding that people's conceptions of the prototypical emotion include a set of antecedents. Thus, some researchers have asked perceivers to choose from a set of emotionally evocative slides the one that they believe the target is viewing.

Accuracy criteria

Whereas we learned in Chapter 3 that it is very difficult to assess the accuracy of personality impressions, the criterion problem is more tractable when measuring the accuracy of perceived emotions. Nevertheless, none of the criteria to be discussed below is foolproof. Measurement artifacts like those that can confound assessments of accuracy in impression formation pose one potential problem. If researchers do not compute differential accuracy scores, then perceivers may appear to be more accurate in identifying a particular emotion simply because they are more likely to guess that emotion.

One accuracy criterion is the target person's *self-report*. Whereas people may not be able to report accurately on their personality traits, it is generally assumed that they know their own emotional states. Although self-reported emotions provide a better criterion for assessing accuracy than self-reported traits, people sometimes do not know their own emotions.

Another option for assessing accuracy is to determine whether the perceiver can identify the *antecedent event* eliciting the emotional response from a set of possible antecedents. A problem with this method is that it requires that the perceiver know not only what emotion the target is experiencing, but also what kind of event would induce that emotion. In so far as the events that induce various emotions differ from person to person, you may accurately perceive someone's emotional state without being able to guess what is making the person feel that way.

The measurement of *concomitant behaviors* may also serve to assess the perceiver's accuracy. For example, the perceiver's judgment may be compared with the target's expressive behaviors or physiological responses. Although the former criteria are frequently used, as described below, existing research has rarely employed the latter. Not only are physiological measures difficult to collect and analyze, but also it is only recently that a clear relationship has been established between specific emotions and specific physiological indicators such as heart rate, skin resistance, and skin temperature (Ekman *et al.* 1983).

Other measures of accuracy in emotion perception parallel those employed in impression-formation research. Thus, the accuracy of the perceiver's predictions about *consequent behaviors* may be determined. Or, the perceiver's judgment may be compared with the *consensus* of others, including those who are expert in reading emotions from face or voice. Such experts may make their judgments with the aid of scoring systems for measuring expressive behavior. These systems have been validated by determining that they differentiate targets who are in different emotion-eliciting situations, predict targets' reports of their emotional experience, and/or allow one to predict what emotional label perceivers will give to a target.

One system for measuring facial expressions is the facial affect scoring technique (FAST) developed by Ekman *et al.* (1971). FAST employs photographic examples to define movements within three facial areas (brow/forehead; eyes/lids; lower face) that theoretically distinguish among six emotions – happiness, sadness, surprise, fear, anger, and disgust (see Figure 4.3). Other methods for measuring facial affect include Ekman and Friesen's (1978) facial action coding system (FACS), Izard's (1979) maximally discriminative facial movement coding system (MAX), and Ermiane and Gergerian's (1978) *Atlas of Facial Expressions*. The *Atlas of Facial Expressions*, like FAST, employs still photographs as coding criteria. It also provides verbal descriptions of the facial behaviors. FACS and MAX, on the other hand, provide video illustrations of the facial movements in addition to other information. FACS is an anatomically based, comprehensive system that codes all observable facial actions. MAX was developed specifically for measuring emotions in infants and young children, and the illustrative photographs and video segments come from the spontaneous expressions of emotions by infants and toddlers.

Figure 4.3   Sample items from the FAST showing surprise

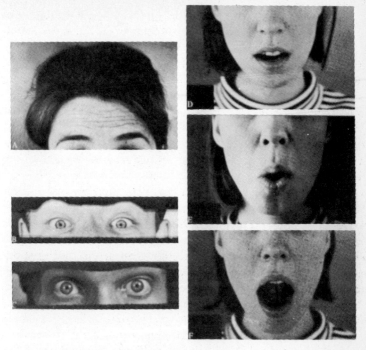

Source: Ekman *et al.* (1982a). Reprinted by permission.

Expressive information provided by targets

Faces

Facial stimuli in emotion-perception research have included schematic drawings and still photographs depicting expressions that are intended to communicate a particular emotion. In some cases, targets are simply asked to pose a particular emotion. In other cases, they are given a particular emotionally evocative scenario to communicate. Sometimes, but not always, methods such as FAST are employed to ensure the validity of the posed expression.

Although posed photographs are frequently employed, they have some serious shortcomings. They may be more exaggerated than spontaneous expressions, and they may also differ in some qualitative respects. Furthermore, we do not usually examine a facial expression for the length of time that people can look at still photos, since real expressions of emotion are quite fleeting. Finally, static faces do not provide the dynamic facial movement information that may be required for the accurate recognition of some emotions.

Videotapes of people who are actually reacting to an emotionally charged stimulus address the problems of posed photographs. Zuckerman *et al.* (1976) created such facial stimuli by videotaping targets while they watched pleasant or stressful films. Buck *et al.* (1972) unobtrusively videotaped target persons as they discussed their reactions to a series of emotionally evocative slides, and Malatesta and her colleagues videotaped targets while they recounted personal experiences that elicited each of several strong emotions (e.g., Malatesta, Izard, Culver and Nicholich 1987).

Although the use of spontaneous expressions has advantages over posed facial expressions, it also has a disadvantage. In the case of posed expressions, the investigator knows what emotion the target is "sending" and can therefore assess whether or not it is accurately perceived. This is more difficult to establish in the case of spontaneous expressions. One solution is to label the emotion according to the slide or film that the target was observing. However, it is possible that various targets react differently to the same stimulus. Another solution is to ask targets what they were feeling, but people may be unwilling or unable to report certain emotions. Furthermore, targets' self-reports may not be available to the researcher who has videotaped spontaneous expressions of emotion in the natural environment rather than the laboratory. A third solution is to use an objective coding system for facial movement, such as FACS or MAX, in order to label the target's emotion. As physiological indicators of emotions become more refined, these too may be used to label a target's spontaneous expressions.

Regardless of the facial stimuli that researchers employ, the question remains as to what specific facial attributes are communicating a particular emotion. One way to answer this question is to determine what emotion is perceived when various parts of the face are masked. Another approach is to use a system such as FAST to create composite faces, in which the emotional expression in various facial areas is manipulated independently. Still another method is to correlate ratings or physical measurements of the target's facial qualities with the perceived emotions.

Voices

A variety of techniques have been employed to investigate what emotion information is communicated by paralinguistic vocal qualities – that is, qualities of speech apart from the actual verbal content. The simplest method is to present speech samples in which targets express a particular emotion within a *standard content*. For example, they might recite the alphabet or read a standard passage in an angry or fearful or joyful voice. This method is akin to the use of posed facial expressions, and it suffers from some of the same problems.

A second method for studying the impact on emotion perception of paralinguistic speech qualities is *randomly spliced speech*. This involves cutting up the speech and randomly pasting it together again. Fortunately, computer technology allows the researcher to do this without literally cutting audiotapes into pieces. The result is that the content becomes unintelligible, while pitch and intensity information is intact. This method can be used with vocalizations that have been produced spontaneously in emotion-eliciting contexts, thus remedying the problem of artificiality in the fixed content method.

A shortcoming of randomly spliced speech is that it scrambles the natural temporal aspects of the speech, such as inflection, pauses, and speed, which may communicate emotion. A third method, which leaves such temporal factors intact, is *content-filtered speech*. This involves removing from the speech all frequencies above approximately 400 Hz, which renders the content of the speech unintelligible, while the natural sequencing and inflection remains. Like the method of randomly splicing speech, this method can be applied to spontaneous emotional vocalizations. A significant drawback, however, is that it removes pitch information as well as voice-quality information, such as shrillness or raspiness.

While randomly spliced speech and content-filtered speech each lose significant vocal information, the combined use of these methods can help untangle the impact of specific cues on emotion perception. For example, if emotion is accurately perceived in content-filtered speech, but not in randomly spliced speech, this would suggest that sequence information, such as speed or inflection, is crucial.

Synthesized speech is another method that can isolate the specific paralinguistic information communicating various emotions. Such speech is generated by computers which can vary one vocal quality at a time or particular combinations of qualities. Thus, for example, one can determine whether vocal intensity in and of itself influences emotion perception when all other speech qualities are held constant.

A fifth method for studying the impact of paralinguistic information on emotion perception is to employ *foreign speech*. This permits the presentation of spontaneous vocalizations in emotional contexts with all paralinguistic information intact, since the content will be masked for listeners who do not speak the language. A drawback of this method is the possibility that paralinguistic indicators of emotions are culturally specific. Thus, if subjects cannot identify the target's emotion, it is not clear whether this reflects a fundamental inability to "read" the emotion in voices or whether it reflects cultural differences in the emotion conveyed by certain paralinguistic qualities. Positive results, on the other hand, will be unambiguous. Still, it will remain for scientists using other methods, including ratings of vocal qualities, acoustic measures, or vocal manipulations such as those mentioned above, to ascertain exactly what specific vocal qualities communicate particular emotions.

Body movement
Like facial expressions and vocal qualities, bodily movements, such as gait, gestures, and postures, may communicate emotions. One technique for manipulating such information is the profile of non-verbal sensitivity (PONS) test developed by Rosenthal *et al.* (1979). This test contains two-second videotaped segments drawn from 20 different scenes enacted by a 24-year-old Caucasian woman. Each segment depicts an affect shown in one of several channels of nonverbal information, including the body from neck to knees, and the face and body down to thighs. (Other channels included in the PONS test are: face alone; content-filtered voice (CF); randomized spliced voice (RS); face plus RS; face plus CF; body plus RS; body plus CF; face and body plus RS; and face and body plus CF.)

The affects depicted are either positive or negative and either dominant or submissive. For example, a negative-dominant scene depicts the target criticizing someone for being late and a positive-submissive segment depicts her expressing gratitude. The perceiver's task is to select from two short written descriptions of the scene the one which is correct. As is true for other manipulations of posed emotion, the generalizability of the PONS test to spontaneous expressions is uncertain. The generalizability of the PONS test is also limited by its use of a single target.

While the PONS test may reveal whether or not particular emotions can be communicated by the body, it was not designed to reveal what specific aspects of bodily movement convey those emotions. To do so requires correlating ratings or measurements of the movement patterns with the emotions that are perceived. Although several systems have been developed for measuring movement patterns (see Rosenfeld 1982, for a review), these notational systems have not been used to measure body movement patterns in emotion-perception research, perhaps because they are laborious to conduct and there are no theoretical principles to guide the selection of movement patterns to measure.

Because movement information is embedded within a particular body, perceptions of a target's emotions may be influenced by body build as well as by movement patterns *per se*. The point-light display methodology described in Chapter 3 addresses this confound by separating the information provided by movement patterns from that provided by other visual cues. Movement patterns are much more salient in the point-light display than when embedded in a full-body videotape, and are thus easier for judges to rate. There are also automated devices available for measuring various motion parameters (e.g., velocities and accelerations) in point-light displays (Gustafsson and Lanshammar 1977).

A system called *proxemics* (Hall 1979) is also pertinent to measuring bodily movements and positions that may influence emotion perception, although this system has been employed largely to study cross-cultural differences in bodily contact norms. Hall's coding dimensions include postural identifiers (prone, standing, sitting, or squatting), orientation (toward others or away from others, measured by direction and angle), kinesthetic factors (capacity for touching), and forms of touching.

Multimodal information

In order thoroughly to identify the expressive information that perceivers utilize in judging emotion, research is required that takes a multimodal approach. The fact that perceivers *can* utilize information in the face or in the voice or in the body does not necessarily imply that they do so when each is combined with other information that may neutralize or even contradict it. Several paradigms have been employed to investigate the relative impact of each modality or "channel" on emotion perception.

One method is to present conflicting expressive information in two different channels to see which has the greatest effect on emotion perception. Another technique is to compare perceptions based on multiple channels with those based on single-channel expressions of the same emotion. These comparisons can reveal whether the emotion that is perceived in a visual channel alone is still perceived when voice information is added and vice versa. Appropriate comparisons can also reveal which channel contributes the most to the perception of particular emotions when all channels are available.

Theories of emotion perception

Evolutionary position

Darwin (1872) argued that the basic expressions of emotion evolved in humans because their adaptive value for social communication promoted species survival. If your friend's facial or vocal expressions communicate fear to you, this may permit you to evade danger and/or to protect your friend. Your friend's emotional expression has thus fostered behaviors that have adaptive consequences for both of you. Similarly, the expression of anger, joy, or other emotions may facilitate adaptive actions. According to Darwin's evolutionary position, individuals who manifest emotional expressions that serve adaptive social interactions have been favored through natural selection – e.g., those who did not clearly display fear were not saved from danger. Individuals who recognize and respond to these emotional expressions would also be favored through natural selection – those who did not recognize fear were themselves more vulnerable to danger, not to mention the greater vulnerability of their offspring.

Although Darwin's theoretical position argues for innate, culturally universal accuracy in emotion perception, he did acknowledge the possibility of error. In particular, he suggested that perceptions could be biased by the perceiver's own emotional state or by the perceiver's expectations. Nevertheless, the evolutionary position is primarily a *structuralist* approach, since the external stimulus information provided in a target's expressive behavior is viewed as the primary determinant of emotion perception.

Cultural relativist position

In contrast to Darwin's evolutionary view, the cultural relativist position holds that emotion perception is learned (see Birdwhistell

1970). Just as verbal expressions have different meanings from culture to culture, so do non-verbal expressions, and the person who looks or sounds afraid in one culture will not necessarily communicate fear in another. This position may be viewed as a *constructivist* approach to emotion perception in the sense that a given culture has imposed meaning on particular expressive behaviors, which is not given by the expressions themselves.

Integrative positions

A middle position in the nature–nurture debate on emotion perception is suggested by Ekman and Friesen's (1975) model of expression production. This model holds that although an emotional stimulus initiates facial expressions that are innately associated with that emotion, the actual expression will also be influenced by *display rules*, which are culturally transmitted rules regarding what emotional expressions are appropriate to display. Thus, people might *modulate* an expression, increasing or decreasing its intensity relative to what they actually feel because the felt emotion is socially unacceptable. Such unacceptability might even lead a person to *mask* the felt emotion – e.g., keeping a "stiff upper lip" – or to *simulate* a different one. Finally, people may *qualify* an expression by adding another expression to comment on the felt one. For example, a person might scowl after expressing fear to communicate contempt for his own weakness. The implication of Ekman and Friesen's model is that in order to perceive an emotion accurately, we must be sensitive to innate and universal expressive features as well as to learned and culturally variable ones.

The ecological approach to social perception proposed by McArthur and Baron (1983) also represents a middle position in the nature–nurture debate. Like the evolutionary position, the ecological approach predicts pancultural accuracy in emotion perception. However, it allows that such accuracy could derive from universal learning experiences as well as from an innate sensitivity to emotional expressions. It further suggests that sensitivity to expressive features depends not only on their relevance to species survival, but also on their relevance to an individual perceiver's goal attainment, which also implicates learning experiences. For example, perceivers may become more attuned to the emotional meaning in expressions of those who are familiar to them, since it is most adaptive to perceive accurately the emotions of those with whom we interact. An implicit assumption in this prediction is that emotional expressions do differ somewhat from person to person, since there would be no advantage to familiarity if they did not. Thus, like Ekman and Friesen's model, the ecological position suggests that in order accurately to perceive an emotion, perceivers must be sensitive to universal expressive features as well as to individually variable ones.

Target person determinants of emotion perception

Research concerning target person determinants of emotion perception has addressed four general questions concerning targets' expressive accuracy: Can people accurately express in their face, voice, body, and/or intermodally the emotion that they intend to communicate? Do people spontaneously express the emotion that they are experiencing in a manner that permits accurate identification? What expressive information conveys a target person's emotion to perceivers? Are there differences among targets in expressive accuracy? Although a variety of target differences have been studied (cf. Buck 1984; Rosenthal *et al.* 1979), space limitations restrict the present review to the demographic characteristics of culture, age, and gender.

In reality, targets' expressive accuracy cannot easily be separated from perceivers' judgmental accuracy. This is because the expressive accuracy of targets is often assessed by determining how reliably their emotions are judged by perceivers. Nevertheless, these two topics are often separated, as in the present chapter. This section will emphasize the influence, or lack thereof, of different targets. The next section, on perceiver determinants of emotion perception, will emphasize the influence, or lack thereof, of different perceivers.

The face

Expressive accuracy
Considerable research has demonstrated that at least six basic emotions can be communicated by facial expressions – happiness, fear, surprise, anger, disgust, and sadness (Ekman *et al.* 1982a). Expressions of these emotions posed in still photographs or in

motion picture films by a variety of targets, including a culturally
isolated group from New Guinea, are accurately identified. An
overview of some of the research demonstrating such accuracy is
provided in Table 4.2. Whereas all six basic emotions are labeled
with better than chance accuracy, most studies find that happiness is
more accurately expressed than sadness or anger, a finding that has
been documented across a large number of targets from various
cultures and age groups (see Ekman 1972; Izard *et al.* 1980; Shimoda
et al. 1978; Zuckerman and Przewuzman 1979). Interestingly,
whereas happy faces are more accurately labeled, an angry face is
more quickly perceived in a crowd of neutral faces (Hansen and
Hansen 1988). This finding may reflect the operation of automatic
information processing in contrast to the conscious processing
operative when expressions are labeled (Bargh 1984).

Research has revealed that spontaneous emotional expressions
can also be identified accurately. Still photographs or brief excerpts
from motion picture films depicting faces as they appeared during a
stress-inducing interview are rated as more unpleasant than faces
photographed during a relief-inducing part of the interview (Ekman
1965; Howell and Jorgenson 1970). Using the slide-viewing
paradigm in which perceivers observe targets' videotaped faces as
they watch and talk about slides designed to elicit affect, Buck *et al.*
(1972; 1974) found that the rated pleasantness of the targets'
emotional responses were significantly correlated with their
self-ratings. Moreover, the targets' facial expressions accurately
communicated the type of slide being viewed.

The accurate identification of spontaneous facial expressions of
emotion also obtains when perceivers are asked to provide discrete
emotion labels rather than dimensional ratings. Wagner *et al.* (1986)
covertly videotaped targets as they watched emotionally loaded
slides, after which targets labeled their own emotional reactions.
Agreement between the targets' own emotional labels and those
given by perceivers who watched the videotapes was highest for
happiness, which is consistent with results for posed emotions.
Significant agreement was also found for anger and disgust, and the
accurate identification of sadness approached significance. Fear and
surprise, on the other hand, were not accurately labeled. This may
reflect a tendency to confuse these two emotions which has been
reported in a number of studies. Such confusion may be explained by
Izard's (1977) suggestion, mentioned earlier, that surprise is a state
that precedes true emotions, becoming transformed into an emotion

Table 4.2   Accuracy studies of posed behavior*

Methodology	Woodworth (1938) Kanner (1931)	Woodworth (1938) Feleky (1914)	Dusenbury & Knower (1938)	D. F. Thompson & Meltzer (1964)	Levitt (1964)	Osgood (1966)	Drag & Shaw (1967)	Kozel & Gitter (1968)	Ekman & Friesen (1965)
Number of stimulus persons	1	1	2	50	50	50 or 5[a]	48	10	6
Number of stimuli for each emotion	1–3	2	2	100	50	5	10	5	2
Method of presenting stimuli	Still	Still	Still	Live	Motion picture film	Live	Live	Motion picture film	Still
Number of observers	409	100	388	4	24	110	4	44	57
Number of judgment categories other than those listed below	b	1	5	2	0	6	3	1	3

Percentage of accurate judgments on:

happy	—	93	100	76	86	55	71	86	65
surprise	76	77	86	—	43	38	68	69	—
fear	75	66	93	74	58	16	62	80	35
anger	32	31	92	60	62	39	42	79	—
sad	33	70	84	52	—	19	49	59	88
disgust/contempt	66	74	91	67	45	50	41	55	0
pleasantness factor	—	—	—	—	—	0.38[c]	—	—	—
intensity factor	—	—	—	—	—	0.32[c]	—	—	—
control factor	—	—	—	—	—	0.50[c]	—	—	—

[a]Although there was a total of 50 stimulus persons, each emotion was posed by only 5 people.

[b]Kanner allowed free labeling; in reanalyzing his results, many of his responses, which were not obviously in one of the categories, were not verified.

[c]These are correlations between intended emotion and observed emotion when the emotion word data were reordered in terms of factor scores.

* *Note:* Accuracy values were calculated by dividing the number of correct category responses given to a particular expression by the total number of responses given.

Source: Ekman *et al.* (1982a). Reprinted by permission.

when the eliciting event is appraised as positive or negative. Perhaps surprise is a frequent precursor of fear.

In contrast to the foregoing evidence for expressive accuracy in spontaneous emotions, Malatesta, Izard, Culver and Nicolich (1987) found that perceivers could not accurately label targets' self-reported emotions from videotapes depicting their faces as they recounted sad, angry, or fearful experiences. On the other hand, perceivers did agree with each other in their labeling of the facial expressions, and these labels concurred with objective measures of the facial expressions made with Izard's MAX system. Thus, the spontaneous facial expressions manifested by targets in this study were reliably different from the emotional experience they were asked to recount, even though their self-rated emotions matched that experience.

A crucial methodological difference between the Malatesta, Izard, Culver and Nicolich study and those that did find expressive accuracy in spontaneous emotions (Wagner *et al.* 1986; Buck *et al.* 1972; 1974) is that targets in the former study thought they were being observed by the experimenter on closed circuit television, while those in the latter studies thought they were in private. A detailed analysis of the expressions manifested by "observed" targets revealed that they were often masked or blended with expressions characteristic of other emotions, perhaps as a consequence of cultural display rules (Malatesta and Izard 1984). Because emotional expressions that are made in private are less influenced by display rules, they may be "purer" and thereby easier to identify. It thus appears that although people *can* communicate various emotions via their spontaneous facial expressions, they may not always do so in the course of experiencing actual emotions in a social interaction.

Expressive information
Shakespeare wrote of "dull-eyed melancholy" (*Perides*, I, ii, 2) and "the contempt and anger of his lip" (*Twelfth Night*, III, i, 159), suggesting that there are specific facial components that give rise to the perception of each emotion. Scientists have confirmed this view. Ekman *et al.* (1971) applied the FAST to 51 photographs representing 28 different targets. All of these photographs had been assigned to one emotion category by at least 70 per cent of observers judging the presence of one or two emotions from a list of six – happiness, sadness, anger, surprise, fear, and disgust. Each photograph was scored with the FAST procedure by masking to reveal only one facial

Table 4.3   Appearance of the face for six emotions

	Brows-forehead	Eyes-lids	Lower face
Surprise	Raised curved eyebrows; long horizontal forehead wrinkles	Wide opened eyes with schlera showing above and often below the iris; signs of skin stretched above the eyelids and to a lesser extent below	Dropped-open mouth; no stretch or tension in the corners of the lips, but lips parted; opening of the mouth may vary
Fear	Raised and drawn together brows; flattened raised appearance rather than curved; short horizontal and/or short vertical forehead wrinkles	Eyes opened, tension apparent in lower lids, which are raised more than in surprise; schlera may show above but not below iris; hard stare quality	Mouth corners drawn back, but not up or down; lips stretched; mouth may or may not be open
Anger	Brows pulled down and inward, appear to thrust forward; strong vertical, sometimes curved forehead wrinkles centered above the eyes	No schlera shows in eyes; upper lids appear lowered, tense and squared; lower lids also tensed and raised, may produce an arched appearance under eye; lid tightening may be sufficient to appear squinting	Either the lips tightly pressed together or an open, squared mouth with lips raised and/or forward; teeth may or may not show
Disgust	Brows drawn down but not together; short vertical creases may be shown in forehead and nose; horizontal and/or vertical wrinkles on bridge of nose and sides of upper nose	Lower eyelids pushed up and raised, but not tensed	Deep nasolabial fold and raising of cheeks; mouth either open with upper lip raised and lower lip forward and/or out, or closed with upper lip pushed up by raised lower lip; tongue may be

Table 4.3   *Continued*

	Brows-forehead	Eyes-lids	Lower face
			visible forward in mouth near the lips, or closed with outer corners pulled slightly down
Sadness	Brows drawn together with inner corners raised and outer corners lowered or level, or brows drawn down in the middle and slightly raised at inner corners; forehead shows small horizontal or lateral curved and short vertical wrinkles in center area, or shows bulge of muscular contraction above center of brow area	Eyes either glazed, with drooping upper lids and lax lower lids, or upper lids are tense and pulled up at inner corner, down at outer corner with or without lower lids tensed; eyes may be looking downward or eyes may show tears	Mouth either open with partially stretched, trembling lips, or closed with outer corners pulled slightly down
Happiness	No distinctive brow-forehead appearance	Eyes may be relaxed or neutral in appearance, or lower lids may be pushed up by lower face action, bagging the lower lids and causing eyes to be narrowed; with the latter, crow feet apparent, reaching from outer corner of eyes toward the hairline	Outer corners of lips raised, usually also drawn back; may or may not have pronounced nasolabial fold; may or may not have opening of lips and appearance of teeth

Source: Ekman (1972). Reprinted by permission.

area and comparing it with the FAST criterion photographs for that area. Table 4.3 summarizes the facial characteristics associated with each of the six emotions. It is interesting to compare the data in this table with those presented in Table 4.1. Whereas many of the responses mentioned in laypersons' descriptions of emotions do indeed differentiate facial expressions of these emotions as assessed by the FAST, some, such as "flushed", "glowing", and "eyes darting" cannot be detected with the FAST procedure.

In an ingenious study of primitive masks from a variety of cultures, Aronoff *et al.* (1988) determined that the facial qualities that communicate anger are characterized by diagonality and angularity. Compared with non-threatening masks, those known to have a threatening social function tended to have more diagonal and angular features, such as vertical lines between the eyebrows, diagonal cheekbone lines, triangular eyes and nose, and pointed chin, beard, and ears. A second study further revealed that diagonal lines and acute angles in and of themselves are perceived as more threatening than straight lines or curvilinear patterns.

Whereas the preceding studies identified static facial qualities that communicate various emotions, Frijda (1953) compared the impact of dynamic and static facial qualities on the accurate identification of spontaneous emotional expressions. This was accomplished by showing perceivers film clips of naturally occurring expressions that the target person had labeled and slides of the same expressions taken from the films. The results revealed considerably greater expressive accuracy for the film clips than the slides, which suggests that dynamic facial cues are important for the identification of spontaneous emotional expressions.

Adapting the point-light technique described above, Bassili (1979) found that dynamic facial information is itself sufficient for the accurate identification of posed emotions even when no information about the shape and position of facial features is discernible. As in research with full-face stimuli, happiness was easier to identify than sadness or fear, though surprise was easiest of all to identify from movement information alone. Bassili's study also elucidated the patterns of facial movement for each emotion, and his results are summarized in Figure 4.4.

Figure 4.4   Movement patterns yielded by six emotions (from time exposures of television displays)

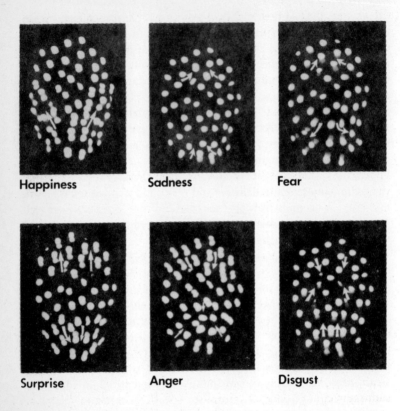

Happiness   **Sadness**   **Fear**

Surprise   **Anger**   **Disgust**

Happiness: Upward displacement of each side of the mouth and the cheeks
Sadness: Slight upward displacement in the chin area and an inward and upward movement of the eyebrows
Fear: Downward and outward movement near the mouth and the same eyebrow movement as sadness
Surprise: Strong upward displacement of the brows coupled with a strong downward displacement of the jaw
Anger: Downward movement in the forehead area and compression in the mouth area
Disgust: Upward movement on the sides of the nose, the cheeks, and the chin

Source: Bassili (1979, p. 2055). Adapted by permission of the American Psychological Association

The voice

Expressive accuracy
Like the emotions posed in facial expressions, those enacted in vocal expressions can be identified. Several studies have shown that targets can accurately communicate a variety of emotions while reciting the alphabet (Davitz and Davitz 1959; Frick 1985). Whereas positive emotions are judged more accurately than negative ones from facial expressions, the reverse has been found for vocal expressions posed in content-free speech (Burns and Beier 1973; Davitz and Davitz 1959). Greater expressive accuracy for negative than for positive emotions holds true for children as well as adults (Fenster *et al.* 1977), and the superior communication of negative expressions appears to be most evident when the target is from a different culture than the speaker (Beier and Zautra 1972; Van Bezooijen *et al.* 1983).

Just as posed facial expressions of emotion may differ from spontaneous ones, so may the intentional portrayal of emotion in some standardized speech content differ from vocal expressions of emotion in everyday life. Unfortunately, the existing literature does not answer the question of whether speakers communicate their emotional state via spontaneous vocal cues and, if so, which emotions are most accurately communicated. Although one study has used naturally occurring vocal expressions, it could not determine the accuracy of perceptions because it did not establish what emotion the speakers were actually experiencing. However, it did demonstrate high interjudge agreement in the perception of anger and sadness in content-filtered naturalistic speech (Soskin and Kauffman 1961).

Expressive information
Efforts to identify what particular vocal qualities communicate what emotions have not met with much success. Individual qualities are not diagnostic, since they tend to be associated with more than one emotion. For example, a louder voice is associated with both happiness and anger. Some attempts to find a defining configuration of qualities for each emotion have also been unsuccessful. Scherer (1979) created a profile for a variety of emotions using five features: loudness, tempo, pitch level, range, and variability. However, even these five features could not adequately discriminate the emotions.

Although anger and sadness had opposite profiles, the profiles for anger and joy were the same (see Table 4.4).

Frick (1985) has suggested that *dynamic* qualities, which have a temporal component, figure importantly in the vocal qualities that communicate various emotions. Consistent with this suggestion, he reports that presenting utterances backwards severely impairs recognition of emotion. Additional evidence for the importance of dynamic qualities is judges' agreement that a distinguishing feature of anger is an irregular up and down inflection, while a downward inflection is unique to sadness, and happiness has an upward inflection (Davitz 1964b).

Scherer (1986) suggested that the key to the vocal differentiation of emotions may be *voice quality*, which is the timbre of the voice. This is what leads us to label a voice as nasal, shrill, harsh, etc. Based on an analysis of the effects of various emotional states on phonation and articulation, Scherer proposed three voice qualities (narrow-wide, lax-tense, and full-thin) that, in combination, can differentiate the basic emotions (see Table 4.5). There is considerable support for his predictions regarding the emotions that will be marked by a tense or lax voice, since these vocal qualities are related to parameters of pitch, intensity, and speech rate that researchers have frequently assessed. However, his predictions regarding the other two voice qualities have not yet been adequately tested.

Gait, posture, and gesture

Expressive accuracy

William James believed that walking alongside a person and observing or mimicking his gait would reveal what the walker was feeling, and Montepare *et al.* (1987) have provided empirical evidence to support this claim. Sadness, anger, and happiness were accurately communicated in the gaits of walkers who were videotaped while they imagined themselves in various emotion-eliciting situations – e.g., the sadness situation involved pretending that they were walking down a hospital corridor after visiting a friend who was in a serious accident.

Sogon and Izard (1987) investigated the communication of emotions in posed body movements. Japanese targets were videotaped from the back as they depicted the emotions of joy, surprise, fear, sadness, disgust, anger and contempt through body movement by

Table 4.4   Results for vocal indicators of emotion

Emotion	Vocal quality				
	Pitch level	Pitch range	Pitch variability	Loudness	Tempo
Joy	High	?	Large	Loud	Fast
Anger	High	Wide	Large	Loud	Fast
Sadness	Low	Narrow	Small	Soft	Slow
Fear	High	Wide	Large	?	Fast
Contempt	Low	Wide	?	Loud	Slow

Source: Scherer (1979, p. 513). Adapted by permission.

imagining themselves in situations designed to elicit each emotion – e.g., fear was enacted by shrinking from the sound of thunder; moving away from a villain; and walking cautiously in a high place. The results revealed that perceivers could identify each of the emotions with considerable accuracy.

Whereas people can deliberately communicate specific emotions in posed body cues, other research suggests that spontaneously occurring emotions may not be specified by the body. In particular, Ekman (1965) found that head cues during a stress interview communicated the particular affect being experienced, whereas body cues communicated only the intensity of affect. It should be noted that this study differed from those which demonstrated expressive accuracy for body cues not only in the spontaneity of the emotional expression, but also in the nature of the stimulus information provided to perceivers. Ekman's perceivers saw still photographs of targets in a seated position, whereas perceivers in the other studies

Table 4.5   Predictions for voice quality indicators of emotion

Emotion	Voice quality		
	Narrow-wide	Lax-tense	Full-thin
Joy	Wide	Medium tense	Medium full
Anger	Narrow	Very tense	Extremely full
Sadness	Narrow	Lax	Thin
Fear	Narrow	Extremely tense	Very thin
Disgust	Very narrow	Slightly tense	Slightly full

Source: Scherer (1986, p. 157). Adapted by permission of the American Psychological Association, Inc.

saw dynamic videotapes of targets in a standing position. Additional research is required to establish more clearly the conditions under which body cues will specify particular emotions.

Expressive information

Although Sogon and Izard did not investigate the postural information that communicated various emotions, ratings of the gait characteristics associated with each emotion in the Montepare *et al.* study revealed that anger was distinguished by heavyfootedness and long strides; happiness was distinguished by a faster pace; and sadness was distinguished by a small arm swing. Wallbott and Scherer (1986b) also reported that seated actors, who were engaged in a dialogue, used less energetic and less active movements when posing sadness than when posing anger or happiness.

Much of the research on posture and gesture had focused on expressive information that influences perceptions of targets' general feelings of liking or disliking rather than perceptions of stronger and more specific emotions like joy or anger. Mehrabian (1972) has found that positive feelings are communicated by greater *immediacy* in posture and gestural cues – i.e., more physical proximity, touching, eye contact, forward lean, and an orientation of the torso toward another. Bull (1987) investigated what sort of postural information communicates targets' feelings of agreement or disagreement. To this end, line drawings were made depicting postures that target persons had manifested while they listened to controversial arguments with which they agreed or disagreed. Perceivers accurately identified a posture with folded arms as signifying disagreement.

Multimodal information

Expressive accuracy

The research discussed thus far has examined the impact on emotion perception of the target's face, voice, *or* body. Yet, in our interactions with others we typically receive information from all of these non-verbal channels as well as the content of a target's speech. An important question thus concerns the accuracy of emotion perception when information from all modalities is present. If all channels are communicating the same emotion, one might expect greater accuracy in real-world encounters than in the more informationally impoverished experimental situations that have been discussed.

Consistent with this argument, multiple-channel accuracy on the PONS test is higher than single-channel accuracy (DePaulo and Rosenthal 1982). On the other hand, if the information communicated by face, voice, body, and/or speech content is inconsistent, as is often the case in naturalistic interactions, then perceivers' accuracy in reading emotions may be overestimated when only a single channel is studied. Even when the information is not inconsistent, the addition of expressive information from "weaker" channels may dilute the effects of "stronger" ones. Thus, when relatively weak audio cues to joy are added to stronger video cues, the expression accuracy of the resultant audiovisual information is lower than for the video channel alone (Wallbott and Scherer 1986b).

Expressive information

Folk wisdom tells us to "believe nothing that we hear and only half of what we see". Do people follow the dictum to trust their ears less than their eyes when they judge emotion from facial and vocal information? Mehrabian and Ferris (1967) addressed this question by creating targets who communicated liking, neutrality, or disliking toward an imagined addressee both in their photographed facial expression and in their taperecorded tone of voice. Although the independent effects of these facial expressions and vocal tones were comparable when perceivers were asked to judge the targets' affect based upon one or the other, facial expression contributed more than tone of voice to perceived affect when the two channels were combined to yield inconsistent information. Other researchers using videotaped facial expressions have also found a "visual primacy effect" when facial and vocal cues are discrepant (DePaulo et al. 1978).

Rather than crossing different facial and vocal expressions to see which channel has the greatest effect on emotion perception, other researchers have compared perceptions based on multiple channels with those based on single-channel expressions of the same emotion. The results using this research paradigm are mixed. Perceptions based on the visual channel alone tend to be more similar to those based on all channels than do perceptions based on only the vocal channel. However, this overall dominance of visual cues depends upon the particular emotion being communicated. Facial cues show the strongest advantage for perceptions of happiness, a somewhat weaker advantage for perceptions of anger and sadness, and a disadvantage for perceptions of fear (Levitt 1964; Burns and Beier

1973). Similarly, accuracy on the PONS test is higher for positive than for negative scenes when the face is shown, while it is higher for negative than for positive scenes when the face is absent (Rosenthal *et al.* 1979). It thus appears that facial cues are relatively more important in the communication of positive than of negative emotions, a finding that is consistent with the tendency for happy facial expressions and negative vocal expressions to be most accurately identified in single-channel studies. Studies using spontaneous, as opposed to posed, affective expressions have also found that the individual channel that best predicts multimodal perceptions depends upon the type of affect being judged (see Krauss *et al.* 1981).

Effects of target culture

The Western stereotype of the Japanese as "inscrutable" finds some validation in cross-cultural studies of their facial and vocal expressiveness. Posed facial expressions of negative emotions by Japanese targets are more difficult for English, Italian, or Japanese perceivers to identify than posed expressions of the same emotions by English or Italian targets (Shimoda *et al.* 1978). Similarly, when American, Israeli, and Japanese speakers expressed emotions by reciting the alphabet in their native languages, the emotional expressions of the Japanese speakers were the most difficult to read (Davitz 1964a).

Whereas it is *negative* emotions that are poorly communicated in the facial expressions of Japanese targets, this is not true for vocal expressions. Indeed, Davitz (1964a) found that anger and sadness were the most accurately communicated emotions in all three cultures. The socialization of Japanese display rules regarding the public expression of negative emotions may be less effective for vocal than for facial expressions because voice tends to be a "leakier" channel, revealing emotions that one is trying to hide (Ekman and Friesen 1969; Rosenthal *et al.* 1979).

Contrary to the view that Italians are highly expressive, while the English are more reserved, the posed facial expressions of Italian targets were no easier to identify than those of the English, regardless of perceiver nationality (Shimoda *et al.* 1978). Posed vocal expressions, on the other hand, have supported the common stereotype that Latins are highly emotional whereas Anglo-Saxons are somewhat cold and aloof. The emotions expressed in Mexicans' content-filtered speech were easier to read by Mexicans and Canadians alike than were those expressed in the speech of Canadians (McCluskey *et al.* 1975).

Subcultural differences in the facial encoding of emotions have been revealed in research comparing black and white Americans. Still photographs of posed expressions enacted by white Americans are more accurately read by both black and white perceivers than those enacted by blacks (Gitter *et al.* 1972). Although this effect held true for overall accuracy, it did not reach significance for individual emotions, and additional research is needed to ascertain exactly which emotions are more clearly expressed by white than black targets.

Whereas the foregoing studies reveal some interesting effects of target culture on the communication of posed emotions, three important questions remain. First, what is the origin of cultural differences in expressive accuracy? Second, what is the nature of the expressive differences across culture? And, third, does target culture influence the expressive accuracy of spontaneous emotions? Little research has addressed these questions, but a study by Ekman (1972) is pertinent to all. Japanese and American subjects' facial behavior was videotaped while they watched a neutral and a stress-inducing film, and FAST was employed to measure the frequency and duration of each movement of the face within three areas. The results revealed that the spontaneous expressive behavior during the stress film was very similar for the two groups when they watched the film alone. On the other hand, when they discussed the film with someone from their own culture, thereby activating cultural display rules, the Japanese subjects masked their negative emotions, while Americans typically did not. Thus, spontaneous expressions may or may not vary with the target's cultural background, depending upon the activation of cultural display rules.

Effects of target gender

Are females more emotionally expressive than males, as common stereotypes would have us believe? Hall (1984) conducted a meta-analysis of 49 studies that investigated sex differences in expressive accuracy using a variety of methods. Although no significant sex differences were revealed in those studies which employed vocal cues, a clear superiority for females was found in the studies employing facial cues. This superiority was obtained for posed and spontaneous emotional expressions, including happiness, love, fear, anger, and surprise.

Developmental research has revealed that sex differences in expressive accuracy vary with age. Expressive accuracy increases in the early childhood years for American females, whereas it *decreases* for males (Buck 1975; 1977; Zuckerman and Przewuzman 1979). This suggests that socialization pressures in the USA encourage boys to inhibit emotional expression in the face just as in other cultures all persons are pressured to inhibit certain facial expressions.

Effects of target age

The Darwinian position regarding the survival value of emotion communication suggests that we should be able to read infants' emotions. However, an experimental test of this hypothesis faces a difficult criterion problem. How can the researcher ascertain whether or not an infant is accurately communicating the intended or felt emotion?

Although there is little systematic evidence regarding the vocal communication of emotion by infants, there is evidence to indicate that they do have the potential accurately to communicate emotions in facial expressions. Within hours after birth, neonates can mimic several facial expressions modeled by an adult in a manner that permits accurate identification of the emotion (Field *et al.* 1982).

Other evidence to indicate that emotional expressions are present from birth rather than learned is provided by research with congenitally blind and deaf children. Although these children have never seen or heard an emotional expression, they exhibit recognizable and situationally appropriate expressions (Eibl-Eibesfeldt 1970a). Also, spontaneous videotaped or still facial expressions produced by infants 1–12 months old are reliably labeled as interest, joy, surprise, sadness, anger, or fear. Not only are infant facial expressions reliably labeled by adults, but also the expressive qualities characterizing their perceived emotions correspond to those predicted by objective coding systems, such as the FAST and MAX, although the correspondence is higher for happiness than for other emotions (Emde *et al.* 1985; Hiatt *et al.* 1979; Izard *et al.* 1980).

Even if infants do mimic or spontaneously produce identifiable facial expressions, the question remains as to whether or not they reveal their emotions in such expressions. In some cases this can be affirmed by the lawful relationship between the expression and certain eliciting stimuli. The fact that a bitter quinine solution elicits the disgust expression in neonates is fairly strong evidence that this expression signifies the same emotion as it does in adults. Similarly, the fact that the caregiver's voice reliably elicits a smile in somewhat older infants whereas an inoculation reliably elicits an angry expression strongly suggests that these expressions signify the respective emotions of happiness and anger for infants, as they do for adults (Izard and Malatesta 1987). On the other hand, the attempt to elicit particular emotions in infants through stimulus situations, such as a stranger's approach and an unexpected event, has sometimes failed to yield the predicted facial expressions even when perceivers agreed in their labeling of the expressions shown (Hiatt et al. 1979). This suggests that certain infant facial expressions may not reflect their emotional state. Alternatively, researchers' expectations regarding what emotion a particular situation would elicit in infants may have been wrong. To sort out these possibilities requires some more objective measure of the infant's emotional state. The physiological measures recently identified by Ekman et al. (1983) may be useful for this purpose.

Studies assessing the expressive accuracy of young children indicate that, like infants, they do convey emotional states via facial expressions. Moreover, they do so with accuracy. Buck (1975) found that preschoolers' facial expressions while watching emotionally evocative slides allowed their mothers and strangers to identify the slide with better than chance accuracy. In addition, mothers' judgments of the pleasantness of their children's facial expressions were positively correlated with the children's ratings of their feelings.

Whereas preschoolers' spontaneous facial expressions accurately communicate their emotions, their posed expressions may be less informative. Indeed, instructing a preschooler to smile is as likely to produce a contorted grimace as a grin, which may be why English-speaking photographers tell their subjects to say "cheese" and Koreans tell them to say "kimchi". Although research investigating developmental changes in the accuracy of posed facial expressions has not included preschoolers, there is evidence to indicate that accuracy does increase throughout the elementary school years, at least for some emotions (Morency and Krauss 1982; Brown and Cunningham 1981). Accuracy of posed vocal expressions also shows developmental changes for some emotions. Although the expressive accuracy of ten-year-olds and of adults did not differ for happiness and anger, fear was communicated more accurately by ten-year-olds, whereas sadness was communicated more accurately by adults (Fenster *et al.* 1977). One possible explanation for these findings is that children's high-pitched voices are better suited to the expression of fear, whereas adults' lower-pitched voices are more adept at expressing sadness. It is also possible that people are most adept at posing familiar emotions, with fear being more familiar to children and sadness more familiar to adults.

Whereas expressive accuracy may show developmental increases in early childhood for certain emotions, Darwin's notion that an individual's expressive habits could leave a permanent imprint on the face suggests that accuracy may decline in later adulthood due to the interfering effects of fixed expressive qualities. Malatesta, Fiore, and Messina (1987) tested this hypothesis by comparing the expressive accuracy of elderly targets who varied in their characteristic emotional style, as measured by a personality test – the differential emotions scale. Neutral facial expressions in these elderly targets were frequently perceived as emotional expressions, and objective measures of these expressions using Izard's MAX system indicated that most targets' neutral poses were not neutral by objective standards. Moreover, there were significant correlations between the targets' emotional style traits and the judges' errors in identifying their posed emotions. Targets whose dominant emotional trait on the differential emotions scale was anger tended to be mistakenly perceived as angry but not mistakenly perceived as sad or fearful or joyful, whereas those whose dominant trait was sadness tended to be mistakenly viewed as sad rather than as expressing some other emotion. It thus appears that years of emotional experience "freezes" the facial muscles into habitual lines and creases. Or, as George Orwell (1949) opined, "at 50, everyone has the face he deserves". However, without a comparison group of young targets who vary in emotional traits, one cannot be certain whether these results do reflect the imprint that a lifetime of expressive habits makes on the face or whether they reflect greater ease in producing an emotional expression that is consistent with one's basic disposition, or both.

Perceiver determinants of emotion perception

Research concerning perceiver determinants of emotion perception has addressed four major questions: Is there sufficient agreement among perceivers from diverse cultures to support Darwin's thesis that basic expressions of emotion are universal to the human species? Is the accurate judgment of emotions manifest at a young enough age to indicate that the ability to read emotions is innate? Do perceivers from some cultural or demographic groups show greater judgment accuracy than those from other groups? Does the cognitive or affective state of the perceiver influence emotion perception?

Cultural universals

Evidence for universal accuracy in judging emotions is provided by the finding that posed facial, vocal, and bodily expressions are similarly labeled across diverse cultures. Significant cross-cultural agreement in perceptions of emotion based on bodily expressions is evidenced by the finding that perceivers representing 20 different countries showed better than chance accuracy on all channels of the PONS test (Rosenthal et al. 1979). Studies of judgment accuracy based on posed vocal expressions also reveal agreement among perceivers from a wide assortment of cultures including the United States, Canada, Israel, Japan, Taiwan, Poland, and the Netherlands (Beier and Zautra 1972; Davitz 1964a; McCluskey et al. 1975; Van Bezooijen et al. 1983). Since many of these studies did not report the effects for individual emotions, it is difficult to conclude with certainty which specific emotions are universally perceived in vocal expressions. The accurate perception of anger and sadness appears to be more universal than the perception of happiness, whereas surprise and fear tend to be universally confused.

Studies of judgment accuracy based on facial expressions have also yielded pancultural agreement. Izard (1969) found high cross-cultural consistency in the labeling of facial expressions as happiness, fear, surprise, anger, disgust, or sadness by perceivers from the USA, England, Germany, Sweden, France, Switzerland, Greece, Japan, and Africa. Other researchers compared perceivers from Japan, Brazil, Chile, Argentina, Malaysia, an isolated New Guinea tribe, and the USA, using posed, photographed facial expressions that were selected with FAST in order to obtain unambiguous single-affect targets. Again, the results revealed strong agreement in the assignment of the faces to the six emotion categories noted above (Ekman et al. 1982b). One exception was that New Guinea perceivers did not discriminate fear and surprise. As noted earlier, fear and surprise are also confused by perceivers from other cultures when judging spontaneous facial expressions or when judging vocal expressions. Finally, a study by Ekman and Friesen (1986) has revealed pancultural agreement in the perception of a seventh emotion in facial expression – contempt.

Cross-cultural agreement in emotion perception is not limited to the dominant emotion expressed by a face. There is also agreement about the second strongest emotion signaled by an expression as well as the relative strength of different expressions of the same emotion. These findings reveal cultural universality in perceptions of subtle differences between facial expressions of emotion as well as in perceptions of the more obvious differences that result from completely different emotions (Ekman *et al.* 1987).

Although there is considerable evidence for pancultural accuracy in the judgment of posed facial expressions, little research has addressed the question of whether spontaneous facial expressions are similarly perceived across cultures. The more subtle information provided in spontaneous displays may reveal cultural differences that do not show up when posed expressions are studied. Indeed, as noted above, within-culture agreement is less reliable for spontaneous, than for posed, facial expressions.

Infants' emotion perceptions

Is it true that "babies are innately prepared to perceive smiles or frowns, soothing tones or harsh inflections, as indications of what others will do next" (Neisser 1976, p. 191)? Methodological barriers make it extremely difficult to test the hypothesis that the ability to perceive emotions is innate. How can one systematically investigate the judgment accuracy of young infants, who cannot be queried regarding their perceptions? One approach has been to employ a habituation paradigm in which researchers determine whether infants will show increased attention to one emotional expression after they have viewed another to the point of bored inattention.

Infants as young as two or three months, and possibly newborns, can discriminate a variety of facial expressions in an habituation paradigm, although it has been noted that the undeveloped visual skills of such young infants suggest that they are responding to changes in particular facial features rather than to the entire expressions (Nelson 1987). At four or five months of age, infants are able to differentiate facial expressions independently of specific features – e.g., the habituation to one target's smiling face generalizes to the smiling faces of other targets. Applying the habituation paradigm to the vocal domain, Caron *et al.* (1988) have also shown that seven-month-old infants can distinguish angry from happy readings of the same script.

Not only can infants discriminate one facial expression from another, but also they can discriminate a mildly fearful from a very fearful face by four months of age and a mildly happy from a very happy face by seven months (Nelson 1987). Although discriminating two happy expressions was a more difficult task for the infants, adults found it more difficult to discriminate the two fearful faces, which may suggest that infants are particularly sensitive to expressions of fear.

The question remains as to what meaning, if any, facial and vocal expressions convey to infants. As what age do children understand that a smile means "happy", that a frown means "sad", and that certain vocal qualities also have affective meaning? One method used to study the meaning that emotional expressions have for infants is to examine their behavioral reactions. Five-month-old infants' recognition of angry facial expressions in the habituation paradigm is sometimes manifested in a tendency to avoid looking at them, which suggests that an anger expression has negative affective significance for the infant (Schwartz *et al.* 1985). More telling evidence for the meaning of facial expressions is provided by research assessing the impact of a mother's facial expression on an infant's willingness to cross a "visual cliff". This is a plexiglass-covered table divided into two halves: a shallow side, which has a patterned surface immediately beneath the plexiglass, and a deep side, which has the same pattern at some varying distance below the plexiglass. Depending on how far below the surface the pattern is placed, it can look like a sudden drop-off, eliciting clear avoidance by the crawling infant who has been placed in the center of the table, or it can merely elicit ambivalent behaviors, reflecting uncertainty as to whether or not to crawl across.

When 12-month-old infants were placed on a visual cliff designed to elicit uncertainty, none of them crossed to the deep side if their mother posed a fearful expression as she stood at the edge of the deep side, whereas three-quarters of them did so if she posed a happy expression. Angry and, to a lesser extent, sad expressions also deterred the infant from crossing the cliff, which suggests that infants may interpret all negative expressions as a warning (Sorce *et al.* 1985).

Another creative method that has been employed to assess infants' understanding of emotional meaning is to see whether they prefer to look at a face whose affect matches that of a concurrent auditory stimulus. For example, do infants look at a smiling rather than a sad face when happy music or an upbeat tone is played, reversing this fixation preference when sad music or a descending tone is played? Recent research reveals that infants do seem to know what kinds of facial expressions of emotion go with what kinds of auditory event, even when the two share no history of co-occurrence but rather are related in a metaphorical sense (Cunningham, 1984; Phillips *et al.* 1988). The presumption underlying this research is that the infants' matching of these two stimuli reflects some understanding of their affective similarity. However, it is possible that an infant could associate the downward lines on a sad face with the downward pitch of a tone without necessarily grasping their affective meaning.

Demographic differences

Age differences

Assessing understanding of the meaning of emotional expressions is less difficult when studying verbal preschoolers than infants, since one can ask the child to label a facial or vocal expression or to match expressions to situations. Of course, the understanding that these tasks reveal could reflect learning as well as an innate attunement to expressive information.

Whereas early research indicated that children did not understand the meaning of most facial expressions until school age, recent paradigms that are less dependent on language skills and/or that use children and infants rather than adults as targets have documented accurate emotion perception by age two. Two-year-olds are able to label accurately infants' spontaneous facial expressions of anger, happiness, sadness, and surprise, as defined by the MAX test. They can also accurately match photographs depicting infants' spontaneous expressions to videotaped vignettes depicting emotion-provoking situations (Riess and Cunningham 1988). Four-year-olds in Buck's slide-viewing paradigm can accurately identify from their peers' facial expressions the emotionally-evocative slide being viewed (Buck 1975), and it is possible that even younger children could do so. Finally, an analysis of the errors that preschoolers make when asked to match faces to emotion labels has revealed that their erroneous choices tend to be faces that are close to the correct one in Russell's (1980) circumplex model of emotion representation, thus revealing more ability to read facial expressions of emotion than a simple accuracy score might suggest (Bullock and Russell 1984).

Although the ability to identify facial expressions is manifest at a very early age, there are also some age-related increases in judgment accuracy. Comparisons of perceivers ranging in age from four to adult reveal age-related increases in the accurate labeling of posed facial expressions of sadness, anger, and surprise, but little if any difference in the accurate labeling of happiness (Brown and Cunningham 1981; Felleman et al. 1983). These developmental differences in the ease of identifying various emotions parallel differences among adults, who identify facial expressions of happiness more accurately than negative emotions.

Evidence for the impact of vocal cues on children's emotion perception is provided by a progressive increase from ages 4 to 12 in the ability to identify the emotions of happiness, sadness, surprise, and anger depicted by an actress reciting the alphabet, with better than chance performance on all emotions occurring by age seven (Dimitrovsky 1964; Fenster et al. 1977; Matsumoto and Kishimoto 1983). Interestingly, the developmental increase in judgment accuracy is most marked for the emotion of fear (Fenster et al. 1977). Thus, the one emotion that children express more accurately than adults is the emotion that they read less accurately, a finding that could reflect variations in the adaptive value of expressing versus reading fear for children versus adults.

A study of children's ability to identify the affective meaning in music provides evidence for an even earlier sensitivity to the rhythm, tempo, pitch, and intensity associated with different emotions. Musical segments that were reliably labeled as happy, sad, angry, or afraid by adults were similarly labeled by children as young as four years old (Cunningham and Sterling 1988). If one assumes that angry music sounds like an angry voice, these results suggest that even preschoolers may be able to decode vocal expressions of emotion if they are given a richer stimulus input than the alphabet.

Other studies indicate that judgment accuracy also increases with age for the emotions portrayed in the PONS test. Between the ages of 9 and 15, there is a significant increase in the accuracy of judging affect in the face, voice, and body. The visual primacy effect discussed in the section on multimodal information (pp. 117–18) also varies with age. The tendency for judgments on the PONS test to be influenced more by facial cues than by discrepant vocal cues increases between the ages of 9 and 15.[3] Moreover, in some situations, children show an audio primacy effect. Specifically, a woman's positive tone of voice has more impact on children's judgments than does her smiling expression, whereas the reverse is true for adults. Interestingly, children did not show this audio primacy effect when judging male targets, and children, like adults, showed a video primacy effect when judging male or female targets with a negative expression or tone of voice (Bugental *et al.* 1970). The overall pattern of results in this study indicates that children are relatively insensitive to a woman's smile, perhaps because mothers are just as likely to smile when giving approval as when criticizing, whereas fathers' facial expressions are related to the positivity of their words (Bugental *et al.* 1971).

Cultural differences

While research has provided strong evidence for cultural universality in the identification of basic emotions from posed facial, vocal, and bodily cues, this research has also revealed some interesting cultural differences in perceivers' recognition accuracy. Table 4.6 shows the percentage of subjects from four culture groups who correctly identified the posed facial expressions of emotion utilized by Izard (1977). Although perceivers from North America and Europe, South America, Japan, and Hong Kong could all identify these emotions, the Japanese sample showed lower recognition accuracy than the other groups for the negative emotion of anger, and both Japanese and Chinese samples showed lower recognition accuracy for disgust and fear than did the other two groups.

Since the faces perceivers judged in the foregoing research were all Westerners, the cultural differences could reflect difficulty in reading negative emotions in targets from another ethnic background rather than cultural differences in the general ability to recognize such emotions. However, research has shown that Japanese perceivers actually show lower recognition accuracy for negative facial expressions of emotion posed by targets from their own culture than for those posed by Americans or Italians. Furthermore, Japanese perceivers do not show lower recognition of happiness in targets from their own or another culture (Shimoda *et al.* 1978). Thus, it appears that Japanese perceivers do indeed have difficulty recogniz-

Table 4.6 Cross-cultural agreement in emotion identification: Percentage of subjects from different cultures who agree on the emotion expressed by Westerners in photographs selected to represent various emotions

Emotion	Cultural group			
	North American and European (N = 503)	South American (N = 956)	Japanese (Tokyo) (N = 60)	Chinese (Hong Kong) (N = 124)
Interest–excitement	78.5	—	71.2	35.5
Enjoyment–joy	96.1	94.5	93.8	97.6
Surprise–startle	84.0	79.3	79.2	66.9
Distress–anguish	68.9	79.8	66.8	61.3
Disgust–contempt	81.8	77.8	55.8	62.1
Anger–rage	85.6	79.0	56.8	96.0
Shame–humiliation	71.3	—	41.2	70.2
Fear–terror	76.4	73.5	58.2	66.9
Average	80.3	80.7	65.4	69.6

Note: Data for North American and European groups were unweighted average of American, English, German, Swedish, French, Swiss and Greek groups; data for South American groups were unweighted average of Mexican, Chilean and Argentinian groups; all data for North American and European groups, South American groups, and Japanese were derived from Izard (1977); percentages of disgust–contempt category were the average of percentages of disgust–revulsion and contempt–scorn for the Hong Kong Chinese.
Source: Chan (1985, p. 688). Reprinted by permission of Elsevier.

ing negative facial expressions of emotion, an effect which may reflect a lack of perceptual experience with such emotions because of Japanese display rules.

As noted earlier, negative facial expressions are more difficult than positive ones for perceivers from all cultures to identify. Interestingly, accuracy in identifying *particular* negative expressions seems to vary across cultures. American children are more likely to choose a sad face for a sad story than Chinese children are, while the Chinese are more likely than Americans to choose an angry face for a story which involves frustration (Borke and Su 1972). The authors attributed these cultural differences to differences in child-rearing practices, which give Chinese children more freedom than Americans to experience their own angry feelings. Research on the development of the ability to identify emotions in vocal information suggests that American children may be intermediate on the dimension of attunement to angry versus sad emotions, with the Japanese most attuned to sadness and the Chinese most attuned to anger (Matsumoto and Kishimoto 1983).

Research comparing the judgment accuracy of black and white Americans has revealed superior performance by blacks judging emotions posed by both black and white targets in still photographs of the head and body (Gitter *et al.* 1972). One explanation for this black advantage is the "oppression hypothesis", which holds that expressive information has greater importance for adaptive actions by those who are relatively powerless. Cultural differences in perceptual experiences with expressive information provide another possible explanation for the greater accuracy of black perceivers. As noted above, white targets are more easily "read" by both black and white perceivers than black targets are. Since the emotional expressions of blacks are more ambiguous than those of whites, the decoding skills of black perceivers may, of necessity, become more finally tuned.

A shortcoming in the evidence concerning cultural differences in the accuracy of judging emotions is the lack of a coherent theory to explain these differences as well as to suggest others that should obtain. Matsumoto (1988) has attempted to conceptualize cultural differences in terms of cultural variations in values as measured by Hofstede (1983). For example, he proposed that the perception of negative emotions, such as anger or fear, will be attenuated in hierarchical cultures which emphasize power differentials because the expression and recognition of such emotions is threatening to the social structure. Additional work along these lines should prove useful in interpreting and predicting cultural differences in emotion perception.

Gender differences

Females not only are easier to read than males are, but also are more accurate judges of others' emotional expressions. They show a small but significant advantage over males on all channels of the PONS test except for randomized spliced speech, an effect that has been replicated for perceivers from grade three through adulthood. This gender effect has also been replicated across a variety of cultures. Such universality suggests that it could reflect an innate superiority of females. However, the "oppression hypothesis" provides an equally plausible explanation, since in most cultures females are in relatively powerless positions.

Consistent with the oppression hypothesis, the female advantage is particularly marked for negative emotions whose detection has the greatest importance for adaptive actions. It is also strongest for the face channel, followed by the body channel with the voice channel showing the smallest gender difference. Also, as girls grow older, their advantage decreases for the voice and body channels, while it increases for the face channel (Rosenthal *et al.* 1979). One explanation that has been offered for variations in the female advantage across channels is that women are more "polite" in their reading of non-verbal cues than men are, refraining from reading those non-verbal cues that are least controllable by the sender (Rosenthal and DePaulo 1979).

A problem with interpreting female superiority on the PONS test is that the target person is a woman. Thus, one could interpret the results as reflecting superior decoding of the emotions of like-sexed targets rather than superior decoding by females. However, a comprehensive review of 125 studies investigating gender differences in judgment accuracy using a variety of methods revealed that the superiority of female perceivers is as great when the targets are male as when they are female. Like the PONS test, these studies reveal female superiority for both facial and vocal cues as well as for perceivers who range in age from preschool to adulthood (Hall 1984).

Cognitive and affective factors

Expectancy effects

Our perceptions of others' emotions invariably take place in a social context, which raises an important question: What happens when the emotion communicated by facial expressions, vocal qualities, and/or body is discrepant with the social context in which these expressive behaviors are manifested? Is a smiling face at a funeral perceived as joy, and a quivering lip at a wedding perceived as sadness? Or do perceivers' expectations about the emotions typically expressed in these contexts cause them to label the smile as nervousness and the quiver as joy?

One study pertinent to the issue of context effects on emotion perception showed perceivers one of two films, both of which began with a child riding a tricycle and culminated with a woman screaming. In one film the intervening scenes suggested an automobile accident while in the other they suggested amiable play between the child and a man. The scream was more likely to be judged as joy or anger in the play version than in the accident version, while it was more likely to be judged as fear in the accident than the play version. However, the effects of context by no means overpowered the expressive behaviors, since the vast majority of perceivers called the scream fear regardless of which film they viewed (Goldberg 1951). Interestingly, this primacy of expression may vary with the gender of the target. Wallbott (1988a) found that context has more impact than facial expression on perceptions of men's emotions, while the reverse is true for perceptions of women's emotions, a finding that may reflect perceivers' awareness of sex differences in expressive accuracy.

Some research has attempted to sort out the relative impact of expectations and expressive behavior by determining what emotion is perceived from the context or expression alone and comparing this to the emotion perceived when both are presented together. Several studies have revealed an "expression primacy" effect when contextual information and facial information are discordant. Thus, when someone looks happy or sad in a situation that makes us expect otherwise, we tend to believe the expressive behavior rather than our expectations. Indeed, there is sometimes a contrast effect whereby a discordant context strengthens the tendency to perceive the emotion suggested by the expressive behavior in isolation (Frijda 1969).

Whether or not we will believe the expressive behavior when someone *sounds* happy or sad in a context that makes us expect otherwise has not been determined. A strong test of the expression primacy hypothesis for vocal information is provided in research investigating the impact of vocal expressions which are discordant with speech content. O'Sullivan *et al.* (1985) found that voice quality did not override the context provide by speech content when perceivers judged the emotions of targets who were telling an interviewer that they had seen a pleasant film when they had actually seen a gory one. However, targets in this study did such a good job of lying that judges could not discriminate honest from deceptive interviews. Since targets' vocal expressions of emotion may not have been discernably negative, the question remains as to what emotion will be perceived in someone who delivers a happy message with a sad voice.

Whether expressive information will overpower the impact of contextually derived expectations or vice versa should depend upon the clarity and intensity of the context and the expression. For example, the relative impact of contextual information is greater when it is presented first and/or in a dynamic visual medium (e.g., videotapes) rather than verbally or in static photographs (Wallbott 1988a; 1988b). It is also likely that contextual information will have a greater effect when expressive information is ambiguous and vice versa (Trope 1986; Trope *et al.* 1988). When the expression and the situation are so strong that a contradiction is noticed, the emotion perceived may depend on how perceivers can most easily resolve the contradiction. Gnepp (1983) found that older children were more likely to resolve it by modifying the significance of the facial expression, suggesting, for example, that true feelings were being masked. Younger children, on the other hand, elaborated the situation to make it congruent with the expression. Wallbott (1988a; 1988b) found that adults also tend to change the meaning of discrepant expressive and contextual information rather than simply weighing one source of information more than the other.

Mood effects

Do we project our own emotional states onto others? Some research suggests that we may. Perceivers who rate themselves as frequently experiencing fear or sadness are more likely to identify posed emotions incorrectly as fear or sadness, respectively (Toner and Gates 1985). More transient affective states also influence emotion perception. When perceivers' moods were manipulated by film clips designed to elicit positive or negative affect, those who experienced a negative mood perceived more sadness in an arguing newlywed couple depicted on film than did those in whom a positive mood had been induced (Zillmann *et al.* 1974). Similarly, when perceivers' emotional states were manipulated by taperecorded messages designed to elicit happiness and disgust, those who were disgusted were more likely to label slides of facial expressions as showing "disgust" than were happy or neutral perceivers. On the other hand, happy perceivers were not more likely to use the label "happy" than were the other groups (Schiffenbauer 1974). The failure of the perceiver's mood to influence the perception of "happiness" was attributed to limitations that the stimulus properties of a face place on the plasticity of judgments. Specifically, the strong connection between a smile and perceived happiness may make it very unlikely that perceivers would label a non-smiling face as happy or a smiling face as anything but happy.

Another limitation to a straightforward effect of the perceiver's mood on emotion perception concerns the target of perception. For example, Feshbach and Feshbach (1963) found that when boys were frightened of receiving a hypodermic injection from an adult male experimenter, they attributed more fearfulness to photographs of young boys and more maliciousness to photographs of men than did non-frightened boys. Thus perceivers sometimes project a complementary emotion onto others rather than their own emotional state (Holmes 1968).

Perceiver–target determinants of emotion perception

A friend of mine could always tell when her husband was irritated by a twitch in his jaw muscle, something that I failed to notice. As children, another friend and her sisters could tell by the color of their father's neck when they had better pipe down in the back seat of the car, a sign that strangers might well overlook. Do such anecdotes reflect a general tendency for people to judge the emotions of family, friends, and/or members of their own social group better than the emotions of strangers?

Some research evidence does reveal greater judgment accuracy for family and friends. Spouses can judge their partner's spontaneous expressions more accurately than strangers can (Sabatelli et al. 1982), and mothers can judge their own children's spontaneous expressions more accurately than strangers can (Buck 1975). Mothers can also judge their own children's posed expressions more accurately than those of other children (Zuckerman and Przewuzman 1979). Similarly, children can tell from spontaneous facial expressions whether their mother or their friend is talking to a friend or to a stranger, whereas they cannot do so for unknown mothers and peers (Abramovich 1977; Abramovich and Daly 1979).

In contrast to the foregoing positive effects of familiarity, adults showed no greater accuracy when judging the spontaneous facial expressions of acquaintances than of strangers (Frijda 1953), and dating couples showed no greater accuracy when judging the spontaneous expressions of their partners than when judging strangers (Sabatelli et al. 1980). Perhaps familiarity effects require more extensive interaction than is provided by acquaintanceship or a non-cohabiting dating relationship. It may also be the case that familiarity is most advantageous when the judgment task is relatively difficult, which may be the case when children are either the perceivers or the targets.

Greater judgment accuracy has been found not only for known than for unknown targets, but also for like-aged than for different-aged targets. When young, middle-aged, and elderly women were videotaped as they recounted past events that had elicited strong feelings of anger, fear, or sadness, the emotions of targets close in age to the perceiver were more accurately identified (Malatesta, Izard, Culver and Nicolich 1987). The advantage in judging the emotions of targets similar in age to oneself may reflect a tendency for people to have more exposure to the emotional expressions of their peers, for those emotional expressions to more closely resemble their own, and/or for those emotional expressions to be more important for adaptive social behavior.

Cross-cultural comparisons have revealed no clear advantage in reading the emotions of targets from one's own culture. Whereas some studies have found more accurate communication of posed vocal expressions within than across cultures (Albas et al. 1976; Beier and Zautra 1972; Van Bezooijen et al. 1983), others have found no differences (Davitz 1964a; McCluskey et al. 1975). Studies investigating perceivers' ability to identify either posed facial expressions or the stimulus-eliciting spontaneous facial expressions have also found no within-culture advantage (Ekman 1972; Shimoda et al. 1978).

One factor that must be considered in interpreting the cross-cultural data is that all but one of these studies employed posed emotional expressions, and the single study using spontaneous expressions recorded them without the target's awareness. Such expressions may be sufficiently strong to negate any advantage of a greater attunement to the expressive information provided by targets from one's own culture. Research investigating the more subtle, spontaneous expressions that occur in social interactions when display rules are operative may reveal that they are more accurately identified by perceivers from the target's own cultural group just as they are more accurately identified by family, friends, and like-aged peers.

Summary and implications

There is strong evidence that six or seven basic emotions are universally perceived in both still and dynamic posed facial expressions. The same emotions may also be universally perceived in posed vocal expressions and body movements, although there is much less research on the latter two modalities. Whereas positive emotions are more accurately identified from facial expressions than negative ones, the reverse seems to be true for vocal expressions. Perhaps this reflects the fact that positive emotions are typically expressed in face-to-face encounters, whereas it is often adaptive to express negative emotions with more distal vocal cues – e.g., a fearful call for help or an angry warning.

Research has identified specific facial configurations that communicate the basic emotions, but it has not yet determined the constellation of vocal qualities or movement qualities that do so. There is also relatively little research investigating spontaneous expressions of emotion. The existing evidence is confined largely to spontaneous *facial* expressions, which can be accurately identified, albeit less reliably than posed ones.

There has been relatively little research investigating the combined effects of face, voice, and/or body on emotion perception. The existing data suggest that facial cues dominate vocal ones in the perception of happiness, whereas vocal cues dominate in the perception of fear. There is also some evidence to indicate that facial cues may dominate contextual ones when these two sources of information are discordant, although the generality of this effect remains to be determined. The contexts that elicit the perception of various emotions also await systematic description.

Some targets are easier to "read" than others, even when emotional expressions are posed. The facial expressions of Western males, who are socialized to hide their emotions, are harder to read than those of females, a gender difference that emerges in late childhood and increases through adolescence. Japanese targets, who are socialized to suppress negative emotions, are harder to read than targets from other cultures when expressing such emotions visually. And elderly adults are harder to read than younger ones, perhaps because the ageing face provides more ambiguous stimulus information.

The ability to read facial expressions of emotion develops at a very early age, and it may be innate. Nevertheless, socialization does seem to have an impact on judgment accuracy. Females, whose socializ-ation stresses social sensitivity, outperform males, and perceivers from cultures that suppress the expression of negative emotions are relatively inept in the recognition of these emotions, at least when expressed in the face. Familiarity with particular targets may also augment the ability to judge their emotions accurately.

Further reading

Buck, R. (1984). *The communication of emotion*. New York: Guilford Press. This book considers the communication of emotion from a variety of perspectives, including species evolution, neuropsychological under-pinnings, individual development, personality differences, and social interaction.

Hall, J. (1984). *Nonverbal sex differences: Communication accuracy and expressive style*. Baltimore, MD: The Johns Hopkins University Press. This book provides a comprehensive review of research concerning gender differences in judgment accuracy and expressive accuracy for facial, vocal, and other nonverbal cues. Various explanations for these gender differences are evaluated.

Nelson, C. A. (1987). The recognition of facial expression in the first two years of life: Mechanisms of development. *Child Development*, 58, 889–909. Research concerning the infant's ability to discriminate, categorize, and understand facial expressions of emotion is reviewed, and experiential and biological contributions to this ability are discussed.

Wallbott, H. G. and Scherer, K. R. (1986). How universal and specific is emotional experience? Evidence from 27 countries on five continents. *Social Science Information*, 25, 763–95. Employing a self-report method-ology, this study documents pancultural similarities in: the non-verbal and physiological reactions accompanying several basic emotions; the perceived characteristics of each emotion such as frequency, duration, intensity, and need for control; and the nature of the events that caused each of the emotions. A sample questionnaire is included.

Notes

1 The topic of deception perception, which is closely related to emotion perception, will not be covered in the present chapter due to space limitations.

2 A dimensional approach is favored by those who view emotional experi-ence as the endpoint of a cognitive process in which degree of pleasure, degree of arousal, and other situational information are integrated to

infer a particular emotion. A categorical approach is preferred by those who view emotional experience as the direct effect of a distinctively patterned bodily reaction to some external stimulus. As noted by Smith and Ellsworth (1985), dimensional and categorical conceptions of emotions are not necessarily mutually exclusive. Rather, various discrete emotions can be conceptualized in terms of their underlying dimensions, just as discrete traits are conceptualized in terms of underlying dimensions.

3 Interestingly, both the PONS accuracy scores and the video primacy effect show a reliable dip at age 13, an effect that may reflect maturational changes in the brain at puberty that affect face perception (DePaulo and Rosenthal 1982).

5 / CAUSAL ATTRIBUTION

Whether we are forming first impressions, perceiving emotions, or engaging in a long-term interpersonal relationship, the question of why people behave as they do often guides our social perceptions and interactions. Indeed trait and emotion labels often serve as causal explanations for observed behaviors. Attribution theorists have assumed that we seek to identify the causes of behavior because such causal knowledge yields a more stable, predictable, and controllable world. For example, I wondered why my college roommate had left me the bed by the window because knowing the cause of this behavior would give me a better sense of what other behaviors to expect. And my high-school friend wondered whether drugs were the cause of her roommate's strange behavior because such causal knowledge might permit some measure of control over their social interactions.

Although attribution theory is concerned both with the antecedents and the consequences of our causal beliefs, only the former topic will be considered in the present chapter. The topic of causal attributions for one's own behavior will also be omitted except when self-attributions are contrasted with attributions for the behavior of others.

The contents of causal attribution

Heider's (1958) "common sense" concepts of causality that were briefly reviewed in Chapter 2 have had a major impact on more recent theories of attribution, which place these concepts into predictive frameworks. A central concept in Heider's analysis is that of *dispositional properties*. He argued that the attribution process often involves inferring unchanging structures and processes of people and the environment – their dispositional properties (e.g., traits, abilities, intentions) – from more observable and variable cues (e.g., overt behaviors, expressions, and verbalizations). Heider noted that the search for dispositional properties is a hierarchical process which begins with the more stimulus-bound recognition of "facts" and gradually goes deeper into the underlying causes of these facts. In this hierarchy, "each previous layer stands to the succeeding one in the relation of raw material to interpretation" (Heider 1958, p. 81). Thus, we may interpret a person's insulting remark as being inadvertent or caused by anger; if anger is perceived, it may, in turn, be attributed to some frustrating event or to a hostile personality; if a hostile disposition is inferred, it may, in turn, be attributed to various biological or environmental causes, such as hormonal imbalances or abusive parents.

Another causal concept proposed by Heider is the *internal versus external causal locus* of an effect, which refers to its origin and governing source. More specifically, Heider differentiated between effects caused by the inanimate environment or by another person (external causes) and those that originate in the actor (internal causes). In the example above, the question of causal locus concerns whether an insulting remark was caused by factors internal to the actor, such as a hostile disposition or insensitivity, or by factors in his external situation, such as a frustrating event. A specific causal locus concept elaborated by Heider is the concept of *can*. He proposed that performance outcomes may be attributed to the internal cause of ability, to the external cause of the difficulty of environmental obstacles, or to both.

Whereas many researchers have studied the causal attributions that are articulated by Heider, others have addressed the question of what kinds of causal attributions people spontaneously make when their responses are not constrained by the investigator and what dimensions of attribution these causes represent. Buss (1978) suggested that the internal–external partition ignores an important distinction between reasons for a behavior (i.e., goals, motives, or intentions) and causes of a behavior. However, reasons can be viewed as one form of internal cause rather than as a separate attributional dimension, since they are beliefs that an actor has about himself, his behavior, or its outcome that cause him to act as he does (Locke and Pennington 1982).

Another alternative to the internal–external dimension was suggested by Kruglanski (1975), who argued for a distinction between endogenous causes (behavior done for its own sake) and exogenous causes (behavior done as a means to an end) when intentional actions are being explained. Although such a partition of causes may make logical sense, research has shown that it does not capture the *psycho*logic (i.e., subjective logic) of the naive attributor (Weiten and Upshaw 1982).

Studies investigating people's performance attributions across diverse cultures have revealed two causal dimensions in addition to internality (Betancourt and Weiner 1982; Meyer 1980; Watkins and Astilla 1984). One of these dimensions is stability – e.g., effort is an internal, unstable cause, whereas ability is an internal, stable cause. The other dimension is controllability – e.g., luck is an unstable, uncontrollable cause, whereas effort is an unstable, controllable cause.

Research exploring attributions within the interpersonal domain has revealed still other dimensions. These findings led Wimer and Kelley (1982) to conclude that the question of what causal distinctions people make must be addressed within specific domains, such as performance. One may have to define domains even more narrowly than this in order to identify adequately perceived causal dimensions, since Anderson (1983) found that different types of performance (interpersonal versus non-interpersonal) generate different causes and different causal dimensions.

Methods for studying causal attribution

Independent variables

A variety of paradigms have been used to elicit causal attributions. A questionnaire methodology, introduced by McArthur (1972), presents subjects with a written description of several responses ostensibly made by other people together with some theoretically relevant information regarding each response. On the basis of this information, subjects are asked to indicate what they think probably caused the response to occur. Although this method lacks ecological validity, it provides a "plausibility test" of a theory (Ross and Fletcher 1985), revealing whether subjects are capable of using theoretically relevant information in the predicted fashion. It also has the advantage of permitting a broad scope of investigation, since each subject can be asked to make attributions for a number of behaviors in the context of various patterns of information. Another common paradigm is to give subjects written accounts of an event that are considerably longer than that provided by the single sentences in the questionnaire method. Research with young children has used a storybook methodology in which verbal descriptions of various behaviors are accompanied by pictorial representations. Still greater realism has been achieved by presenting audio- or videotapes of posed behaviors or social interactions. Finally, some researchers have studied causal attributions for real life events by relying on subjects' recall of social interactions. This method has permitted the study of people's causal attributions for a wide range of significant behaviors including child abuse, depression, marital conflict, academic achievement, sports performance, and adjustment to life-threatening illness.

Dependent variables

The dependent measures that have been used to assess causal attributions reflect the content dimensions discussed above. Researchers testing hypotheses derived from Heider's concept of dispositional causes have typically assessed causal attributions by asking subjects to rate the actor's traits or attitudes to see if the perceived dispositions correspond to the actor's observed behavior. Researchers testing hypotheses derived from Heider's concept of causal locus have asked subjects to assign causality to internal causes (e.g., the actor) or to external causes (e.g., the target of action or the external circumstances). The assignment of causality to various loci has been assessed through a forced choice among alternatives, the allocation of a percentage value to each alternative representing its relative importance in causing the effect, ratings of each alternative on independent scales, and ratings on a single bipolar scale reflecting an internal–external dimension. The latter measuring instrument is congruent with Heider's suggestion that the more a person is seen as causing an event, the less causal influence the environment will be perceived to exert and vice versa. However, this reciprocal relationship does not always hold and a single bipolar scale is not equivalent to two independent ratings of internal and external causes (Miller *et al.* 1981).

A shortcoming in measures of causal loci is that they fail to reveal the *type of cause* within a given locus. For example, although "internal" attribution has typically been equated with "dispositional trait" attribution, there are a variety of other internal causes of behavior, such as attitudes, goals, emotions, and habits (Ross and Fletcher 1985). Ratings of causal loci also fail to identify the *specific* trait, attitude or goal that caused the behavior in question – and it has been argued that such concrete causes may be more typical of people's spontaneous attributions than are abstract causal loci (Read 1987).

Research has sometimes addressed the ambiguity of causal loci measures by giving each causal locus a specific name. In particular, when performance attributions are assessed, subjects typically are asked to assign causality to the person's ability, the task difficulty, luck, or effort. One problem with such measures is that different perceivers may ascribe the same cause to different loci. For example, some people view luck as a cause internal to the actor and others view it as an external cause. Researchers who examine luck attributions in order to test the hypothesis that inconsistent performance will yield attribution to the external circumstances may fail to support this hypothesis, not because it is wrong, but because some subjects view luck as an internal cause. Thus, hypotheses bearing on the locus of causal attribution may not be well tested by ratings of specific causes that do not specify an explicit locus. A solution to this problem is to have subjects rate each cause on a causal dimension scale which assesses how they perceive the cause of a performance outcome in terms of locus of causality, stability, and controllability dimensions (Weiner 1983; Russell *et al.* 1987).

The choice of causal dimension scales is itself problematic. Given the variety of dimensions identified in research exploring the contents of causal attributions it would seem advisable to begin the study of causal attributions within a given domain with pilot research containing open-ended questions. From the open-ended data, one can then design the appropriate structured attribution scales, which, because of superior validity and reliability, are better than open-ended questions for testing hypotheses regarding those factors that influence causal attributions (e.g., Elig and Frieze 1979; Russell *et al.* 1987).

Critics of the attribution measures discussed above have questioned whether or not people spontaneously make causal attributions of any kind. To address this issue, researchers have investigated spontaneous attributional activity using a variety of inventive techniques such as the analysis of explanations for interpersonal problems offered by people writing to newspaper advice columns and subjects' verbalizations as they think aloud during or after some task. These studies reveal that spontaneous attributional activities are ubiquitous, and that unexpected events and failures elicit more attributional activity than do expected events and successes (Weiner 1985). It should be emphasized that these studies were limited to modern, Western cultures, primarily the United States. Whether or not causal attributions are as commonplace in other cultures remains to be determined. Bond (1983) has suggested that attributional activity may be more common in individualistic cultures that encourage domination over nature and role flexibility, because predicting and controlling others' behavior is more problematic and more valued in such cultures. The nature of the events which elicit attributional activity may also vary across contexts and cultures (Antaki and Naji 1987).

Correspondent inference theory

Correspondent inference theory (Jones and Davis 1965) is concerned primarily with the question of whether a person's behavior will be attributed to his or her disposition rather than to accidental or extenuating factors. An attribution or inference is "correspondent" when the disposition attributed to an actor "corresponds to" the behavior from which this disposition is inferred. Thus, attributing a generous disposition to the roommate who gave me the bed near the window would be a correspondent inference inasmuch as the behavior and the disposition can be similarly labeled as "generous". On the other hand, attributing my roommate's behavior to compliance with the housemother's instructions would not be a correspondent inference.

According to Jones and Davis, a precondition for a correspondent inference is the attribution of intentionality, and they specify two conditions for the attribution of intent: the actor must be perceived as having *knowledge* that the act would have the observed effects; the actor must be perceived as having the *ability* to produce the observed effects. The theory does not actually focus on factors that affect the attribution of knowledge and ability. Rather, it focuses on those factors that influence the attribution of a correspondent disposition, once intentionality is attributed. Due to its assumption of intentionality, correspondent inference theory is applicable only to voluntary actions, not to what have been called "occurrences", which are events that are "in some significant degree independent of the will" (Kruglanski 1975). Several factors hypothesized to yield correspondent inference are discussed below along with pertinent research evidence.[1]

Choice and social desirability

Much of the research bearing on correspondent inference theory has focused on the effects that choice and social desirability have on perceivers' tendency to infer people's attitudes from their behavior. According to the theory, when people's attitude statements could reflect the influence of external constraints – e.g., when these statements are socially desirable or when the person has been assigned a particular position in a debate rather than freely choosing it – then perceivers should not attribute to them "corresponding" internal attitudes. On the other hand, when people express a particular attitude with no apparent constraints – e.g., when they have the choice to state any attitude and/or the expressed attitude is socially undesirable – then corresponding attitudes should be attributed to them. Recall, for example, my college friend who made disparaging remarks about her father. Such statements would be attributed to a negative attitude toward her father both because they were freely made and also because they are socially undesirable. One is fairly confident that socially undesirable remarks reflect true attitudes because they are made despite possible aversive consequences, such as social disapproval. On the other hand, positive remarks about one's father may be attributed to social norms rather than to the speaker's true attitude.

Several studies have provided evidence consistent with the foregoing theoretical predictions. When an applicant for an astronaut job expressed extraverted inclinations even though he knew that extraversion was undesirable in astronauts, he was perceived as more affiliative – i.e., more extraverted – than an applicant for a submarine job who showed the same extraverted behavior but knew that extraversion was socially desirable for submariners. In short, extraverted behavior is more apt to be perceived as corresponding to a target's true disposition when it is socially undesirable, and the same is true for introverted behavior (Jones et al. 1961).

Behavior is also more apt to be perceived as corresponding to a target's true disposition when it is freely chosen. When a student attending college in the northern United States freely chose to make a pro-segregation speech, he was perceived to have much stronger pro-segregation attitudes than when he was assigned this position in a debate or when he chose to make an anti-segregation speech (Jones and Harris 1967). An unexpected finding, however, is the occurrence of correspondent attribution under conditions of no choice: subjects estimated the college student to have stronger pro-segregation opinions when he made a pro-segregation speech than when he made an anti-segregation speech even though they knew that these positions were assigned in a debate.

The tendency to infer attitudes from speeches or essays that are not freely chosen is hard to suppress. It occurs when subjects' themselves have just written essays under conditions of no choice, when the actor's speech is explicitly described as having been written by someone else, and even when the perceiver is the one who tells the actor what to say (Gilbert and Jones 1986; Jones 1979). Such effects occur for trait inferences as well as for attitudinal inferences. When subjects interacted with a clinical psychology graduate student who employed a friendly or aloof consulting style, their impressions of her friendliness corresponded to her behavior even when they had been explicitly told that she was required to employ a particular style (Napolitan and Goethals 1979).

The foregoing findings have been taken as evidence for Heider's (1958, p. 54) assertion that "behavior engulfs the field" – i.e., that behavior has such salient properties that situational constraints may be partly or completely ignored. More recently, this phenomenon has been labeled the *fundamental attribution error*, which is defined as a "general tendency to overestimate the importance of personal ... factors relative to environmental influences" (Ross 1977, p. 184).

Non-common effects

Jones and Davis (1965) propose that correspondent attribution is more likely when an action produces effects that differ from those which would have resulted from another action. This prediction is based on the assumption that the distinctive, or non-common, effects will be perceived as indicative of the actor's goals and preferences – i.e., his or her disposition. Support for the principle of non-common effects has been provided in studies in which subjects read about targets who had selected one of several behavioral alternatives. When the alternatives had many common effects, subjects were less likely to infer attitudes that corresponded to the particular choice that was made. For example, subjects read about a student who had to choose one of four programs of study, and picked one that included a course in computer programming, sociology of ageing, organic chemistry, and African literature. For some subjects, the chosen program was the only one that included computer programming, whereas for others two or more of the programs included this course. Subjects were much more likely to infer that the student wanted to take a course in computer programming when it was a non-common effect than when getting this course was an effect common to many of the alternative programs under consideration (Ajzen and Holmes 1978).

It should be noted that the impact of non-common effects on trait attributions has been documented only in situations in which subjects were explicitly told the number and nature of the non-common effects. This, of course, is not the situation faced by perceivers in everyday life. If you witness your friend choose a program of study, you must acquire considerable information before performing a non-common effects analysis of this choice. First you must decide what other possible programs of study have been forgone. For most college students, this would be a very large number. Next you must determine how many non-common effects accompany the chosen program. Moreover, you must be able to label these non-common effects if you are to make a correspondent inference. For example, if you manage to determine that a computer programming course is a non-common effect, you still have to decide what it is about this course that made your friend choose it before you can make a correspondent inference. If the "effect" is "greater interest value", then you will make the correspondent inference that your friend likes computer programming. However, if the effect is "an easy teacher", then you willl make a different inference. And, if the effect is "fulfilling a science requirement", then you might not make a correspondent inference at all. Because the determination of non-common effects is such a difficult task, their number and nature may rarely be a useful source of information for causal attributions.

Hedonic relevance and personalism

Jones and Davis (1965) propose two motivational factors that foster a correspondent inference: hedonic relevance and personalism. Hedonic relevance is high when perceivers have a strong emotional response to the action, and personalism is high when perceivers see the consequences of the action as intended for them. The greater the hedonic relevance or personalism, the more likely perceivers are to make a correspondent attribution. Presumably these factors increase correspondent attribution because they focus perceivers' attention on a particular non-common effect, namely the effect of an action on them. Thus, when Nina makes disparaging remarks about her father, her father is more apt to make the correspondent inference that she dislikes him than is a dispassionate observer who may be attentive to a variety of effects produced by Nina's remarks that could militate against a correspondent inference.

The results of a study by Jones and DeCharms (1957) support the hypothesis that the greater the hedonic relevance of an act, the more likely it is to yield a correspondent inference. Subjects rated the motivation of an actor who failed to earn a reward because of poor performance on a series of problem-solving tasks. For some subjects, the actor's failure also deprived them of the reward (high hedonic relevance) whereas for others it did not. Subjects who suffered as a consequence of the actor's poor performance rated him as less competent than did those who did not suffer, thus reflecting a more correspondent inference under conditions of high hedonic relevance.

Other research that may be viewed as supporting the hedonic relevance hypothesis concerns attributions of responsibility for an accident. Although there are some exceptions, considerable research reveals a small but significant tendency for perceivers to attribute more irresponsibility to the perpetrator of an accident when consequences, such as property damage, are severe (Burger 1981; Shaver 1970; Walster 1966). This effect has an analogue in the developmental research literature, where it has been found that young children attribute more naughtiness to actors whose actions have more negative consequences, regardless of the actors' intentions (Costanzo and Fraenkel 1988). Although a variety of explanations for these effects have been suggested, one possibility is that severe consequences are more emotionally disturbing to the perceiver – i.e., hedonically relevant – and thus more likely to yield the correspondent attribution of irresponsibility.

Hedonic relevance may increase correspondent inferences about the victim as well as the perpetrator of an emotionally unsettling event. Specifically, there is a well-documented tendency to "blame the victim" who suffers severe consequences more than one who suffers only mild ones. Thus, a rape victim was seen as more personally responsible for the event when she was either a virgin or a married woman than when she was a divorcee, whom subjects viewed as less respectable and thus suffering less severe consequences (Jones and Aronson 1973).

"Blaming the victim" effects have been explained in terms of people's motivation to believe in a *just world* where good things happen to good people and bad things happen to bad people (Lerner 1980). According to this theory, the rape of a virgin or married woman threatens the belief in a just world more than the rape of the "less respectable" divorcee, with the result that subjects feel the need to justify the rape of the former victims by finding fault with their actions. Often perceivers cannot rationalize an injustice by attributing behavioral responsibility, in which case they tend to derogate an innocent victim's personal characteristics, such as likeability and attractiveness.

Whether hedonic relevance will increase correspondent inferences about the perpetrator or the victim depends in part upon the person with whom the perceiver identifies. Those who anticipate being in an accident-prone situation where they themselves might be victimized attribute responsibility to the perpetrator of a past accident, whereas those who anticipate that they might perpetrate an accident derogate the victim (Burger 1981; Chaikin and Darley 1973).

Covariation theory

Kelley's (1967) covariation model derives from Heider's distinction between causal loci. As such, it is concerned primarily with the question of whether the cause of some behavior will be located in the actor (internal attribution) or in the environment (external attribution). However, Heider's bipolar division of the causal space is extended to include two types of environmental cause: the external target to which a response is made, and the external circumstances surrounding the behavior. Thus, within Kelley's model, the question of interest is whether an insulting remark should be attributed to the provocation of a target, to irritating circumstances, or to the actor's

disposition. The covariation principle holds that "the effect is attributed to that condition which is present when the effect is present and
which is absent when the effect is absent" (Kelley 1967, p. 194).
Unlike correspondent inference theory, the question of causal locus
in Kelley's covariation theory is pertinent to involuntary occurrences
as well as to voluntary actions.

Kelley proposed that perceivers operate as naive scientists, interpreting a given behavior, such as an insulting remark, in the context
of information gathered from experiment-like variation of conditions. Three conditions are varied. One is the targets toward which
the response may be directed, which yields *distinctiveness* information – i.e., whether or not the insult is delivered to other
targets. A second condition is the actors who may respond to a given
target, which yields *consensus* information – i.e., whether or not
other actors insult the target. The third condition is time or modalities of interaction with the target, such as before and after the
interactants have had their morning coffee (time) or during a dinner
party and during a card game (modalities). Varying these conditions
yields *consistency* information – i.e., whether or not the insult is
delivered whenever and however the target is presented.

According to the covariation principle, if my college friend, Nina,
repeatedly insults her father (high consistency), rarely insults anyone
else (high distinctiveness), and if many others also insult her father
(high consensus), then Nina's behavior will be attributed to causes in
her father, with whom the behavior covaries. This is a *target*
attribution. On the other hand, if Nina repeatedly insults her father
(high consistency), also insults many other men (low distinctiveness),
and if few others also insult Nina's father (low consensus), then the
behavior will be attributed to Nina, with whom it covaries. This is an
actor attribution. (It should be noted that in the attribution literature, the term "person attribution" is often used rather than "actor
attribution", and "stimulus" or "entity" attribution is often used in
place of "target attribution".) Both of the foregoing examples
involve attribution to a stable cause – in either the actor or the target.
Attribution to the particular circumstances in which the response
occurred, an unstable cause, is proposed to occur when the response
shows low consistency.

In an extension of Kelley's model, Pruitt and Insko (1980) differentiated *comparison-object consensus* from *target-object consensus*.
Whereas consensus information in Kelley's model concerns whether
or not others insult Nina's father (target-object consensus), compari-

son-object consensus concerns whether or not others show the same pattern of insulting behavior as Nina does toward other men. It is predicted that Nina's response is more apt to be attributed to causes in her father when other people respond to other men like she does and to causes in Nina when others respond differently to other men.

Although the covariation model predicts when causal attribution will be made to the actor, the target, or the temporary circumstances, it does not predict what specific circumstance or actor or target disposition will be inferred. Thus, the covariation information that yields a "circumstance" attribution cannot predict whether perceivers will attribute Nina's disparaging remarks to feeling sick or tired or losing a card game or some other temporary circumstances. Similarly, the covariation information that yields an "actor" attribution cannot predict whether perceivers will attribute Nina's disparaging remarks to her hostility, her insensitivity or some other stable disposition. Correspondent inference theory, on the other hand, does attempt to predict what specific disposition will be inferred, although, as noted above, the non-common effects analysis utilized for this purpose is difficult to implement.

McArthur (1972) tested Kelley's covariation model using a questionnaire methodology. Subjects were presented with one sentence descriptions of various responses representing emotions, accomplishments, opinions, and actions – e.g., Sue is afraid of the dog; George translates the sentence incorrectly. Each behavior was accompanied by high or low consensus information (Almost everyone / Hardly anyone who sees the dog is afraid of it); high or low distinctiveness information (Sue is not / is afraid of almost every other dog); and high or low consistency information (Sue has almost always / almost never been afraid of this dog). Subjects were asked to attribute each response to characteristics of the actor, the target, the circumstances, or to some combination thereof. The results provided strong support for predictions derived from Kelley's model. Research by Pruitt and Insko (1980) has also provided support for predictions derived from their extension of this model. The effects of covariation information on attributions have been replicated in other cultures including Korea (Cha and Nam 1985) as well as for children as young as four years of age (Divitto and McArthur 1978; Higgins and Bryant 1982; Sedlak and Kurtz 1981).

Research investigating causal attributions for performance by Weiner and his colleagues has also provided evidence for the impact of covariation information. Low consistency in performance yields attributions for success or failure to the unstable causes of luck or effort (circumstance attribution), whereas high consistency yields attributions to the stable causes of task difficulty (target attribution) or ability (actor attribution). Whereas covariation of performance with time affects the stability of causal attributions, without regard to their internality, covariation of performance with the actor affects their internality. If an actor succeeds or fails on a task and most others perform differently (low consensus information), then performance is attributed to the internal causes of ability and effort, whereas if most others perform similarly (high consensus information), then performance is attributed to the external cause of task difficulty (Read and Stephan 1979; Weiner *et al.* 1972).

Whereas the foregoing studies demonstrate that perceivers can use covariation information, they do not reveal whether or not perceivers will actually seek covariation information through experiment-like variations of conditions. Cordray and Shaw (1978) found that perceivers do spontaneously detect and utilize information regarding the covariation of effort and success when making causal attributions for the test performance of a videotaped target. And Major (1980) found that when perceivers are given the option of requesting several instances of consensus, distinctiveness, and consistency information before making a causal attribution, most examine all three types. However, they sample only a limited portion of the available information, and there is a marked preference for consistency information over distinctiveness and consensus as well as less utilization of consensus information than either distinctiveness or consistency. It remains for future research to ascertain the impact of these sources of information on causal attributions in naturalistic situations.

Causal schemas

Kelley (1973) noted that perceivers often make causal attributions in the absence of the complete complement of information that is specified in his covariation model. He further proposed that they do so by invoking various causal schemas, which are people's conceptions about what information is indicative of what cause and what causes contribute to what effects.

Schemas for actor, target, and circumstance causes

One set of causal schemas is the pattern of consensus, distinctiveness, and consistency information that people assume to exist when the cause of some effect is the actor, the target, or the circumstances. Kelley proposed that whatever covariation information is available is compared with these patterns and a response is attributed to the causal pattern with which the available information is most consistent. As can be seen in Table 5.1, high consensus information is unique to the schema for causes in the target. As such, it is proposed that perceivers who have only high consensus information will attribute causality to the target because that information is consistent only with the schema for target causes. Similarly, perceivers who have low distinctiveness information and nothing else will attribute causality to the actor because that information fits the schema for actor causes. And, low consistency information, which fits the schema for circumstance causes, will by itself elicit attribution to the circumstances.

A study by Orvis *et al.* (1975) provided support for the existence of actor, target, and circumstance causal schemas. Subjects who were given only partial covariation information – e.g., high consensus *or* low distinctiveness *or* low consistency – made inferences about the other information variables that were consistent with a particular causal schema. For example, those who were given only high consensus information inferred that distinctiveness and consistency were also high (the target cause schema) while those who were given only low distinctiveness information inferred that consensus was low and consistency was high (the actor cause schema). In addition, when subjects were asked to make a causal attribution based on partial information without inferring the values of other information, they

Table 5.1 Information patterns for three causal attributions

	Information pattern		
Attribution	Consensus	Distinctiveness	Consistency
Target (Stimulus)	High	High	High
Actor (Person)	Low	Low	High
Circumstance	Low	High	Low

Source: Orvis *et al.* (1975, p. 607). Reprinted by permission of the American Psychological Association.

tended to choose the cause implied by the schema which the known information matched.

According to Kelley (1973), causal schemas may permit a causal attribution even on the basis of a single observation of the response with no covariation information at all. For example, simply knowing that "John laughs at the comedian" may yield causal attribution to the comedian, and simply knowing that "Sue is afraid of the ant" may yield causal attribution to Sue. This is possible because, having observed similar effects before, perceivers have developed expectancies regarding the covariation information that exists for a given effect and these schemas influence their causal judgments. Thus most people would expect high consensus and high distinctiveness for John's laughter at the comedian (a target cause schema) and low consensus and low distinctiveness for Sue's fear of the ant (an actor cause schema). People are also more apt to expect success than failure – i.e., they assume higher consistency for success – and this may contribute to the tendency for success to be attributed more to stable causes in the actor than failure is. Failure evokes the schema for circumstance causes, whereas success evokes the schema for actor causes.

Expectancies about covariation information derived from group stereotypes may also affect performance attributions. The stereotype that men are more competent than women may cause successful performance by a man and failure by a woman to be viewed as consistent with their past behavior, which could contribute to the well-documented tendency for such performance outcomes to be attributed to ability and inability, respectively. A man's success or a woman's failure evokes the schema for actor causes. On the other hand, sex stereotypes may cause a man's failure and a woman's success to be viewed as inconsistent with their past behavior, which could contribute to the tendency for these performance outcomes to be attributed to unstable causes, such as effort or luck. A man's failure or a woman's success evokes the schema for circumstance causes (Deaux and Emswiller 1974; Etaugh and Brown 1974). Similar attributional effects have been demonstrated for other group stereotypes (Hewstone *et al.* 1982).

Linguistically based schemas

Why do you like your best friend? Why do you visit her? People typically list causes in their friend in response to the first question (e.g., She is kind and intelligent) and causes in themselves in response to the second (e.g., I enjoy being with her). This finding represents a tendency for different categories of verbs to evoke different causal schemas. State verbs, expressing emotional or cognitive states (e.g., like, hate), tend to evoke target attributions, whereas action verbs, expressing manifest, observable behaviors (e.g., visit, help) evoke actor attributions both in adults (Brown and Fish 1983; McArthur 1972) and in children as young as five years old (Lalljee *et al.* 1983).

One possible explanation for verb effects on causal attributions is that different verbs trigger different inferences about consensus and distinctiveness information – i.e., state verbs elicit an assumed information pattern that corresponds to a target causal schema, whereas action verbs elicit an assumed information pattern that corresponds to an actor causal schema. Another explanation for verb effects is that different types of verbs imply different behavioral contexts (Fiedler and Semin 1989). Events communicated by state verbs, such as "Esther likes Harry", are assumed to be preceded by the target's behaviors (e.g., Harry helps Esther), and to be followed by the actor's behaviors (e.g., Esther visits Harry). The temporal order of events within this context implicates the target, Harry, as the cause of liking. On the other hand, events communicated by action verbs, such as "Esther helps Harry", are assumed to be preceded by the actor's behaviors (e.g., Esther likes Harry) and to be followed by the target's behaviors (e.g., Harry likes Esther). The temporal order of these assumed events implicates the actor, Esther as the cause of helping.

Schemas for multiple sufficient and multiple necessary causes

Whereas some behaviors have a strong tendency to elicit actor, target, or circumstance causal schemas, others may not. In these cases, Kelley (1973) proposes that perceivers who lack covariation information will consider plausible internal and external causes suggested by their past experiences, and various causal schemas may be invoked in an effort to choose among these causes.

A *multiple sufficient causes schema* is invoked when any one of several causes is perceived as sufficient to produce the effect. In this situation, the knowledge that one such cause is present throws into question the presence of another. The perceiver consequently applies the *discounting principle*, which specifies that the role of a given cause is discounted if other plausible causes are also present. Because external causes are typically more salient and easily verified, internal causes are more apt to be discounted. Discounting effects are analogous to the prediction from correspondent inference theory that dispositional causes will not be inferred when the actor has external pressures to perform a particular behavior.

Consider, for example, the effect of Nina insulting her brother. This effect would probably evoke a multiple sufficient causes schema, in which the perceiver would consider the possibility that Nina is a hostile person or that her brother has provoked her. If the perceiver happens to know that her brother insulted her, causes internal to Nina, such as a hostile disposition, would probably be discounted. This tendency to discount internal causes varies with the level of skill required to produce some effect. The presence of an external cause is less likely to yield discounting of internal causes for socially or intellectually skilled behaviors than for less skilled behaviors. Thus, when an actor's behavior conforms to social pressures, this does not dissuade perceivers from inferring dispositional causes for highly intellectual or highly extraverted behaviors, though it does yield discounting of internal causes for non-intellectual or introverted behaviors (Messick and Reeder 1974; Reeder *et al.* 1977).

A reciprocal principle to discounting, proposed by Kelley (1973), is the *augmentation principle*. Whereas discounting occurs when some effect is observed in the presence of a known cause that facilitates that effect, *augmentation* occurs when an effect is observed in the presence of a known inhibitory cause that acts to suppress the effect. Augmentation is analogous to the prediction from correspondent inference theory that dispositional causes will be more strongly inferred when the actor's behavior is socially undesirable. The fact that the effect occurs despite an inhibitory cause augments the perceived strength of other plausible facilitating causes. For example, if Nina insults her father, whose status would typically inhibit such behavior, the perceiver will infer either more extreme hostility or provocation than he would if she insulted her brother. Consistent with Kelley's predictions, the presence of an inhibitory cause for some behavior (e.g., paying very high fees to join a backpacking club) does enhance the perceived strength of a facilitating cause (e.g., the actor's motivation to join the club) (Kruglanski *et al.* 1978).

Another schema proposed by Kelley is the *multiple necessary causes schema* in which more than one cause must be present if the effect is to occur. Kelley suggests that this schema is evoked for extreme or unusual effects, and, consequently, such effects will not lead to discounting. Contrast the example of Nina insulting her brother with the more extreme effect of Nina punching him in the face. This effect would evoke a multiple necessary causes schema in which the perceiver would assume that both an external provocation and an internal hostile disposition are necessary to produce the effect. In this case, knowing that Nina's brother had insulted her would not lead to discounting of possible causes in Nina.

Cunningham and Kelley (1975) tested the prediction that perceivers are more likely to utilize a multiple necessary causes schema for explaining extreme effects than more moderate ones. They presented subjects with a variety of interpersonal effects in questionnaire format, such as "Phil dominates Bill", asking them to rate the extent to which the effect was caused by Phil, by Bill, or by both. The extremity of an effect was manipulated by including an adverb like "completely" or "slightly" in the sentence. As predicted, more extreme effects were attributed to causes in both people – i.e., multiple causes – more often than less extreme effects, for which one of the causes was discounted.

Several studies have investigated developmental trends in the ability to apply schemas for multiple sufficient and multiple necessary causes (see Sedlak and Kurtz 1981, for a review). Whereas even five-year-olds make use of a multiple necessary causes schema for extreme effects (Kun 1977), children of this age do not reliably apply the discounting principle as predicted by the schema for multiple sufficient causes. In one study, subjects of different ages listened to stories about two children, one of whom was either rewarded for playing with a toy or ordered to do so (external causes) and one of whom played with the toy under no external pressure. Subjects were then asked which child wanted to play with the toy, a measure of attribution to internal causes. College students chose the unconstrained child, thus demonstrating the discounting of internal causes in the children for whom external causes were known. In contrast, kindergartners showed no reliable tendency to choose the unconstrained child as the more internally motivated (Smith 1975).

A subsequent study demonstrated that young children's responses to this attribution task are not random, but rather reflect use of an *additivity principle* in lieu of the predicted discounting principle. That is, a higher proportion of kindergartners attributed to a target child the internal cause of wanting to play with a toy when there was a known external cause (the mother's command or offer of a reward) than when there was not. Thus, young children perceive external constraints as adding to the strength of internal motives. With age, use of the additive principle decreased and use of the discounting principle increased (Karniol and Ross 1976). Young children's use of an additive principle has also been found in research on their attributions for success. Whereas adults who have information about a target's performance often infer an inverse relationship between ability and effort, discounting one if the other is known to be present, young children infer a direct relationship and attribute more effort to successful people with high ability than to those with low ability (Kun 1977).

Interestingly, children's failure to apply the discounting principle varies with the particular causes in question, and they are more apt to discount internal causes when the external constraint is physical than when it is social. Specifically, young children show greater discounting of internal causes for a target's choice of toys when the external cause is the physical inaccessibility of a certain toy than when it is an adult's admonition not to play with it (Costanzo et al. 1974).

This finding suggests that children's failure to apply the discounting principle does not represent a failure in their logical reasoning per se. Indeed, discounting is not necessarily more logical, since there need not be an inverse relationship between internal and external causes. The fact that a child does not play with a forbidden toy does not imply that she wants to play with it. It just means that one cannot be certain. The results of the Costanzo et al. study further suggest that the discounting process requires learning what factors serve as behavioral constraints, and that physical constraints are understood before social ones. Accordingly, Karniol and Ross (1979) found that the ability to perceive a behavioral inducement as manipulative increased the likelihood of discounting. Subjects who reported that a target's mother offered him cake because she wanted him to play with one toy rather than another were more likely to show discounting than those who reported that she offered cake because she was nice. Moreover, hearing someone ascribe manipulative intent to a reward increased the likelihood of discounting among subjects who had previously shown additivity in their causal attributions.

The impact on causal attributions of learned assumptions about various causes is revealed in cross-cultural as well as developmental research. Japanese mothers attribute their children's poor mathematics performance more to lack of effort than American mothers do, whereas American mothers make stronger attributions to lack of ability and poor instruction (Holloway *et al.* 1986). These findings may reflect the superior performance of Japanese children in mathematics (Husen 1967) or, alternatively, they may reflect cultural differences in basic assumptions about the contribution of effort and ability to successful performance on difficult tasks. American adults assume that effort will make more of a difference for persons with high than with low ability (Anderson and Butzin 1974), whereas Indian adults (and perhaps Japanese, as well) take the more egalitarian view that effort makes as much of a difference for persons with low as with high ability (Gupta and Singh 1981). It is worth noting that an emphasis on effort as the cause of poor performance could foster the mathematical superiority of Japanese children, since the attribution of failure to unstable causes improves subsequent performance (Weiner *et al.* 1972).

The fact that discounting varies with the content of the attribution problem and depends upon the learning of certain culturally specific causal rules suggests that it may be inappropriate to view causal schemas as abstract cognitive structures. Indeed, this criticism of the schema construct was made by Fiedler (1982), who further argued that causal schemas have been used in a circular way. Specifically, he argued that the existence of a schema must be demonstrated independently of relationships between stimulus input and causal judgments if the schema is to be more than merely a summary label for those relationships. For example, he suggested that independent evidence of different schemas for moderate and extreme effects could be reflected in differences in the learning or recall of sentences describing such effects. While not rejecting the concept of causal schemas, Fiedler concluded that the research evidence had not provided convincing evidence for their existence.

Temporal order, perceptual organization, contiguity, and similarity

Einhorn and Hogarth (1986) have noted that people utilize several cues to causality in addition to covariation. One of these is *temporal order*, which is essential for determining which of two factors that covary is a cause and which is an effect. Temporal order seems like a straightforward cue, and indeed, children as young as three years old can utilize it to identify causes (Sedlak and Kurtz 1981). However, McArthur (1980) has noted that temporal order can actually be difficult to discern in ongoing social interactions.

Consider a dynamic social interaction, such as bickering between husband and wife. Each spouse's behavior may be perceived as both cause and effect: the husband reacts to his wife by withdrawing, that reaction causes a nagging reaction in the wife, which in turn causes the husband to withdraw, which causes the wife to nag, and so on. The temporal order of nagging and withdrawing that is perceived may vary with how perceivers segment this interaction chain into perceptual units – its *perceptual organization*. Moreover, the power of certain stimuli to draw attention may cause the perceiver to pick up the visually or vocally salient person's influence on the non-salient person, rather than vice versa. Thus, the husband may segment the interaction as "she nags, I withdraw, she nags, I withdraw", because his wife's behavior is more salient to him than his own – he can see her, but not himself. The wife, on the other hand, may segment the interaction as "he withdraws, I nag, he withdraws, I nag". Outside observers may segment the interaction as the husband does if they take the husband's perspective or if the wife's appearance or voice is very attention-getting – e.g., if she is fat or shrill – whereas observers may segment the interaction as the wife does if the husband is more salient.

Figure 5.1 is a schematic depiction of salience effects on perceptual segmentation. Imagine that O and o are two actors engaged in a social interaction. The behavioral exchanges tend to be perceptually organized into units reflecting the causal influence of O on o rather

Figure 5.1   Segmentation of a dyadic interaction into causal influence units as a function of the actors' salience

O====o----O=== o --- O===o ---O=== o-----O

o-----O====o ---- O====o---- O=== o ---O=== o

O ==== o   Is the causal influence of the salient actor on the non-salient actor.

o-----O   Is the causal influence of the non-salient actor on the salient actor.

Source: McArthur (1980, p. 512). Reprinted by permission of Sage Publications, Inc.

than into units reflecting the causal influence of o on O, regardless of who actually begins the interaction. As a consequence, the salient actor may be seen as exerting more causal influence than the non-salient actor even though their actual influence is equal (McArthur 1980).

Another cue discussed by Einhorn and Hogarth (1986) is *contiguity*. The extent to which events are contiguous in time and space is an important cue to physical causality for children as well as adults (Michotte 1963; Sedlak and Kurtz 1981), and it seems reasonable to propose that it would be an important cue to social causality as well. You are more apt to attribute your friend's bad mood to the exam she took today than to the one she took last week.

Some empirical evidence for the impact of contiguity on perceptions of social causality is provided in Heider and Simmel's (1944) classic animated film, which depicts two triangles and a circle moving in and out of a square enclosure with a "door". The cues of temporal and spatial contiguity as well as velocity and direction of movement that are provided in this film give rise to impressions about behavior and its causes. Specifically, viewers perceive a bully (a large triangle) chasing after a victim (a circle), whom someone else (a small triangle) is trying to protect. These three "characters" are perceived to be running in and out of a house; barring the door; breaking it down; and ultimately the bully is perceived to deliberately destroy the house. Bassili (1976) addressed the question of exactly what movement qualities yield the perception of social causality by systematically varying the movements of two geometric objects. He found that any temporal contingency between the changes in direction of two objects yields the perception that they are interacting with each other, whereas a temporal contingency that increases the spatial proximity of the two objects creates the perception of intentionality.

When contiguity cues are absent, the attribution of causality requires that the perceiver become a "storyteller", creating a *causal chain* which links some cause to an intermediate effect which in turn causes the final effect (Einhorn and Hogarth 1986; Read 1987). Interestingly, there is some evidence to indicate that when two causes are equally relevant, the earlier one in a chain of events is attributed greater importance than the later one, even though the latter has more temporal contiguity with the effect. Thus, a history of fights and conflicts is perceived as a more significant cause of divorce than extramarital sexual relations when the conflict causes the extramarital sex, which in turn causes the divorce, than when the extramarital sex causes the conflict, which in turn causes the divorce (Vinokur and Ajzen 1982).

The attribution of causality also requires some *conceptual link* between cause and effect. In order to attribute a couple's divorce to conflict or to extramarital sex, you need to view these events as possible causes of divorce. This link can be likened to a schema regarding plausible causes, which may be based upon past experience and world knowledge or an innate predisposition to perceive certain causal links. Classical conditioning experiments have demonstrated that the plausibility of causes as well as their contiguity is necessary for a cause–effect association. Thus, the pairing of a rabbit with a loud noise conditioned little Albert to fear rabbits, whereas the pairing of a block of wood with a loud noise did not condition him to fear the block of wood. Albert perceived a rabbit as a plausible cause of loud noise, but not a wooden block. Similarly, rats in a classical conditioning paradigm learn to associate gastro-intestinal illness with a novel-tasting food, but not with audiovisual cues (Garcia and Koelling 1966). Organisms seem "prepared" to detect some causal relations, but not others (Seligman and Hager 1972).

The perceived *similarity* between cause and effect – the "resemblance criterion" – may sometimes provide the conceptual link needed for causal attribution. However, this is not always an accurate cue. For example, Nisbett and Ross (1980) noted that physical similarity between disease symptoms and cures was the basis for certain erroneous medical theories, such as attributing the cure of jaundice to a brilliant yellow substance. In the realm of social causes, the cue of similarity may also be employed erroneously, although here the similarity is more likely to be metaphorical than physical, as when negligent (childlike) crimes are attributed to babyfaced adults (Berry and Zebrowitz-McArthur 1988). Despite such examples of erroneous inferences, the similarity between various possible causes and an effect can be a valid cue to causality. It makes sense to attribute an upset stomach to something that was ingested, an inference that is fostered by physical similarity between cause and effect. And it often makes sense to attribute large effects to large causes. Whereas a difficult exam may be of appropriate magnitude to explain your friend's bad mood, you would probably be correct to look for a "bigger" cause to explain the "bigger" effect of a suicide attempt.

Actor–observer attribution differences

Causal locus

Consistent with the foregoing analysis of the effects of perceptual organization on causal attribution, Jones and Nisbett (1972) proposed that actor–observer differences in attentional focus will yield systematic differences in causal attributions for the actor's behavior. More specifically, they suggested that observers tend to attribute an actor's behavior to internal causes because their attention is focused on the actor, who is salient or "figural" against the ground of the situation. Actors, on the other hand, attribute their own behavior to external causes because they attend to their environment and the people within it who, for them, are salient or figural.

The predicted actor–observer attribution difference was demonstrated by Storms (1973). Moreover, this difference was reversed when the attentional focus of actors and observers was manipulated through videotapes such that each saw the interaction from the other's perspective. More direct evidence for a perceptual organization explanation of actor–observer attribution differences has been provided by Swann *et al.* (1987) who assessed actors' and observers' segmentation of a social interaction. Observers segment the interaction in terms of the causal influence that an actor's behavior has on their own as evidenced by their tendency to recall more "actor's statement–own statement" verbal exchanges than "own statement–actor's statement" exchanges. Moreover, this perceptual organization is accompanied by the observers' tendency to attribute the actor's behavior more to the type of person he is (internal causes) than to their own behaviors (external causes).

Interestingly, the tendency for observers to segment a social interaction in terms of the causal influence that the actor's behavior has on their own is reduced when they are attempting to control the actor's behavior. Specifically, when observers were trying to influence an actor's beliefs, they correctly recalled more "own statement–actor's statement" verbal segments than vice versa, and this change in perceptual organization was accompanied by a tendency to attribute the actor's behavior *less* to the type of person he is than to their own eliciting behaviors. Several other studies have found that when observers are encouraged to empathize with an actor, their causal attributions for the actor's behavior are less dispositional than those of non-empathizing observers (see Howe 1987; Regan and

Totten 1975; Wolfson and Salancik 1977). However, these effects may reflect observers' adoption of the motivations and psychological perspective of the actor rather than merely reflecting adoption of the actor's visual perspective (Fiske *et al.* 1979).

Although many studies support the view that the differing visual perspectives of actors and observers yields a basic tendency for people to attribute their own behavior to external causes while attributing the behavior of others to internal dispositions (see Watson 1982, for a review of this literature), Jones and Nisbett (1972) noted that informational differences between actors and observers may also contribute to this effect. In particular, the actor is likely to assess the cause of her own behavior by comparing it to previous behaviors, and, because these are typically variable, she is more apt to make a situational than a dispositional attribution. Observers, on the other hand, are likely to compare an actor's behavior to that of other actors, and because they are typically variable, observers are more inclined to make a dispositional than a situational attribution.

Actor–observer differences in information about the actor's past behaviors may at times counteract the perceptually-based actor–observer difference in causal attribution (Eisen 1979; Monson and Snyder 1977). Thus, extraverts attribute their own extraverted behavior more to dispositional causes than observers do, presumably because the extraverts know that their past behavior is *not* variable (Monson and Hesley 1982). Since research investigating informational differences between actors and observers has employed methods that do not tap the influence of their divergent visual perspectives, the question remains as to whether or not such differences will obscure the perceptually-based actor–observer difference when differences in visual perspective are also present.

Dispositional inferences

If there is a general tendency to perceive other people's behavior as more internally caused than our own, then not only may we be more likely to infer a particular trait from another person's behavior, but also we may perceive a greater number of traits in others than in ourselves. Evidence to support this prediction has been provided in studies which asked subjects to describe themselves and others (see Nisbett *et al.* 1973). The greater propensity to attribute traits to others has been documented for practically the entire English lexicon of trait terms (Goldberg 1978). Moreover, people are more likely to view the behavior of others as more reflective of their traits and less dependent upon the situation than their own behavior is, regardless of how well they know or like those others, and this effect obtains even when subjects are given a variety of response options regarding the descriptiveness of a trait, such as "uncertain" and "moderately descriptive" (Goldberg 1981b).[2]

The tendency to attribute more traits to others than ourselves could derive from a greater perceptual focus on their behaviors than on our own, with resulting correspondent trait inferences. This tendency could also reflect less awareness of the variability of others' behavior than of our own. Evidence that such informational factors do contribute to the actor–observer difference in trait attribution is provided by the finding that increased familiarity with others, which should increase awareness of variability in their behavior, does increase the tendency to view their behavior as depending upon the situation as opposed to reflecting their traits (Goldberg 1981b).

Attribution biases

Attribution bias is the tendency to favor one cause over another when explaining some effect. Such favoritism may result in causal attributions that deviate from predictions derived from rational attributional principles, like covariation. The actor–observer difference in causal attribution is one example of attribution bias, since the actor and the observer each favor a particular cause when explaining the actor's behavior. Research has documented a number of additional attribution biases, which are described below.

The illusory causation effect

The effect of visual perspective on actor–observer differences in causal attributions has an analogue in observers' attributions for the behavior of actors who elicit varying degrees of visual attention. For example, when perceivers watched two people interacting in a getting-acquainted conversation, they tended to see the person who was facing them as causing the behavior of the person who sat with his back to them rather than vice versa (Taylor and Fiske 1975). This tendency to attribute causality to physically salient actors has been dubbed the "illusory causation effect" (McArthur 1980). Other research has varied the degree to which perceivers attend to particular people by manipulating their physical qualities. When an actor conversed with someone who was brightly lit, moving, wearing a boldly striped shirt, or who formed a *Gestalt* "unit" with others present by virtue of similar clothing or gender, then the actor's behavior was attributed more to external causes – i.e., the salient target – than when he conversed with someone who was dimly lit, stationary, wearing a grey shirt, or who did not form a "unit" with others present (McArthur and Post 1977). A salient voice can also produce an illusory causation effect. When an actor conversed with a partner whose voice was slightly louder than his own, perceivers tended to attribute the actor's behavior to causes in the salient-voiced partner (Robinson and McArthur 1982).

The tendency to attribute an actor's behavior to the causal influence of perceptually salient interaction partners has interesting implications for our assignment of responsibility for social conflicts. Indeed, an aggressor's behavior is attributed more to causes in the victim when attention is drawn to the victim by virtue of a novel appearance – a leg brace or red hair – than when these physical attributes are not apparent (McArthur and Solomon 1978). Although high personal involvement in a social interaction can reduce the magnitude of such perceptual salience effects (Borgida and Howard-Pitney 1983), the fact that they obtain for a novel physical attribute as inconsequential as red hair suggests that such effects may be very widespread. They may also occur at a very young age, since children are more sensitive to visually than to verbally represented causal influences (Kassin *et al.* 1980; Kassin and Pryor 1985). More generally, the documentation of illusory causation effects suggests that causal attributions are often made with much less thought and conscious information processing than is implied by the correspondent inference and covariation theories.

Egocentric attributions

When people are engaged in a close interpersonal relationship or interacting with someone on a joint project, they more readily recall their own contributions, and this biased recall is positively related to a tendency to take more credit or blame for the outcome than is attributed to others (Ross and Sicoly 1979; Ross 1981; Thompson and Kelley 1981). Thus, if two roommates are asked how much of the cleaning they do, each may take credit for 75 per cent of the work, and if they are asked how much they contribute to the clutter in their room, each may assume the lion's share of responsibility for the mess. This phenomenon has been labeled the "egocentric bias" in casual attributions (Ross and Sicoly 1979).

It should be noted that egocentric attributions are not necessarily in conflict with the proposal that actors attribute their own behavior to external causes. Egocentric attributions pertain to attributions of responsibility rather than attributions to internal versus external causes. Thus, for example, two roommates may each report that they make 75 per cent of the mess (egocentric attributions of responsibility). However, if asked why they make a mess, their own behavior may be attributed to external causes – working on big art projects – while their roommate's behavior may be attributed to internal causes – a lazy disposition.

Underutilization of consensus and the false consensus effect

Early research testing Kelley's (1967) covariation model revealed that consensus information had a weaker impact on causal attributions than either distinctiveness or consistency (McArthur 1972). Although subsequent studies demonstrated that modifications in the content or format of consensus information can considerably strengthen its effects (Kassin 1979; Hewstone and Jaspars 1983), Nisbett and Borgida (1975) found surprisingly weak effects when they asked university students to explain the behavior of a participant in a psychology experiment. This participant, like most others, had agreed to tolerate a high level of electric shock. However, knowledge of the actual behavior of most participants (consensus information) did not affect subjects' causal attributions for his behavior. Thus, subjects who were told that 16 out of 34 participants had tolerated the highest possible level of shock were no more likely to make situational attributions for the behavior of a participant who had done likewise than were subjects who had been given no consensus information at all.

Nisbett and Borgida (1975) attributed their findings to the fact that people's judgments are less responsive to the dull and abstract baserates that constitute consensus information than they are to the more vivid information about the behavior of a concrete target person. On the other hand, Wells and Harvey (1977) argued that Nisbett and Borgida's failure to obtain effects for consensus information reflected shortcomings in its manipulation. More specifically, they suggested that subjects may have viewed the available consensus information as unrepresentative of the population inasmuch as it was very discrepant with most people's expectations. Although the modal subject in the shock study tolerated the highest level of electric shock, naive subjects estimated that most participants would tolerate only a moderate level. A replication of the Nisbett and Borgida study in which subjects were explicitly told that the consensus information was based on a random sample of participants revealed significant effects for consensus that did not obtain when sampling information was not provided. However, it should be noted that information about the target person was less vivid in this study than it had been in Nisbett and Borgida's original research, which could also have augmented the impact of the abstract consensus information (Nisbett and Ross 1980).

The need to bolster consensus information with sampling information when it conflicts with subjects' prior expectations is related to the phenomenon of *false consensus effects*. This is the tendency for people to assume that there is high consensus for their own past or expected behaviors (Marks and Miller 1987; Ross *et al.* 1977; van der Pligt 1984). The consequence of the false consensus effect for causal attributions is that perceivers are prone to attribute an effect to the cause with which their own response covaries. Perceivers will consequently be less responsive to consensus information when they have experienced a target directly than when they have not, since the direct experience can generate egocentric consensus information that conflicts with consensus information from other sources (Feldman *et al.* 1976; Hansen and Donoghue 1977; Higgins and Bryant 1982; Kulik and Taylor 1980). Assume, for example, that your friend raves to you about a particular professor, and that you find consensual support for his reaction among other students. You are more likely to attribute these evaluations to the professor's scintillating lectures if you have never had a course with him than if you have had a course which you found very boring. It should be noted that the use of your own response as a basis for estimating the degree of consensual support for your friend's response would be a rational strategy if you did not have access to other students' evaluations. Thus, egocentrically generated consensus information should be called a *false* consensus effect only if you weight your own response more than that of another, randomly chosen student (Dawes 1989).

The fundamental attribution error

As noted earlier, the tendency for perceivers to make correspondent inferences about an actor's disposition or attitude from his behavior despite strong environmental constraints has been called the fundamental attribution error – "the tendency to underestimate the impact of situational factors and to overestimate the role of dispositional factors in controlling behavior" (Ross 1977, p. 183). Although there is considerable evidence for such effects (Jones and Harris 1967; Jones 1979), there are also conditions under which people overestimate the role of *situational* causes. In particular, Quattrone (1982) found that when perceivers were sensitized to the possibility of environmental constraints on an actor's behavior, they perceived these constraints as causing the actor's behavior even though it was totally explicable in terms of the actor's stated prior attitude.

Other evidence that has been offered in support of the fundamental attribution error includes the finding that attributions to causes in the actor are more frequent than attributions to causes in the target. For example, when covariation information is held constant, effects such as "Sue is afraid of the dog" and "George translates the sentence incorrectly" are more likely to be attributed to causes internal to Sue and George than to external causes in the dog or the sentence (McArthur 1972). However, the fact is that attributions to causes in the actor do *not* exceed attributions to external causes when attribution to the *circumstances* is considered in addition to target attributions. Moreover, the most frequent category of attributions is mixed causes in the actor and the environment, which does not support the fundamental attribution error (Howe 1987; McArthur 1972).

Further evidence that the fundamental attribution error may not be so "fundamental" is provided by the finding that it is culturally specific. In a replication of McArthur's (1972) study, Korean perceivers showed a target attribution bias rather than an actor attribution bias when no covariation information was provided. That is, attributions to external causes, such as the dog or the sentence, were higher than attributions to actors, such as Sue or George (Cha and Nam 1985). Hamilton *et al.* (1983) have reported analogous effects for Japanese perceivers whose attributions of responsibility for acts of harmdoing gave less weight than Americans to intentionality information and greater weight to information about the influence of an external party. Similarly, Miller (1984) found that whereas Americans were more likely to explain deviant behaviors in terms of personal dispositions than in terms of external constraints, Hindus showed a reverse trend. Interestingly, young children in the USA also show an external attribution bias (Ruble *et al.* 1979; Higgins and Bryant 1982). The cultural divergence in the frequency of actor attributions has been attributed to the fact that the Japanese and Hindus place greater emphasis than Americans on role obligations (Hamilton *et al.* 1983; Miller 1984) and that "beliefs in free will are mostly alien to the Koreans" (Cha and Nam 1985, p. 179). The developmental divergence may similarly reflect the impact of children's relatively low level of autonomy on their perceptions of social causality.

Another source of evidence for the fundamental attribution error has been actor–observer differences in causal attribution. The assumption that actors' attributions for their own behavior are more accurate than observers' attributions (Jones and Nisbett 1972; Monson and Snyder 1977) implies that a tendency for observers to make more dispositional attributions than actors do reflects the fundamental attribution error. However, the tendency for observers to make more dispositional attributions is not so "fundamental". It is most pronounced for negative behaviors and may be absent or even reversed for positive ones (see Cunningham *et al.* 1979; Eisen 1979). This impact of behavioral positivity on actor–observer differences in attribution can be interpreted within a non-motivational, information-processing model as well as a motivational one (Miller and Ross 1975; Bradley 1978). Thus, people may be less likely to attribute their own than another's failure to internal causes because this enhances their self-esteem (a motivational explanation) or because they know that their own failures are unusual whereas their successes are not (a cognitive explanation).

Not only does the tendency for observers to make more dispositional attributions vary with the behavior in question, but also, when the effect does occur, it may not necessarily be an "error". The concept of attributional error requires some standard of accuracy against which to compare people's attributions, and establishing such a standard is often an impossible task inasmuch as most behaviors can be reasonably linked to more than one causal force. Thus the fact that actors and observers make different attributions need not imply that either one is mistaken, and it certainly does not imply that the observer's dispositional attribution is the erroneous one (Funder 1982). A person may do something because of inducements from the external environment. At the same time, she may be responsive to those inducements because of her internal states or traits. As such, it is typically reasonable to attribute behavior to external causes or to internal ones, although an interactive attribution may be the most reasonable of all. And, as noted above, at least some research has revealed that when perceivers are given the opportunity to make interactive attributions, they favor these over attributions to causes only in the actor.

Hilton (1989) has further suggested that actor–observer differences may sometimes reflect conversational norms rather than any erroneous disregard of environmental causes by observers. Thus, the question "Why does Joann major in Psychology?" may be taken by Joann to mean "Why did you choose Psychology versus some other major?", which yields attributions to target characteristics, whereas it may be taken by an outside observer to mean "Why did Joann choose Psychology whereas others do not?", which yields attributions to actor characteristics. The divergent construals of the question by actors and observers are explained in terms of what information they have at their disposal and their consequent assumptions about what the questioner wants to know.

Trope's (1986) two-stage model of dispositional attribution provides additional evidence that observers may not have any "fundamental" tendency to disregard the impact of external factors on an actor's behavior. According to this model, the causal attribution process involves both the *identification* of an actor's behavior and situation, and *dispositional inferences* from whatever behavior and situation have been identified. Research testing this model reveals that evidence for the fundamental attribution error may actually reflect the effects of situational and behavioral cues on identification processes followed by appropriate dispositional inferences. For example, a perceiver may recognize that an actor was provoked into insulting someone and take into account this provocation when inferring the actor's dispositional hostility. At the same time, however, the provocation may result in the identification of greater anger in that actor than would be perceived were the provocation absent. The net result may be the attribution of as much dispositional hostility to the provoked as to the non-provoked actor.

In sum, the fundamental attribution error is best viewed as a bias toward attributing an actor's behavior to dispositional causes rather than as an attributional error. This bias may be limited to adults in Western societies and it may be most pronounced when they are constrained to attribute behavior to a single cause. Finally, it may reflect processes other than a fundamental tendency to ignore situational influences on behavior.

Summary and implications

People frequently seek to understand the causes of an actor's behavior, and they make a variety of attributions which vary in causal locus – internal to the actor versus external – and in descriptive correspondence with the actor's overt behavior. Consistent with a constructivist, "theory-driven" view of social perception, a number of perceiver characteristics influence causal attributions. These include perceivers' expectations regarding their own behavior, their affective reactions to the behavior to be explained, their causal schemas, and their perspective – i.e., whether they are explaining their own or another person's behavior.

Characteristics of the actor and the behavior to be explained also influence causal attributions, as predicted by "data-driven" theories of social perception. An actor's physical salience, the nature of an actor's behavior, the distinctiveness of its effects, its consistency over time and its distinctiveness across targets all influence causal attributions. The social context in which a behavior occurs is also a significant factor. Explicit social pressures, implicit social norms, and the behavior of others all have an effect on attributions for an actor's behavior.

Despite the considerable research concerning the effects on causal attributions of perceiver characteristics as well as qualities of the actor and the behavior, there are notable gaps in this literature. There is a need for a more comprehensive catalogue of the specific categories of behavior that evoke various perceiver schemas. There is also a need for research regarding the impact on casual attributions of specific qualities of an actor's appearance or non-verbal behavior, each of which could influence attributions by virtue of perceived similarity between cause and effect. More generally, research is needed to articulate the kinds of events, actors, and dispositions that are perceived as plausible causes for various effects, by virtue of either their "resemblance" or some other principles. This is necessary for theoretical predictions to go beyond abstract causal loci to concrete causes. Research investigating the joint influence on attributions of the perceiver and the actor whose behavior is to be explained is also needed, although studies of attributions in ongoing relationships have begun to fill this gap (see Fincham *et al.* 1987; Grigg *et al.* 1989).

Theories of causal attribution take as their starting point the assumption that people operate as naive scientists in their efforts to understand the causes of behavior. Although research testing attribution theories has affirmed the application of logical principles such as covariation and discounting, attributional bias has been a recurrent theme. Biases include the fundamental attribution error, victim blaming, sex-stereotyped attributions, the illusory causation effect, egocentric attributions, and the false consensus effect.

Whether these biases are construed as reflecting motivational or cognitive influences, their existence has been taken as evidence that the attributor does not fare too well as a "naive scientist" in search of the true causes of behavior. However, as noted in Chapter 3, *bias* need not imply error. For example, the fundamental attribution error may reflect an efficient, automatic process of dispositional inference from behavior that, on the average, yields accurate perceptions by perceivers who are too cognitively busy to make conscious corrections based on situational causes (Gilbert 1989). Perhaps the most appropriate basis for evaluating causal attributions is in terms of the consequences they have for behavior. Do they fulfill the function of causal attributions that theorists have posited – the creation of a more stable, predictable, and controllable social world? Research on the *consequences* of causal attributions suggests that they often do. (See Kelley and Michela 1980, for a review of this work.)

Further reading

Jones, E. E., Kanouse, D. E. Kelley, H. H., Nisbett, R. E., Valins, S. and Weiner, B. (eds) (1972). *Attribution: Perceiving the causes of behavior.* Morristown, NJ: General Learning Press. A classic collection of papers by distinguished attribution theorists, treating a variety of topics including actor–observer differences, performance attributions, linguistic bases of attribution, and causal schemata.

Kassin, S. M. and Pryor, J. B. (1985). The development of attribution processes. In J. B. Pryor and J. D. Day, *The development of social cognition*. (pp. 3–34). New York: Springer-Verlag. Research on the development of causal attribution is reviewed with attention to the role of temporal order, contiguity, perceptual salience, covariation, discounting, augmentation, and content-specific knowledge. It is argued that developmental changes may reflect changes in experientially based or culturally transmitted knowledge as well as cognitive maturational processes.

Miller, J. G. (1984). Culture and the development of everyday social explanation. *Journal of Personality and Social Psychology*, **46**, 961–78. Causal explanations for prosocial and deviant behaviors offered by American and Hindu adults and children reveal contrasting developmental changes in the two cultures, and it is argued that attribution theories need to give greater weight to the social acquisition of causal knowledge.

Trope, Y. (1986). Identification and inferential processes in dispositional attribution. *Psychological Review*, **93**, 239–57. This paper presents a two-stage model of social perception in which the first stage is the identification (categorization) of an actor's behavior and situational and historical context, and the second stage is the application of causal schemas to infer the actor's personal disposition from the identifications that have been made.

Notes

1 Modifications to correspondent inference theory proposed by Jones and McGillis (1976) will not be discussed inasmuch as they have not been well integrated into the research literature.

2 When people are given the option of attributing opposite traits to self and others (e.g., attributing both "seriousness" *and* "carefreeness") rather than rating self and others on bipolar trait scales (e.g., serious to carefree), they attribute more traits to themselves (Sande *et al.* 1988). Since attributing two opposite traits to the self is tantamount to saying that one's own behavior depends on the situation, these findings do not negate the conclusion that we perceive others to have more traits than ourselves when traits are defined as stable predispositions to respond in a particular way across a variety of situations.

6 / TOWARD AN INTEGRATIVE THEORY OF SOCIAL PERCEPTION

In the introductory chapter to this book, I recalled my early desire to write a novel about my perceptions of the people in my college residence hall. Although the scant resemblance of this book to the novel I had fantasied may be attributable to my lack of literary talent, the causal role of the research literature should not be discounted. As noted by an eminent social perception theorist: "the topics in social psychology read more like a Sears and Roebuck catalogue than like a novel. They provide a listing of items of possible interest to the reader rather than a story with a plot, development of characters, and so on" (Kelley 1983, p. 8). This characterization of social psychology topics in general is equally pertinent to the specific social perception topics covered in this book. The absence of a storyline is manifested in several ways.

Shortcomings in the social perception story

First, there is inadequate integration within each topic. Kurt Lewin, sometimes called the father of modern social psychology, stressed that behavior is a function of the *person* and the *environment* (e.g., Lewin 1936). Although the research literature did allow a consideration of environmental (the target person) as well as person (the perceiver) determinants of social perception within each chapter of this book, these two influences have typically been treated in isolation from one another. For example, research has examined the impact on impression formation of the perceiver's schemas (person effects) and the target's appearance (environment effects), but rarely their joint effects. Without some theoretical integration of these two influences on social perceptions, a proper story cannot be told.

A second gap in the story that I have been able to tell is that the phenomena of social perception have rarely been integrated into the life of a behaving social being. The actions of the perceiver have a significant impact on what is perceived, and this fact is often overlooked in social perception research, which typically treats the perceiver as a passive recipient of information provided by an experimenter. Moreover, experimentally manipulated information is often a far cry from the dynamic, multimodal information provided by target persons in real social interactions.

A third shortcoming in social perception research is the scant attention paid to the cultural context of the perceiver. This disregard reflects researchers' emphasis on social perception *processes* as opposed to *contents*, coupled with the assumption that processes are universal. However, the cross-cultural research that has been re-viewed in this book reveals that parochial assumptions about social perception processes may well be wrong. Consider Westerners' tendency to describe others in terms of their traits and to perceive their behavior as being caused more by personal than environmental influences – the fundamental attribution error. This has been attri-buted, in part, to the inherently greater perceptual salience of "figural" people than their environmental background. But the fact that the fundamental attribution error is not manifested in other cultures raises doubts about the ability of this social perception process to explain the effect. Similarly, consider the tendency for Westerners' trait impressions to be influenced by an actor's physical appearance. Although this has been attributed to culturally learned stereotypes, doubts about the explanatory value of this social percep-tion process are raised by the finding of very similar appearance-based stereotypes in a variety of cultures. The fact is that conclusions about the universality or the cultural specificity of social perception phenomena can be drawn only when cross-cultural comparisons of the *contents* of social perception are made. And such comparisons are needed to clarify the story of the *processes* that underlie these phenomena.

Developmental comparisons, like cross-cultural ones, have been neglected in certain areas of social perception research, although they can be very informative. Indeed, developmental studies of gender differences in emotion perception (such as Rosenthal *et al.* 1979) have shed light on the determinants of gender differences among adults, and developmental studies of causal attribution phenomena, such as discounting (see Sedlak and Kurtz 1981), have illuminated the determinants of discounting among adults. Similarly, studies of developmental changes in impression formation or the contents of social perception may clarify the origins and functions of adult perceptions. Ideally, developmental comparisons should be coupled with cross-cultural ones. For instance, it was long assumed that Western adults' use of abstract trait descriptors, in contrast to Western children's use of more concrete ones, reflected more sophisticated inferential abilities among adults. Only when developmental research was conducted in other cultures did it become apparent that social perceptions do not necessarily develop from the concrete to the abstract, but may also develop from the simple to the complex (Miller 1984). This fact implicates different processes underlying the contents of social perception than had formerly been assumed.

Another shortcoming in the social perception story is that there is inadequate integration across topics. Despite the wealth of theory and data pertaining to the contents of social perception, impression formation, emotion perception, and causal attribution, there is little to integrate these domains of social perception. Yet surely they are interrelated. For example, it is widely assumed that the descriptive categories that people use in their social perceptions and the organizational structure of these categories will influence impression formation. However, the research literature has rarely linked perceivers' implicit personality theories, person types, and so on, to their impressions of specific targets. Similarly, causal attributions for a target's behavior are influenced by perceptions of the target's emotional state while performing the behavior (see Lowe and Kassin 1980), and by stereotyped impressions of the target's social group (see Hewstone *et al.* 1982). Yet the link between causal attribution and emotion perception or trait perception has only recently been formalized (Trope 1986). And although trait perceptions may often rest on the perception of recurrent emotional states, the research literatures on emotion perception and impression formation rarely intersect. An integrative theory must draw connections between these various domains if we are to tell a proper story about social perception.

In sum, a truly integrative theory must place social perceptions within a behavioral, cultural and developmental framework, specifying how characteristics of the perceiver and the social environment

jointly influence the contents of social perception, impression formation, emotion perception, and causal attributions, and how these
various components of social perception influence each other. Only
then will there be a plot to the story of social perceptions.

Tenets of the ecological theory

An ecological theory of social perception, proposed by McArthur
and Baron (1983), specifies a number of concepts that may help to
provide the integration needed to transform the catalogue of social
perception research into a story. This theory draws on theories of
object perception (see Gibson 1979; Shaw *et al.* 1982), and has
several distinguishing features.

First, social perception is integrated into the life of a behaving
social being via the assumption that "perceiving is for doing" and
that social perception serves an *adaptive function* either for the
survival of the species or for the goal attainment of individuals. This
emphasis on the adaptive function of social perception focuses
attention on the intrinsic connection between action and perception,
which, as noted above, has been given insufficient consideration in
traditional theories. It also focuses attention on the contents of
perception – what people need to perceive in order to function – as
opposed to the processes of perception, which are the focus of more
traditional theoretical approaches.

A second component of the ecological position is its emphasis on
the perception of social *affordances*. Affordances are defined by
Gibson (1979, p. 127) as what the environment "offers the animal,
what it provides or furnishes, either for good or ill". A more poetic
and vivid indication of what Gibson means by affordance is provided
by his quotation from Koffka: "Each thing says what it is . . . a fruit
says 'eat me'; water says 'drink me'; thunder says 'fear me'; and
woman says 'love me'" (Gibson 1979, p. 138). Although Gibson
emphasizes the objective reality of affordances, he also emphasizes
their emergence from the interaction of qualities of the environment
and qualities of the perceiver. A fruit affords eating by some perceivers but not others, and a woman affords loving by some perceivers but not others. The affordance concept thus facilitates the
integration of perceiver and target effects on social perceptions.

A third tenet of the ecological theory is that the external stimulus
environment provides *structured information* that reveals its afford-

ances. This information is often contained in *events*, which are multimodal, dynamic changes over space and time – e.g., to learn whether or not someone affords domination may require observing the person in a social interaction. This emphasis on dynamic and temporally extended stimulus information has several implications for our view of social perception. First, it provides a needed balance to the constructivist perspective that currently dominates many areas of research. Second, it encourages the study of social perception in more naturalistic contexts than those of the typical research paradigm. Third, it implies a perceiver whose perceptions are informed by an active interaction with the social environment. Finally, it explains certain erroneous perceptions as resulting from impoverished stimulus information.

A fourth hallmark of the ecological theory is that the detection of social affordances depends upon the perceivers' *attunements* – that is, the particular stimulus information to which they attend. Attunements may be innate or they may be conditioned by the perceivers' social goals, behavioral capabilities, or perceptual experience. Perceptual errors may occur when an attunement to certain information configurations is overgeneralized – e.g., an attunement to the configuration of an infant's face is overgeneralized to babyfaced adults, yielding stereotyped impressions of their traits (Berry and McArthur 1986). Like the assumption that social perceptions serve an adaptive function, the concept of attunement places social perceptions into the life of a whole human being with a personal history and a social context.

Applications of the ecological theory

In this section, I will briefly describe some potential contributions of the ecological theory to our understanding of the contents of social perception, impression formation, emotion perception, and causal attributions. These potential contributions are meant to be illustrative rather than exhaustive.

The contents of social perception

The affordance concept provides a common denominator that can integrate perceiver variations in the frequency of various kinds of person descriptors. Specifically, the effects of perceiver culture, gender, and age on person descriptors may reflect variations in the categories that communicate adaptively significant affordances. The trait descriptors favored by Westerners may communicate social affordances such as who will help them or who will dominate them, while social role descriptors may communicate the same social affordances to perceivers in other cultures (see Miller 1984). The interpersonal interaction descriptors favored by females may communicate the social affordance of who is fun to be with, while the non-social activity descriptors that are favored by males may communicate the same affordance to them (see Korten 1974). Similarly, the traits pertaining to dominance that are emphasized by younger children may communicate for them the affordance of who is fun to be with, while the traits pertaining to prosocial behaviors that older children favor may communicate the same affordance to them (Livesley and Bromley 1973). The affordance concept may also integrate variations in person descriptor categories as a function of the target person. For example, the finding that trait descriptors are more common for friends than for strangers, for whom more contextual descriptors are generated (Fiske and Cox 1979), may reflect the fact that what our friends afford us depends upon their traits, while the same affordance from strangers depends upon the social context in which we interact with them.

A more general implication of the affordance concept for research on the contents of social perception is that a clearer understanding of these contents may be provided by studies that ask people to describe their social interactions with others rather than simply to describe others, an instruction that does not readily elicit perceived affordances. The ecological theory also suggests that our understanding of the contents of social perception will be enhanced by a consideration of the perceivers' interaction goals, since variations in such goals across perceivers or targets may yield variations in the perceived affordances.

Impression formation

The concept of affordance also has implications for research on impression formation. For one thing, it may provide a way to resolve questions concerning the accuracy of impressions. Rather than reflecting qualities of the perceiver or the perceived, impressions may reflect the affordances of the perceived for the perceiver. And, although it is difficult if not impossible to find a criterion for validating perceived traits, behavioral evidence can validate perceived affordances. If someone is perceived to afford domination, one can determine the accuracy of this perception by ascertaining whether that person can indeed be dominated by the perceiver. However, if someone is perceived as dominant, then any instance of dominating or not dominating can neither confirm nor disconfirm this trait ascription.

The assumption that social perceptions serve an adaptive function and the corollary that erroneous perceptions may reflect the overgeneralization of some highly adaptive perceptual attunement have implications for stereotypic impressions of targets with particular physical qualities. For example, the impression that leadership qualities are lacking in adults who are babyfaced, short, or fat (see Chapter 3) may reflect the overgeneralization of the very adaptive impression that such qualities are lacking in short and chubby babies. Other erroneous impressions may similarly reflect the overgeneralization of adaptive attunements that, on the average, yield accurate perceptions rather than reflecting fundamentally flawed social perception processes, as has often been assumed.

The ecological theory's emphasis on dynamic stimulus information as the source of social perceptions holds promise for filling a glaring gap in impression-formation research, namely what *behaviors* influence impressions. For example, research using the point-light methodology has revealed that impressions of a person's power are influenced by the way he walks, and it has identified the pattern of gait characteristics that influence perceived power (Montepare and Zebrowitz-McArthur 1988b). Additional investigations of social stimulus information, using this and other methods, will determine the influence of other non-verbal behaviors on impressions.

Emotion perception

Like research on impression formation and the contents of social perception, research on emotion perception may be enriched by the affordance concept. Specifically, emotional expressions may be viewed as specifying social affordances such as "approach me" or "avoid me" or "help me" rather than simply as "happy" or "angry" or "afraid". Indeed, emotions are associated with specific states of action readiness (Frijda *et al.* 1989). Moreover, a fearful or angry face not only signals that the environment affords danger but also facilitates appropriate adaptive actions by the perceiver (see Lanzetta and Orr 1981).

Research investigating the effects of perceiver and target variables on emotion perception may find more integration than heretofore if consideration is given to the affordances of a particular expression for a particular perceiver. Consider, for example, the finding that New Guinea perceivers do not differentiate posed expressions of surprise and fear, whereas Western perceivers do (Ekman 1972). Rather than reflecting cultural variations in the perceiver or perceived, this result may reflect a tendency for the expressions of surprise and fear to specify the same affordance in a primitive culture, namely danger, while often specifying different affordances in modern cultures.

The ecological emphasis on the information value of dynamic, multimodal stimulus information may stimulate research that can fill some significant gaps in our knowledge of emotion perception. Although it has been determined that vocal qualities convey particular emotions, the precise nature of those vocal qualities has not been ascertained in research on static qualities, such as average pitch and loudness (see Chapter 4). An investigation of dynamic vocal qualities that have a temporal component, such as changes in pitch over time, may answer the question of how the voice communicates various emotions.

Research incorporating the ecological emphasis on the information value of multimodal stimulus information should also increase our understanding of emotion perception. Multimodal expressions may yield higher accuracy in the identification of spontaneous emotional expressions than does face or voice or gesture alone. And in so far as perceiver and target effects on emotion recognition reflect weaknesses in one communication modality, such effects may be diminished when multimodal expressions of emotion are investigated. Also pertinent to the accuracy of emotion perception in real life is the concept of attunement. Subtle, spontaneous expressions of emotion may be more easily read by perceivers who have had considerable perceptual experience with a target person than by strangers in laboratory research.

Research on emotion perception has largely ignored information provided by the eliciting situation. Moreover, the research that has been done has addressed the question of whether contextual cues can outweigh expressive ones rather than the question of what kinds of contexts elicit the perception of various emotions. Yet perceivers' conceptions of various emotions do incorporate antecedent conditions (see Schwartz and Shaver 1987), and it seems likely that their perceptions of various emotions will be responsive to the presence of these conditions. The context in which an emotion occurs is intimately tied to the affordances that it specifies. For example, a fearful expression observed in a rollercoaster rider specifies different affordances than a similar expression observed in an airplane pilot. The ecological emphasis on identifying the affordances specified by various emotional expressions will necessarily focus research attention on the social context that elicits those expressions.

Causal attributions

It is perhaps no accident that the two causal loci that have been emphasized in research on the layman's causal attributions for behavior – the person and the environment – parallel scientific psychology's explanations for human behavior. However, it was argued in Chapter 5 that causal attributions to the person or to the environment are less reasonable than interactive ones. The concept of *affordance* captures the interactive influence of the person and the environment on behavior, and research on causal attributions may do well to replace the concept of internal versus external locus of causality with an affordance concept. If perceivers are allowed to express their perceptions of social causality in terms that reflect the emergence of social events from qualities in the person *and* the environment, researchers may find less evidence of attributional bias.

Research on causal attributions has largely ignored two factors that Heider (1958) argued were central to the perception of intentionality – equifinality (engaging in a variety of behaviors, all of which are a means to the same end), and exertion (showing behavioral effort in producing some effect). The ecological emphasis on the information value of dynamic, temporally extended stimulus information is relevant to the perception of equifinality and effort. Kinematic stimulus information can yield the perception of several behaviors characterized by equifinality, including *chasing*, *fighting*, *protecting*, and *destroying* (Heider and Simmel 1944; Bassili 1976). Kinematic stimulus information can also specify exertion. Perceivers accurately judge physical effort from the speed, direction, and/or smoothness of body movements depicted in point-light displays (Runeson and Frykholm 1981), and the non-verbal expression of effort influences causal attributions for an athlete's performance (Lowe and Kassin 1980). Further research investigating the precise nature of human movements that yield the perception of equifinality and exertion will enhance our ability to predict the perception of intentionality. A method that may be useful in this regard identifies informative points in the behavior stream by having observers indicate when one meaningful action ends and a different one begins (Newtson 1976). Such research is germane to the argument that a central attributional problem is to explain extended sequences of behavior, relating actions in a sequence to one another so as to elucidate the plans and goals of the actor (Read 1987).

Summary and implications

It has been argued that social perception research lacks sufficient integration, and an ecological theory of social perception (McArthur and Baron 1983) has been offered as a framework that can provide at least some of the needed links between: the person and environmental determinants of social perceptions; the social perceptions and actions, social context, and developmental history of the perceiver; and the various facets of social perception.

The ecological approach differs in a number of respects from the constructivist approach which has dominated the field of social perception in recent years. One notable difference is that the constructivist approach stresses the internal organization and structuring of social information, while the ecological approach stresses the organization and structure that is provided in the external stimulus information. The fact is that both internal and external structures exist, and each may exert an influence on social perceptions. An integration of these approaches may be provided by viewing the internal structures as attunements that have developed from perceptual experiences with the external structures. Thus, rather than constructing social reality, the internal structures may reflect that reality. At the same time, these structures may guide the deployment of attention to one or another aspect of a multifaceted external world, thereby exerting their own influence on social perceptions. Finally, the resultant external stimulus information feeds back into the internal structures, modifying them as appropriate. And so the cycle continues. In short, internal structures and external structures are both cause and effect in the social perception process. Unfortunately most researchers have chunked this interaction chain so that they focus only on the causal influence of internal or external structures, a bias reminiscent of the tendency to attribute causality to the most salient person in a two-person interaction. Hopefully, future research will better integrate the internal and external influences on social perception so that a better story can be told.

Further reading

Bond, M. H. (ed.) (1988). *The cross-cultural challenge to social psychology.* Cross-cultural research and methodology series, Vol. 11. Newbury Park, CA: Sage. This book contains a collection of papers which discuss the promise and pitfalls of cross-cultural research in social psychology. The cross-cultural perspective is also applied to several content areas, including causal attributions, impression formation, and person concepts.

Higgins, E. T. and Parsons, J. E. (1983). Social cognition and the social life of the child: stages as subcultures. In E. T. Higgins, D. N. Ruble and W. W. Hartup (eds), *Social cognition and social development: A sociocultural perspective.* Cambridge: Cambridge University Press, pp. 15–62. A parallel is drawn between cultural and developmental effects on social perception. Social-life features that distinguish each life phase for North American children are described and related to age-related changes in social concepts and social information processing. Cross-cultural and demographic differences in the social-life phases of children are also related to differences in the development of social perception.

McArthur, L. Z. and Baron, R. M. (1983). Toward an ecological theory of social perception. *Psychological Review,* 90, 215–47. The assumptions and advantages of the ecological approach (Gibson, 1979; Shaw *et al.,* 1982) are enumerated, its applicability to social perception is documented, and some implications for research on impression formation, emotion perception, causal attribution, and accuracy are discussed.

Neisser, U. (ed.) (1987). *Concepts and conceptual development: Ecological and intellectual factors in categorization.* Cambridge: Cambridge University Press. Many of the essays in this book take an ecological approach to concepts and conceptual development, stressing the interrelationship of intellectual (internal) and perceptual (external) contributions. Although the focus is on conceptions of the physical world, the basic principles have relevance for conceptions of the social environment as well.

REFERENCES

Abramovitch, R. (1977). Children's recognition of situational aspects of facial expression. *Child Development*, 48, 459–63.

Abramovitch, R. and Daly, E. M. (1979). Inferring attributes of a situation from the facial expressions of peers. *Child Development*, 50, 586–9.

Addington, D. W. (1968). The relationship of selected vocal characteristics to personality perception. *Speech Monographs*, 35, 492–503.

Ajzen, I. (1988). *Attitudes, personality, and behavior*. Chicago: The Dorsey Press.

Ajzen, I. and Holmes, W. H. (1978). Uniqueness of behavioral effects in causal attribution. *Journal of Personality*, 44, 98–108.

Albas, D. C., McCluskey, K. W. and Albas, C. A. (1976). Perception of the emotional content of speech: A comparison of two Canadian groups. *Journal of Cross-Cultural Psychology*, 7, 481–90.

Alley, T. R. (1983). Growth-produced changes in body shape and size as determinants of perceived age and adult caregiving. *Child Development*, 54, 241–8.

Allport, G. W. (1937). *Personality: A Psychological Interpretation*. New York: Henry Holt.

Allport, G. W. and Odbert, H. S. (1936). Trait names: A psycholexical study. *Psychological Monographs*, 47 (171).

Andersen, S. M. and Klatzky, R. L. (1987). Traits and Social Stereotypes: Levels of categorization in person perception. *Journal of Personality and Social Psychology*, 53, 235–46.

Anderson, C. A. (1983). The causal structure of situations: The generation of plausible causal attributions as a function of type of event situation. *Journal of Experimental Social Psychology*, 19, 185–203.

Anderson, N. H. (1981). *Foundations of information integration theory*. New York: Academic Press.

Anderson, N. H. and Butzin, C. A. (1974). Performance = Motivation ×

Ability: An integration theoretical analysis. *Journal of Personality and Social Psychology*, 30, 598–604.

Antaki, C. and Naji, S. (1987). Events explained in conversational "because" statements. *British Journal of Social Psychology*, 26, 119–26.

Archer, D. and Akert, T. (1977). Words and everything else: Verbal and nonverbal cues in social interpretation. *Journal of Personality and Social Psychology*, 35, 443–9.

Arcuri, C. (1982). Three patterns of social categorization in attribution memory. *European Journal of Social Psychology*, 12, 271–82.

Argyle, M., Shimoda, K. and Little, B. (1978). Variance due to persons and situations in England and Japan. *British Journal of Social and Clinical Psychology*, 17, 335–7.

Aron, A. (1988). The matching hypothesis reconsidered again: Comment on Kalick and Hamilton. *Journal of Personality and Social Psychology*, 54, 441–6.

Aronoff, J., Barclay, A. M. and Stevenson, L. A. (1988). The recognition of threatening social stimuli. *Journal of Personality and Social Psychology*, 54, 647–55.

Asch, S. (1946). Forming impressions of personality. *Journal of Abnormal and Social Psychology*, 41, 258–90.

Asch, S. (1958). The metaphor: A psychological inquiry. In R. Taguiri and L. Petrullo (eds), *Person perception and interpersonal behavior*. Stanford, CA: Stanford University Press, pp. 86–94.

Ashmore, R. D. (1981). Sex stereotypes and implicit personality theory. In D. L. Hamilton (ed.), *Cognitive processes in stereotyping and interpersonal behavior*. Hillsdale, NJ: Erlbaum, pp. 37–81.

Assor, A., Aronoff, J. and Messe, L. A. (1981). Attribute relevance as a moderator of the effects of motivation on impression formation. *Journal of Personality and Social Psychology*, 41, 789–96.

Bar-Hillel, M. and Fischhoff, B. (1981). When do base rates affect predictions? *Journal of Personality and Social Psychology*, 41, 671–80.

Bargh, J. A. (1984). Automatic and conscious processing of social information. In R. S. Wyer and T. K. Srull (eds), *Handbook of Social Cognition*, Vol. 3. Hillsdale, NJ: Erlbaum, pp. 1–43.

Bargh, J. A., Bond, R. N., Lombardi, W. J. and Tota, M. E. (1986). The additive nature of chronic and temporary sources of construct accessibility. *Journal of Personality and Social Psychology*, 50, 869–78.

Bassili, J. N. (1976). Temporal and spatial contingencies in the perception of social events. *Journal of Personality and Social Psychology*, 33, 680–5.

Bassili, J. N. (1979). Emotion recognition: The role of facial movement. *Journal of Personality and Social Psychology*, 37, 2049–58.

Battistich, V. A. and Aronoff, J. (1985). Perceiver, target, and situational influences on social cognition: An interactional analysis. *Journal of Personality and Social Psychology*, 49, 788–98.

Beach, L. and Wertheimer, H. (1961). A free response approach to the study of person cognition. *Journal of Abnormal and Social Psychology*, **62**, 367–74.

Beier, E. G. and Zautra, A. J. (1972). Identification of vocal communication of emotions across cultures. *Journal of Consulting and Clinical Psychology*, **39**, 166.

Berman, J. S. and Kenny, D. A. (1976). Correlational bias in observer ratings. *Journal of Personality and Social Psychology*, **34**, 263–73.

Berry, D. S. and McArthur, L. Z. (1986). Perceiving character in faces: The impact of age-related craniofacial changes on social perception. *Psychological Bulletin*, **100**, 3–18.

Berry, D. S. and Zebrowitz-McArthur, L. (1988). What's in a face? Facial maturity and the attribution of legal responsibility. *Personality and Social Psychology Bulletin*, **14**, 23–33.

Berscheid, E., Graziano, W., Monson, T. and Dermer, M. (1976). Outcome dependency: Attention, attribution, and attraction. *Journal of Personality and Social Psychology*, **34**, 978–89.

Berscheid, E. and Walster, G. (1974). Physical attractiveness. In L. Berkowitz (ed.), *Advances in Experimental Social Psychology* (Vol. 7). New York: Academic Press, pp. 157–215.

Betancourt, H. and Weiner, B. (1982). Attributions for achievement-related events, expectancy, and sentiments. *Journal of Cross-Cultural Psychology*, **13**, 362–74.

Birdwhistell, R. L. (1970). *Kinesics and context*. Philadelphia: University of Pennsylvania Press.

Block, J., Weiss, D. S. and Thorne, A. (1979). How relevant is a semantic similarity interpretation of personality ratings? *Journal of Personality and Social Psychology*, **37**, 1055–74.

Bond, M. H. (1972). Effect of an impression set on subsequent behavior. *Journal of Personality and Social Psychology*, **24**, 301–5.

Bond, M. H. (1979). Dimensions used in perceiving peers: Cross-cultural comparisons of Hong Kong, Japanese, American and Filipino university students. *International Journal of Psychology*, **14**, 47–56.

Bond, M. H. (1983). A proposal for cross-cultural studies of attribution. In M. Hewstone (ed.), *Attribution theory: Social and functional extensions*. Oxford: Blackwell, pp. 144–57.

Bond, M. H. (1987). Old wine in new skins: Impressions about others can be disconfirmed by social reality. *Psychologia*, **30**, 39–43.

Bond, M. H. and Cheung, T. S. (1983). College students' spontaneous self-concept: The effect of culture among respondents in Hong Kong, Japan, and the United States. *Journal of Cross-Cultural Psychology*, **14**, 153–71.

Bond, M. H. and Forgas, J. P. (1984). Linking person perception to behavior intention across cultures: The role of cultural collectivism. *Journal of Cross-Cultural Psychology*, **15**, 337–52.

Borgida, E. and Howard-Pitney, B. (1983). Personal involvement and the robustness of perceptual saliance effects. *Journal of Personality and Social Psychology*, **45**, 560–70.

Borke, H. and Su, S. (1972). Perception of emotional responses to social interactions by Chinese and American children. *Journal of Cross-Cultural Psychology*, **3**, 309–14.

Bornstein, R. F., Leone, D. R. and Galley, D. J. (1987). The generalizability of subliminal mere exposure effects: Influence of stimuli perceived without awareness on social behavior. *Journal of Personality and Social Psychology*, **53**, 1070–9.

Bradley, G. W. (1978). Self-serving biases in the attribution process: A re-examination of the fact or fiction question. *Journal of Personality and Social Psychology*, **36**, 56–71.

Braithwaite, U. A. (1986). Old age stereotypes: Revealing contradictions. *Journal of Gerontology*, **41**, 353–60.

Brewer, M. B. (1988). A dual process model of impression formation. In T. K. Srull and R. S. Wyer, Jr (eds), *Advances in Social Cognition*, Vol. 1. Hillsdale, NJ: Lawrence Erlbaum, pp. 1–36.

Brewer, M. B. (1979). In-group bias in the minimal intergroup situation: A cognitive-motivational analysis. *Psychological Bulletin*, **86**, 307–24.

Broverman, I. K., Vogel, S. R., Broverman, D. M., Clarkson, F. E. and Rosenkrantz, P. S. (1972). Sex-role stereotypes: A current appraisal. *Journal of Social Issues*, **28**, 59–78.

Brown, A. and Cunningham, J. G. (1981). Developmental interactions in the production and interpretation of affective facial expression. Paper presented at the meeting of the Society for Research on Child Development, Boston.

Brown, B. L. (1980). The detection of emotion in vocal qualities. In H. Giles, P. W. Robinson and P. Smith (eds), *Language: Social Psychological Perspectives*. Oxford: Pergamon.

Brown, P. J. and Turner, J. C. (1979). The criss-cross categorization effect in intergroup discrimination. *British Journal of Social and Clinical Psychology*, **18**, 371–83.

Brown, R. and Fish, D. (1983). The psychological causality implicit in language. *Cognition*, **14**, 233–74.

Bruner, J. S. (1951). Personality dynamics and the process of perceiving. In R. R. Blake and G. V. Ramsey (eds), *Perception: An approach to personality*. New York: Ronald, pp. 121–47.

Buck, R. (1975). Nonverbal communication of affect in children. *Journal of Personality and Social Psychology*, **31**, 644–53.

Buck, R. (1977). Nonverbal communication of affect in preschool children: Relationships with personality and skin conductance. *Journal of Personality and Social Psychology*, **35**, 225–36.

Buck, R. (1984). *The Communication of Emotion*. New York: Guilford Press.

Buck, R., Miller, R. E. and Caul, W. F. (1974). Sex, personality, and physiological variables in the communication of affect via facial expression. *Journal of Personality and Social Psychology*, 30, 587–96.

Buck, R. W., Savin, V. J., Miller, R. E. and Caul, W. F. (1972). Communication of affect through facial expressions in humans. *Journal of Personality and Social Psychology*, 23, 362–71.

Bugental, D. E., Kaswan, J. W., Love, L. R. and Fox, M. N. (1970). Child versus adult perception of evaluative messages in verbal, vocal, and visual channels. *Developmental Psychology*, 2, 367–75.

Bugental, D. E., Love, L. R. and Gianetto, R. M. (1971). Perfidious feminine faces. *Journal of Personality and Social Psychology*, 17, 314–18.

Bull, P. E. (1987). *Posture and Gesture*. Oxford: Pergamon Press.

Bullock, M. and Russell, J. A. (1984). Preschool children's interpretation of facial expressions of emotion. *International Journal of Behavioral Development*, 7, 193–214.

Burger, J. M. (1981). Motivational biases in the attribution of responsibility for an accident: A meta-analysis of the defensive-attribution hypothesis. *Psychological Bulletin*, 90, 496–512.

Burns, K. L. and Beier, E. G. (1973). Significance of vocal and visual channels in the decoding of emotional meaning. *Journal of Communication*, 23, 118–30.

Bush, L. E. (1972). Empirical selection of adjectives denoting feelings. *JSAS Catalogue of Selected Documents in Psychology*, 2, 67.

Buss, A. R. (1978). Causes and reasons in attribution theory: A conceptual critique. *Journal of Personality and Social Psychology*, 36, 1311–21.

Buss, D. M. (1989). Sex differences in human mate preferences: Evolutionary hypotheses tested in 37 cultures. *Behavioral and Brain Sciences*, 12, 1–49.

Caldwell, M. A. and Peplau, L. A. (1982). Sex differences in same-sex friendship. *Sex Roles*, 8, 721–32.

Cantor, N. and Mischel, W. (1979). Prototypes in person perception. In L. Berkowitz (ed.) *Advances in Experimental Social Psychology*. New York: Academic Press, pp. 3–52.

Caron, A. J., Caron, R. F. and MacLean, D. J. (1988). Infant discrimination of naturalistic emotional expressions: The role of face and voice. *Child Development*, 39, 604–16.

Carpenter, S. L. (1988). Self-relevance and goal directed processing in the recall and weighting of information about others. *Journal of Experimental Social Psychology*, 24, 310–32.

Catrambone, R. and Markus, H. (1987). The role of self-schemas in going beyond the information given. *Social Cognition*, 5, 349–68.

Cattell, R. B. (1957). *Personality and motivation structure and measurement*. Yonkers-on-Hudson, NY: World Book Co.

Cha, J.-H. and Nam, K.-D. (1985). A test of Kelley's cube theory of attribution: A cross-cultural replication of McArthur's study. *Korean Social Science Journal*, 12, 151–80.

Chaikin, A. L. and Darley, J. M. (1973). Victim or perpetrator: Defensive attribution of responsibility and the need for order and justice. *Journal of Personality and Social Psychology*, 25, 268–75.

Chan, D. W. (1985). Perception and judgment of facial expressions among the Chinese. *International Journal of Psychology*, 20, 681–92.

Chapman, L. J. (1967). Illusory correlation in observational report. *Journal of Verbal Learning and Verbal Behavior*, 6, 151–5.

Clark, M. S. and Isen, A. M. (1982). Toward understanding the relationship between feeling states and social behavior. In A. Hastorf and A. Isen (eds), *Cognitive social psychology*. New York: Elsevier North-Holland.

Clark, M. S., Milberg, S. and Ross, J. (1983). Arousal cues arousal-related material in memory: Implications for understanding effects of mood on memory. *Journal of Verbal Learning and Verbal Behavior*, 22, 633–49.

Clifford, M. M. and Walster, E. (1973). Research note: The effects of physical attractiveness on teacher expectations. *Sociology of Education*, 46, 248–58.

Clore, G. L., Ortony, A. and Foss, M. A. (1987). The psychological foundations of the affective lexicon. *Journal of Personality and Social Psychology*, 53, 751–66.

Cordray, D. S. and Shaw, J. I. (1978). An empirical test of the covariation analysis in causal attribution. *Journal of Experimental Social Psychology*, 14, 280–90.

Costanzo, P. R. and Fraenkel, P. (1988). Social influence, socialization, and the development of social cognition. In N. Eisenberg (ed.), *Advances in Developmental Psychology*. New York: John Wiley.

Costanzo, P. R., Grumet, J. F. and Brehm, S. S. (1974). The effects of choice and source of constraint on children's attributions of preference. *Journal of Experimental Social Psychology*, 10, 352–364.

Costrich, N., Feinstein, J., Kidder, L., Marecek, J. and Pascale, L. (1975). When stereotypes hurt: Three studies of penalties for sex-role reversals. *Journal of Experimental Social Psychology*, 11, 520–530.

Crocker, J., Hannah, D. B. and Weber, R. (1983). Person memory and causal attributions. *Journal of Personality and Social Psychology*, 44, 55–66.

Cronbach, L. J. (1955). Processes affecting scores on 'understanding of others' and 'assumed similarity'. *Psychological Bulletin*, 52, 177–93.

Cunningham, J. D. and Kelley, H. H. (1975). Causal attribution for interpersonal events of varying magnitude. *Journal of Personality*, 43, 74–93.

Cunningham, J. D., Starr, P. A. and Kanouse, D. E. (1979). Self as actor, active observer, and passive observer: Implications for causal attributions. *Journal of Personality and Social Psychology*, 37, 1146–52.

Cunningham, J. G. (1984). Nonverbal affective communication in early development. Invited address to Developmental Research Group, Department of Psychology, Harvard University.

Cunningham, J. G. and Sterling, R. S. (1988). Developmental change in the understanding of affective meaning in music. *Motivation and Emotion*, 12, 399–413.

Cunningham, M. R. (1986). Measuring the physical in physical attractiveness: Quasi-experiments on the sociobiology of female facial beauty. *Journal of Personality and Social Psychology*, 50, 925–35.

Darley, J. M., Fleming, J. H., Hilton J. L. and Swann, W. B. (1988). Dispelling negative expectancies: The impact of interaction goals and target characteristics on the expectancy confirmation process. *Journal of Experimental Social Psychology*, 24, 19–36.

Darwin, C. (1872). *The expression of emotions in man and animals.* London: John Murray.

Davitz, J. R. (1964a). Minor studies and some hypotheses. In J. R. Davitz (ed.), *The communication of emotional meaning.* New York: McGraw-Hill, pp. 143–54.

Davitz, J. R. (1964b). Personality, perceptual, and cognitive correlates of emotional sensitivity. In J. R. Davitz (ed.), *The communication of emotional meaning.* New York: McGraw-Hill, pp. 57–68.

Davitz, J. R. and Davitz, L. J. (1959). The communication of feelings by content-free speech. *Journal of Communication*, 9, 6–13.

Dawes, R. M. (1989). Statistical criteria for establishing a truly false consensus effect. *Journal of Experimental Social Psychology*, 25, 1–17.

Deaux, K. and Emswiller, T. (1974). Explanations of successful performance on sex-linked tasks: What is skill for the male is luck for the female. *Journal of Personality and Social Psychology*, 29, 80–5.

Deaux, K. and Lewis, L. L. (1984). Structure of gender stereotypes: Interrelationships among components and gender label. *Journal of Personality and Social Psychology*, 46, 991–1005.

Deaux, K. and Taynor, J. (1973). Evaluation of male and female ability: Bias works two ways. *Psychological Reports*, 32, 261–2.

DeJong, W. (1988). Personal communication.

DeJong, W. and Kleck, R. E. (1986). The social psychological effects of overweight. In C. P. Herman, M. P. Zanna and E. T. Higgins (eds), *Physical appearance, stigma, and social behavior: The Ontario Symposium*, Vol. 3. Hillsdale, NJ: Erlbaum, pp. 65–88.

DePaulo, B. M. and Rosenthal, R. (1982). Measuring the development of sensitivity to non-verbal communication. In C. E. Izard (ed.), *Measuring emotions in infants and children.* Cambridge: Cambridge University Press, pp. 208–47.

DePaulo, B. M., Rosenthal, R., Eisenstat, R. A., Rogers, P. L. and Finkelstein, S. (1978). Decoding discrepant nonverbal cues. *Journal of Personality and Social Psychology*, 36, 313–23.

Dermer, M. and Thiel, D. L. (1975). When beauty may fail. *Journal of Personality and Social Psychology*, 31, 1168–76.

Deschamps, J. C. and Doise, W. (1978). Crossed category memberships in intergroup relations. In H. Tajfel (ed.), *Differentiation between social groups: Studies in the social psychology of intergroup relations.* European Monographs in Social Psychology. London: Academic Press.

Deutsch, F., Clark, M. E. and Zalenski, C. M. (1983). Is there a double standard of ageing? Paper presented at the 54th Meeting of the Eastern Psychological Association, Philadelphia, PA, April.

Dimitrovsky, L. (1964). The ability to identify the emotional meaning of vocal expressions at successive age levels. In J. R. Davitz (ed.), *The Communication of emotional meaning.* New York: McGraw-Hill, pp. 69–86.

Dion, K. K. (1972) Physical attractiveness and evaluation of children's transgressions. *Journal of Personality and Social Psychology,* 24, 207–13.

Divitto, B. and McArthur, L. Z. (1978). Developmental differences in the use of distinctiveness, consensus, and consistency information for making causal attributions. *Developmental Psychology,* 14, 474–82.

Dornbusch, S. M., Hastorf, A. H., Richardson, S. A., Muzzy, R. E. and Vreeland, R. S. (1965). The perceiver and perceived: Their relative influence on categories of interpersonal perception. *Journal of Personality and Social Psychology,* 1, 434–40.

Dovidio, J. F. and Gaertner, S. L. (1986). Prejudice, discrimination and racism: Historical trends and contemporary approaches. In J. F. Dovidio and S. L. Gaertner (eds), *Prejudice, discrimination, and racism.* Orlando, FL: Academic Press, pp. 1–34.

Drag, R. M. and Shaw, M. E. (1967). Factors influencing the communication of emotional intent by facial expressions. *Psychometric Science,* 8, 137–8.

Duncan, S. L. (1976). Differential social perception and attribution of intergroup violence: Testing the lower limits of stereotyping of blacks. *Journal of Personality and Social Psychology,* 34, 590–8.

Dusenbury, D. and Knower, F. H. (1938). Experimental studies on the symbolism of action and voice: In a study of the specificity of meaning in facial expression. *Quarterly Journal of Speech,* 24, 424–35.

Dutton, D. G. and Aron, A. P. (1974). Some evidence for heightened sexual attraction under conditions of high anxiety. *Journal of Personality and Social Psychology,* 30, 510–17.

Eagly, A. H. (1987). *Sex difference in social behavior: A social role interpretation.* Hillsdale, NJ: Lawrence Erlbaum.

Easterbrook, J. A. (1959). The effect of emotion on cue utilization and the organization of behavior. *Psychological Review,* 66, 183–201.

Eibl-Eibesfeldt, I. (1970a). *Ethology: The biology of behavior.* New York: Holt, Rinehart & Winston.

Eibl-Eibesfeldt, I. (1970b). The expressive behavior of the deaf and blind born. In M. von Cranach & I. Vine (eds), *Non-verbal behavior and expressive movements.* London: Academic Press.

Einhorn, H. J. and Hogarth, R. M. (1986). Judging probable cause. *Psychological Bulletin*, **99**, 3–19.

Eisen, S. V. (1979). Actor–observer differences in information inference and causal attribution. *Journal of Personality and Social Psychology*, **37**, 261–2.

Ekman, P. (1965). Differential communication of affect by head and body cues. *Journal of Personality and Social Psychology*, **2**, 726–35.

Ekman, P. (1972). Universals and cultural differences in facial expressions of emotion. In J. Cole (ed.), *Nebraska Symposium on Motivation, 1971*, Vol. 19. Lincoln: University of Nebraska Press, pp. 207–82.

Ekman, P. and Friesen, W. V. (1965). Progress Report to the National Institute of Mental Hearth, Bethesda, MD.

Ekman, P. and Friesen, W. V. (1969). Non-verbal leakage and cues to deception. *Psychiatry*, **32**, 88–106.

Ekman, P. and Friesen, W. V. (1975). *Unmasking the face*. Englewood Cliffs, NJ: Prentice-Hall.

Ekman, P. and Friesen, W. V. (1978). *The facial affect coding system (FACS)*, Palo Alto, CA: Consulting Psychologists Press.

Ekman, P. and Friesen, W. V. (1986). A new pan-cultural facial expression of emotion. *Motivation and Emotion*, **10**, 159–68.

Ekman, P., Friesen, W. V. and Ellsworth, P. (1982a). Does the face provide accurate information? In P. Ekman (ed.), *Emotion in the human face*, 2nd edn. Cambridge: Cambridge University Press, pp. 56–97.

Ekman, P., Friesen, W. V. and Ellsworth, P. (1982b). What are the similarities and differences in facial behavior across cultures? In P. Ekman (ed.), *Emotion in the human face*, 2nd edn. Cambridge: Cambridge University Press, pp. 128–44.

Ekman, P., Friesen, W. V. and Tomkins, S. S. (1971). Facial affect scoring technique (FAST): A first validity study. *Semiotica*, **3**, 37–58.

Ekman, P., Friesen, W. V., O'Sullivan, M., Chan, A., Diacoyanni-Tarlatzis, I., Heider, K., Krause, R., LeCompte, W. A., Pitcairn, T., Ricci-Bitti, P. E., Scherer, K., Tomita, M. and Tzavaras, A. (1987). Universals and cultural differences in the judgments of facial expressions of emotion. *Journal of Personality and Social Psychology*, **53**, 712–17.

Ekman, P., Levenson, and Friesen, W. V. (1983). Autonomic nervous system activity distinguishes among emotion. *Science*, **221**, 1208–10.

Elig, T. W. and Frieze, I. H. (1979). Measuring causal attributions for success and failure. *Journal of Personality and Social Psychology*, **37**, 621–34.

Ellyson, S. L. and Dovidio, J. F. (1985). *Power, dominance, and nonverbal behavior*. New York: Springer Verlag.

Emde, R. N., Izard, C., Huebner, R., Sorce, J. F. and Klinnert, M. (1985). Adult judgments of infant emotions: Replication studies within and across laboratories. *Infant Behavior and Development*, **8**, 79–88.

Ermiane, R. and Gergerian, E. (1978). *Atlas of facial expressions; Album des expressions du visage.* Paris: La Pensée Universelle.

Etaugh, C. and Brown, B. (1974). Perceiving the causes of success and failure of male and female performers. *Developmental Psychology*, 11, 103.

Feingold, A. (1988). Matching for attractiveness in romantic partners and same sex friends: A meta-analytic and theoretical critique. *Psychological Bulletin*, 104, 226–35.

Feldman, N. S., Higgins, E. T., Karlovac, M. and Ruble, D. N. (1976). Use of consensus information in causal attributions as a function of temporal presentation and availability of direct information. *Journal of Personality and Social Psychology*, 34, 694–8.

Feldman, N. S. and Ruble, D. N. (1981). Development of person perception: cognitive and social factors. In S. S. Brehm, F. M. Kassin and F. X. Gibbons (eds) *Developmental social psychology: Theory and research.* New York: Oxford University Press, pp. 191–206.

Feleky, A. M. (1914). The expression of the emotions. *Psychological Review*, 21, 33–41.

Felleman, E. S., Barden, R. C., Carlson, C. R., Rosenberg, L. and Masters, J. C. (1983). Children's and adults' recognition of spontaneous and posed emotional expressions in young children. *Developmental Psychology*, 19, 405–13.

Fenster, C. A., Blake, L. K. and Goldstein, A. M. (1977). Accuracy of vocal emotional communication among children and adults and the power of negative emotions. *Journal of Communication Disorders*, 10, 301–14.

Feshbach, S. and Feshbach, N. (1963). Influence of the stimulus object upon the complementary and supplementary projection of fear. *Journal of Abnormal and Social Psychology*, 66, 498–502.

Fiedler, K. (1982). Causal schemata: Review and criticism of research on a popular construct. *Journal of Personality and Social Psychology*, 42, 1001–13.

Fiedler, K. and Semin, G. R. (1989). On the causal information conveyed by different interpersonal verbs. The role of implicit sentence context. *Social Cognition*, 6, 21–39.

Field, T. M., Woodson, R., Greenberg, R. and Cohen, D. (1982). Discrimination and imitation of facial expressions in neonates. *Science*, 218, 179–81.

Fincham, F. D., Beach, S. R. and Baucom, D. H. (1987). Attribution processes in distressed and nondistressed couples: 4. Self-partner attribution differences. *Journal of Personality and Social Psychology*, 52, 739–48.

Fiske, S. T. (1980). Attention and weight in person perception: the impact of negative and extreme behavior. *Journal of Personality and Social Psychology*, 38, 889–906.

Fiske, S. T. and Cox, M. G. (1979). Person concepts: The effect of target familiarity and descriptive purpose on the process of describing others, *Journal of Personality*, 47, 136–61.

Fiske, S. T. and Neuberg, S. L. (1990). A continuum of impression formation from category-based to individuating processes: Influences of information and motivation on attention and interpretation. In M. P. Zanna (ed.), *Advances in experimental social psychology*, Vol. 23. New York: Academic Press.

Fiske, S. T. and Taylor, S. E. (1984). *Social cognition*. Reading, MA: Addison-Wesley.

Fiske, S. T., Taylor, S. E., Etcoff, N. L., & Laufer, J. K. (1979). Imaging, empathy, and causal attribution. *Journal of Experimental Social Psychology*, 15, 356–77.

Fong, G. T. and Markus, H. (1982). Self-schemas and judgments about others. *Social Cognition*, 1, 191–205.

Forgas, J. P. and Bower, G. H. (1988). Affect in social and personal judgments. In K. Fiedler and J. P. Forgas (eds), *Affect, cognition and social behaviour*. Toronto: Hogrefe International Publishers.

Frable, D. E. S. (1987). Sex-typed execution and perception of expressive movement. *Journal of Personality and Social Psychology*, 53, 391–6.

Frick, R. W. (1985). Communicating emotion. The role of prosodic features. *Psychological Bulletin*, 97, 412–29.

Frijda, N. H. (1953). The understanding of facial expression of emotion. *Acta Psychologica*, 9, 294–362.

Frijda, N. H., Kuipers, P. and ter Schure, E. (1989). Relations among emotion, appraisal, and emotional action readiness. *Journal of Personality and Social Psychology*, 57, 212–28.

Funder, D. C. (1982). On the accuracy of dispositional versus situational attributions. *Social Cognition*, 1, 205–22.

Funder, D. C. (1987). Errors and mistakes: Evaluating the accuracy of social judgment. *Psychological Bulletin*, 101, 75–90.

Funder, D. C. and Colvin, C. R. (1988). Friends and strangers: Acquaintance, agreement, and the accuracy of personality judgment. *Journal of Personality and Social Psychology*, 55, 149–58.

Garcia, J. and Koelling, R. A. (1966). Relation of cue to consequence in avoidance learning. *Psychonomic Science*, 4, 123–4.

Garner, W. (1986). Interactions of stimulus and organism in perception. In S. H. Hulse and B. F. Green, Jr (eds), *One hundred years of psychological research in America*. Baltimore, MD: Johns Hopkins University Press.

Gibson, J. J. (1979). *The ecological approach to visual perception*. Boston: Houghton Mifflin.

Gifford, R. and O'Connor, B. (1987). The interpersonal circumplex as a behavior map. *Journal of Personality and Social Psychology*, 52, 1019–26.

Gilbert, D. T. (1989). Thinking lightly about others: Automatic components of the social inference process. In J. S. Uleman and J. A. Bargh (eds), *Unintended thought: Limits of awareness, intention, and control.* New York: Guilford.

Gilbert, D. T. and Jones, E. E. (1986). Perceiver induced constraint: Interpretations of self-generated reality. *Journal of Personality and Social Psychology,* 50, 269–80.

Giles, H. (1979). Ethnicity markers in speech. In K. Scherer and H. Giles (eds), *Social markers in speech.* Cambridge: Cambridge University Press, pp. 251–90.

Gitter, A. G., Black, H. and Mostofsky, D. (1972). Race and sex in the perception of emotion. *Journal of Social Issues,* 28, 63–78.

Gnepp, J. (1983). Children's social sensitivity: Inferring emotions from conflicting cues. *Developmental Psychology,* 19, 805–14.

Goldberg, H. D. (1951). The role of "cutting" in the perception of motion pictures. *Journal of Applied Psychology,* 35, 70–1.

Goldberg, L. R. (1978). Differential attribution of trait-descriptive terms to oneself as compared to well-liked, neutral and disliked others: A psychometric analysis. *Journal of Personality and Social Psychology,* 36, 1012–28.

Goldberg, L. R. (1981a). Language and individual differences: The search for universals in personality lexicons. In L. Wheeler (ed.), *Review of personality and social psychology,* Vol. 2. Beverly Hills, CA: Sage.

Goldberg, L. R. (1981b). Unconfounding situational attributions from uncertain, neutral, and ambiguous ones: A psychometric analysis of descriptions of oneself and various types of others. *Journal of Personality and Social Psychology,* 41, 517–52.

Goldberg, L. R. (1982). From Ace to zombie: Some explorations in the language of personality. In C. D. Spielberger and J. N. Butcher (eds), *Advances in personality assessment,* Vol. 1. Hillsdale, NJ: Lawrence Erlbaum.

Goldberg, P. A. (1968). Are women prejudiced against women? *Transaction,* 4, 28–30.

Goldman, E. and Lewis, P. (1977). Beautiful is good: Evidence that the physically attractive are more socially skillful. *Journal of Experimental Social Psychology,* 13, 125–30.

Gregor, T. (1979). Short people. *Natural History,* 88, 14–19.

Griffitt, W. (1970). Environmental effects on interpersonal affective behavior: Ambient effective temperature and attraction. *Journal of Personality and Social Psychology,* 15, 240–4.

Grigg, F., Fletcher, G. J. O. and Fitness, J. (1989). Spontaneous attributions in happy and unhappy dating relationships. *Journal of Social and Personal Relationships,* 6, 61–8.

Gupta, M. and Singh, R. (1981). An integration-theoretical analysis of cultural and developmental differences in attribution of performance. *Developmental Psychology*, 17, 816–25.

Gustafsson, L. and Lanshammer, H. (1977). *ENOCH: An integrated system for measurement and analysis of human gait.* Uppsala, Sweden: Institute of Technology.

Guthrie, G. M. and Bennett, A. B., Jr (1971). Cultural differences in implicit personality theory, *International Journal of Psychology*, 6, 305–12.

Guthrie, R. D. (1976). *Body hot spots: The anatomy of human social organs and behavior.* New York: Van Nostrand Reinhold.

Hall, E. T. (1979). *Handbook for proxemic research.* Washington, DC: Society for the Anthropology of Visual Communication.

Hall, J. (1984). *Nonverbal sex differences: Communication accuracy and expessive style.* Baltimore, MD: The Johns Hopkins University Press.

Hamilton, D. L. and Gifford, R. K. (1976). Illusory correlation in inter-personal perception: A cognitive basis of stereotype judgments. *Journal of Experimental Social Psychology*, 12, 392–407.

Hamilton, D. L. and Zanna, M. P. (1974). Context effects in impression formation: Changes in connotative meaning. *Journal of Personality and Social Psychology*, 29, 649–54.

Hamilton, V. L. and Sanders, J. with Y. Hosoi, Z. Ishimura, N. Matsubara, H. Nishimura, N. Tomita and K. Tokoro (1983). Universals in judging wrongdoing: Japanese and Americans compared. *American Sociological Review*, 48, 199–211.

Hansen, C. M. and Hansen, R. D. (1988). Finding the face in the crowd: An anger superiority effect. *Journal of Personality and Social Psychology*, 54, 917–24.

Hansen, R. D. and Donoghue, J. M. (1977). The power of consensus: information derived from one's own and other's behavior. *Journal of Personality and Social Psychology*, 35, 294–302.

Harkness, A. R., DeBono, K. G. and Borgida, E. (1985). Personal involve-ment and strategies for making contingency judgments: A stake in the dating game makes a difference. *Journal of Personality and Social Psychology*, 49, 22–32.

Harris, M. J. and Rosenthal, R. (1985). Mediation of Interpersonal expectancy effects: 31 meta-analyses. *Psychological Bulletin*, 97, 363–86.

Hastorf, A. H. and Cantril, H. (1954). They saw a game: A case study. *Journal of Abnormal and Social Psychology*, 49, 129–34.

Hastie, R. & Park, B. (1986). The relationship between memory and judgment depends on whether the judgment task is memory-based or on-line. *Psychological Review*, 93, 258–68.

Hatfield, E. and Sprecher, S. (1986). *Mirror, mirror . . . : The importance of looks in everyday life.* Albany: State University of New York Press.

Heider, F. (1944). Social perception and phenomenal causality. *Psychological Review*, 51, 358–74.

Heider, F. (1958). *The psychology of interpersonal relations*. New York: Wiley.

Heider, F. and Simmel, M. (1944). An experimental study of apparent behavior. *American Journal of Psychology*, 57, 243–59.

Hewstone, M. and Jaspars, J. (1983). A re-examination of the roles of consensus, consistency, and distinctiveness: Kelley's cube revisited. *British Journal of Social Psychology*, 22, 41–50.

Hewstone, M., Jaspars, J. and Lalljee, M. (1982). Social representations, social attribution and social identity: the intergroup images of "public" and "comprehensive" schoolboys. *European Journal of Social Psychology*, 12, 241–69.

Hiatt, S. W., Campos, J. J. and Emde, R. N. (1979). Facial patterning and infant emotional expressions: Happiness, surprise, and fear. *Child Development*, 50, 1020–35.

Higgins, E. T. and Bargh, J. A. (1987). Social cognition and social perception. *Annual Review of Psychology*, 38, 369–425.

Higgins, E. T. and Bryant, S. L. (1982). Consensus information and the fundamental attribution error: The role of development and in-group versus out-group knowledge. *Journal of Personality and Social Psychology*, 43, 889–900.

Higgins, E. T., King, G. A. and Mavin, G. H. (1982). Individual construct-accessibility and subjective impressions and recall. *Journal of Personality and Social Psychology*, 43, 35–47.

Higgins, E. T., Rholes, W. S. and Jones, C. R. (1977). Category accessibility and impression formation. *Journal of Experimental Social Psychology*, 13, 141–54.

Hilton, D. J. (1989). Conversational processes and causal explanation. *Psychological Bulletin*.

Hoffman, C., Mischel, W. and Mazze, K. (1981). The role of purpose in the organization of information about behavior: Trait-based vs. goal-based categories in person cognition. *Journal of Personality and Social Psychology*, 40, 211–25.

Hofstede, G. (1983). Dimensions of natural cultures in fifty countries and three regions. In J. Deregowski, S. Dziurawiec and R. Annis (eds), *Expiscations in cross-cultural psychology*. Lisse, Netherlands: Swets & Zeitlinger. Holloway, S. D., Kashiwagi, K., Hess, R. D. and Azuma, H. (1986). Causal attributions by Japanese and American mothers and children about performance in mathematics. *International Journal of Psychology*, 21, 269–86.

Holloway, S. D., Kashiwagi, K., Hess, R. D. and Azuma, H. (1986). Causal attributions by Japanese and American mothers and children about performance in mathematics. *International Journal of Psychology*, 21, 269–86.

Holmes, D. S. (1968). Dimensions of projection. *Psychological Bulletin*, 69, 248–68.

Howe, G. W. (1987). Attributions of complex cause and the perception of marital conflict. *Journal of Personality and Social Psychology*, 53, 1119–28.

Howell, R. J. and Jorgenson, E. C. (1970). Accuracy of judging emotional behavior in a natural setting—A replication. *Journal of Social Psychology*, 81, 269–70.

Husen, T. (1967). *International study of achievement in mathematics: A comparison of twelve countries.* New York: Wiley.

Istvan, J., Griffitt, W. and Weidner, G. (1983). Sexual arousal and the polarization of perceived sexual attractiveness. *Basic and Applied Social Psychology*, 4, 307–18.

Izard, C. E. (1969). The emotions and emotion constructs in personality and culture research. In R. B. Cattell (ed.), *Handbook of Modern Personality Theory*. Chicago: Aldine.

Izard, C. E. (1977). *Human emotions.* New York: Plenum Press.

Izard, C. E. (1979). *The maximally discriminative facial movement coding system.* Newark: Instructional Resources Center, University of Delaware.

Izard, C. E., Huebner, R. R., Risser, D., McGinnes, C. and Dougherty, L. M. (1980). The young infant's ability to produce discrete emotion expressions. *Developmental Psychology*, 16, 132–40.

Izard, C. E. and Malatesta, C. Z. (1987). Perspectives on emotional development I: Differential emotions theory of early emotional development. In J. D. Osofsky (ed.), *Handbook of infant development*, 2nd edn. New York: John Wiley, pp. 494–554.

Johnson, D. F. and Pittenger, J. B. (1984). Attribution, the attractiveness stereotype and the elderly. *Developmental Psychology*, 20, 1168–72.

Jones, C. and Aronson, E. (1973). Attribution of fault to a rape victim as a function of respectability of the victim. *Journal of Personality and Social Psychology*, 26, 415–19.

Jones, E. E. (1979). The rocky road from acts to dispositions. *American Psychologist*, 34, 107–17.

Jones, E. E. and Davis, K. E. (1965). From acts to dispositions: The attribution process in person perception. *Advances in Experimental Social Psychology*, Vol. 2. New York: Academic Press, pp. 220–66.

Jones, E. E., Davis, K. E. and Gergen, K. J. (1961). Role playing variations and their informational value for person perception. *Journal of Abnormal and Social Psychology*, 63, 302–10.

Jones, E. E. and DeCharms, R. (1957). Changes in social perception as a function of the personal relevance of behavior. *Sociometry*, 20, 75–85.

Jones, E. E. and Goethals, G. R. (1972). Order effects in impression formation: Attribution context and the nature of the entity. In E. E. Jones, D. E. Kanouse, H. H. Kelley, R. E. Nisbett, S. Valins and B. Weiner (eds), *Attribution: Perceiving the causes of behavior*. Morristown, NJ: General Learning Press, pp. 27–46.

Jones, E. E. and Harris, V. A. (1967). The attribution of attitudes. *Journal of Experimental Social Psychology*, 3, 1–24.

Jones, E. E. and McGillis, D. (1976). Correspondent inferences and the attribution cube: A comparative reappraisal. In J. H. Harvey, W. J. Ickes and R. F. Kidd (eds), *New directions in attribution research*. Vol. 1. Hillsdale, NJ: Erlbaum.

Jones, E. E. and Nisbett, R. E. (1972). The actor and the observer: Divergent perceptions of the causes of behavior. In E. E. Jones, D. E. Kanouse, H. H. Kelley, R. E. Nisbett, S. Valins, and B. Weiner (eds), *Attribution: Perceiving the causes of behavior*. Morristown, NJ: General Learning Press, pp. 79–94.

Jones, E. E., Rock, L., Shaver, K. G., Goethals, G. R. and Ward, L. M. (1968). Pattern of performance and ability attribution: An unexpected primacy effect. *Journal of Personality and Social Psychology*, 10, 317–40.

Jones, E. E., Schwartz, J. and Gilbert, D. T. (1984). Perceptions of moral expectancy violation: The role of expectancy source. *Social Cognition*, 2, 273–93.

Jones, J. M. (1983). The concept of race in social psychology: From color to culture. In L. Wheeler and P. Shaver (eds), *Review of Personality and Social Psychology*, Vol. 4. pp. 117–49. Beverly Hills, CA: Sage.

Jones, J. M. (1986). Cultural differences in temporal perspectives: Instrumental and expressive behaviors in time. In J. McGrath (ed.), *Research on time: Studies toward a social psychology of time*. Beverly Hills, CA: Sage, pp. 117–49.

Jussim, L., Coleman, L. M. and Lerch, L. (1987). The nature of stereotypes: A comparison and integration of three theories. *Journal of Personality and Social Psychology*, 52, 536–46.

Kahneman, D. and Tversky, A. (1973). On the psychology of prediction. *Psychological Review*, 80, 237–51.

Kalick, S. M. and Hamilton, T. E., III (1986). The matching hypothesis re-examined. *Journal of Personality and Social Psychology*, 51, 673–82.

Kanner, L. (1931). Judging emotions from facial expressions. *Psychological Monographs*, 41 (3, whole no. 186).

Karniol, R. and Ross, M. (1976). The development of causal attributions in social perception. *Journal of Personality and Social Psychology*, 34, 455–64.

Karniol, R. and Ross, M. (1979). Children's use of a causal attribution schema and the inference of manipulative intentions. *Child Development*, 50, 463–8.

Kassin, S. M. (1979). Consensus information, prediction and causal attribution: A review of the literature and issues. *Journal of Personality and Social Psychology*, 37, 1966–81.

Kassin, S. M., Lowe, C. A. and Gibbons, F. X. (1980). Children's use of the discounting principle: A perceptual approach. *Journal of Personality and Social Psychology*, 39, 719–28.

Kassin, S. M. and Pryor, J. B. (1985). The development of attribution processes. In J. B. Pryor and J. D. Day (eds), *The development of social cognition*. New York: Springer-Verlag, pp. 3–34.

Katz, D. and Braly, K. W. (1933). Racial stereotypes of 100 college students. *Journal of Abnormal and Social Psychology*, 28, 280–90.

Katz, I. (1981). *Stigma: A social psychological analysis*. Hillsdale, NJ. Lawrence Erlbaum.

Keating, C. F. (1985). Human dominance signals: The primate in us. In S. L. Ellyson and J. F. Dovidio (eds), *Power, dominance, and nonverbal behavior*. New York: Springer-Verlag, pp. 89–108.

Keith, J. (1985). Age in anthropological research. In R. H. Binstock and E. Shanas (eds), *Handbook of aging and the social sciences*. New York: Van Nostrand Reinhold, pp. 231–63.

Kelley, H. H. (1950). The warm–cold variable in first impressions of persons. *Journal of Personality*, 18, 431–9.

Kelley, H. H. (1967). Attribution theory in social psychology. In D. Levine (ed.), *Nebraska Symposium on Motivation*, Vol. 15. Lincoln: University of Nebraska Press, pp. 192–238.

Kelley, H. H. (1973). The processes of causal attribution. *American Psychologist*, 28, 107–28.

Kelley, H. H. (1983). The situational origins of human tendencies: A further reason for the formal analysis of structures. *Personality and Social Psychology Bulletin*, 9, 8–30.

Kelley, H. H. and Michela, J. L. (1980). Attribution theory and research. *Annual Review of Psychology*, 31, 457–501.

Kelly, G. A. (1955) *The psychology of personal constructs*. New York: W. W. Norton.

Kenny, D. and Albright, L. (1987). Accuracy in interpersonal perception: A social relations analysis. *Psychological Bulletin*, 102, 390–402.

Kenrick, D. T. and Funder, D. C. (1988). Profiting from controversy. Lessons from the person–situation debate. *American Psychologist*, 43, 23–34.

Kimmel, D. C. (1988). Ageism, psychology and public policy. *American Psychologist*, 43, 175–8.

Kite, M. E. and Johnson, B. T. (1988). Attitudes toward older and younger adults: A meta-analysis. *Psychology and Aging*, 3, 233–44.

Klayman, J. and Ha. Y. W. (1987). Confirmation, disconfirmation, and information in hypothesis testing. *Psychological Review*, 94, 211–28.

Korten, F. F. (1974). The influence of culture and sex on the perception of persons. *International Journal of Psychology*, 9, 31–44.

Kozel, N. J. and Gitter, A. G. (1968). *Perceptions of Emotion: Differences in Mode of Presentation, Sex of Perceiver, and Role of Expressor*. (Tech. Rep. 18) Boston: Boston University.

Kozlowski, L. T. and Cutting, J. E. (1977). Recognizing the sex of a walker from a dynamic point-lights display. *Perception and Psychophysics*, 21, 575–80.

Kramer, E. (1963). Judgment of personal characteristics and emotions from nonverbal properties of speech. *Psychological Bulletin*, 60, 408–20.

Krauss, R. M., Apple, W., Morency, N., Wenzel, C. and Winton, W. (1981). Verbal, vocal, and visible factors in judgments of another's affect. *Journal of Personality and Social Psychology*, 40, 312–20.

Krueger, J. and Rothbart, M. (1988). Use of categorical and individuating information in making inferences about personality. *Journal of Personality and Social Psychology*, 55, 187–95.

Kruglanski, A. W. (1975). The endogenous–exogenous partition in attribution theory. *Psychological Review*, 82, 387–406.

Kruglanski, A. and Freund, T. (1983). The freezing and unfreezing of lay inferences: Effects on impressional primacy, ethnic stereotyping, and numerical anchoring. *Journal of Experimental Social Psychology*, 19, 448–68.

Kruglanski, A. W., Schwartz, J. M., Maides, S. and Hamel, I. Z. (1978). Covariation, discounting, and augmentation: towards a clarification of attributional principles. *Journal of Personality*, 46, 176–89.

Kuiper, N. A. (1981). Convergent evidence for the self as a prototype: The 'inverted-U RT effect' for self and other judgments. *Personality and Social Psychology Bulletin*, 7, 438–43.

Kulik, J. A. and Taylor, S. E. (1980). Premature consensus on consensus? Effects of sample-based versus self-based consensus information. *Journal of Personality and Social Psychology*, 39, 871–9.

Kulka, R. A. and Kessler, J. B. (1978). Is justice really blind: The influence of litigant physical attractiveness on judicial judgment. *Journal of Applied Social Psychology*, 7, 855–68.

Kun, A. (1977). Development of the magnitude-covariation and compensation schemata in ability and effort attribution of performance. *Child Development*, 48, 862–73.

Lalljee, M., Watson, M. and White, P. (1983). Some aspects of the explanations of young children. In J. Jaspars, F. D. Fincham and M. Hewstone (eds), *Attribution theory and research: Conceptual, developmental and social dimensions*. London: Academic Press, pp. 165–92.

Langer, E. and Abelson, R. P. (1974). A patient by any other name . . . : clinician group differences in labeling bias. *Journal of Consulting and Clinical Psychology*, 42, 4–9.

Langlois, J. H. (in press). The origins and functions of stereotypes based on facial appearance. In R. A. Eder (ed.), *Developmental perspectives in craniofacial problems*. New York: Springer-Verlag.

Lanzetta, J. T. and Orr, S. P. (1981). Stimulus properties of facial expressions and their influence on the classical conditioning of fear. *Motivation and Emotion*, 5, 225–34.

Lee, H. O. and Boster, F. J. (in press). Speech rate and perceptions of source credibility: A cross-cultural comparison study. *Journal of Cross-Cultural Psychology*.

Leeper, R. (1935). A study of a neglected portion of the field of learning – the development of sensory organization. *Journal of Genetic Psychology*, 46, 41–75.

Lerner, M. J. (1980). *The belief in a just world: A fundamental delusion*. New York: Plenum.

Levitt, E. A. (1964). The relationship between abilities to express emotional meanings vocally and facially. In J. R. Davitz (ed.), *The communication of emotional meaning*. New York: McGraw-Hill, pp. 87–100.

Levy, R. I. (1983). The emotions in comparative perspective. In K. R. Scherer and P. Ekman (eds), *Approaches to emotion*. Hillsdale, NJ: Erlbaum, pp. 397–412.

Lewicki, P. (1983). Self-image bias in person perception. *Journal of Personality and Social Psychology*, 45, 384–93.

Lewicki, P. (1984). Self-schema and social information processing. *Journal of Personality and Social Psychology*, 47, 1177–90.

Lewin, K. (1936). *A Dynamic Theory of Personality*. New York: McGraw Hill.

Liggett, J. C. (1974). *The human face*. New York: Stein & Day.

Linville, P. W. (1982). The complexity–extremity effect and age-based stereotyping. *Journal of Personality and Social Psychology*, 42, 193–211.

Linville, P. W. and Jones, E. E. (1980). Polarized appraisals of outgroup members. *Journal of Personality and Social Psychology*, 38, 689–703.

Livesley, W. J. and Bromley, D. B. (1973). *Person perception in childhood and adolescence*. London: John Wiley.

Locke, D. and Pennington, D. (1982). Reasons and other causes: Their role in attribution processes. *Journal of Personality and Social Psychology*, 42, 212–23.

Locksley, A., Borgida, E., Brekke, N. and Hepburn, C. (1980). Sex stereotypes and social judgment. *Journal of Personality and Social Psychology*, 39, 821–31.

Lowe, C. A. and Kassin, S. (1980). A perceptual view of attribution: Theoretical and methodological implications. *Personality and Social Psychology Bulletin*, 6, 532–41.

Lutz, C. (1982). The domain of emotion words on Ifaluk. *American Ethnologist*, 9, 113–28.

Mace, K. C. (1972). The "overt-bluff" shoplifter: Who gets caught? *Journal of Forensic Psychology*, 4, 26–30.

Major, B. (1980). Information acquisition and attribution processes. *Journal of Personality and Social Psychology*, 39, 1010–23.

Major, B., Cozzorelli, C., Testa, M. and McFarlin, D. (1988). Self-verification versus expectancy confirmation in social interaction: The impact of self-focus. *Personality and Social Psychology Bulletin*, **14**, 346–59.

Malatesta, C. Z., Fiore, M. J. and Messina, J. J. (1987). Affect, personality, and facial expression characteristics of older people. *Psychology and Aging*, **2**, 64–9.

Malatesta, C. Z. and Izard, C. E. (1984). The facial expression of emotion: Young, middle-aged, and older adult expressions. In C. Z. Malatesta and C. E. Izard (eds), *Emotion and Adult Development*. Beverly Hills, CA: Sage, pp. 253–73.

Malatesta, C. Z., Izard, C. E., Culver, C. and Nicolich, M. (1987). Emotion communication skills in young, middle-aged, and older women. *Psychology and Aging*, **2**, 193–203.

Malatesta, C. Z. and Haviland, J. M. (1982). Learning display rules: The socialization of emotion expression in infancy. *Child Development*, **53**, 991–1003.

Manis, M., Nelson, T. and Shedler, J. (1988). Stereotypes and social judgment: Extremity, assimilation, and contrast. *Journal of Personality and Social Psychology*, **55**, 28–36.

Marks, G. and Miller, N. (1987). Ten years of research on the false-consensus effect: An empirical and theoretical review. *Psychological Bulletin*, **102**, 72–90.

Markus, M. (1977). Self-schemata and processing information about the self. *Journal of Personality and Social Psychology*, **35**, 63–78.

Martindale, A. E. and Martindale, C. (1988). Metaphorical equivalence of elements and temperaments: Empirical studies of Bachelard's theory of imagination. *Journal of Personality and Social Psychology*, **55**, 836–48.

Matsumoto, D. (1988). Cultural influences on the perception of emotion. *Journal of Cross-Cultural Psychology*, **20**, 92–105.

Matsumoto, D. and Kishimoto, M. (1983). Developmental characteristics in judgments of emotion from nonverbal vocal cues. *International Journal of Intercultural Relations*, **7**, 415–24.

Mayer, J. D. and Bower, G. H. (1986). Learning and memory for personality prototypes. *Journal of Personality and Social Psychology*, **51**, 473–92.

McArthur, L. A. (1972). The how and what of why: Some determinants and consequences of causal attribution. *Journal of Personality and Social Psychology*, **22**, 171–93.

McArthur, L. Z. (1980). Illusory causation and illusory correlation: Two epistemological accounts. *Personality and Social Psychology Bulletin*, **6**, 507–19.

McArthur, L. Z. (1981). What grabs you? The role of attention in impression formation and causal attribution. In E. T. Higgins, C. P. Herman and M. P. Zanna (eds), *Social cognition: The Ontario Symposium*, Vol. 1. Hillsdale, NJ: Erlbaum, pp. 201–46.

McArthur, L. Z. (1982). Judging a book by its cover: A cognitive analysis of the relationship between physical appearance and stereotyping. In A. Hastorf and A. Isen (eds), *Cognitive social psychology*. New York: Elsevier North-Holland, pp. 149–211.

McArthur, L. Z. and Apatow, K. (1983–4). Impressions of babyfaced adults. *Social Cognition*, 2, 315–42.

McArthur, L. Z. and Berry. D. S. (1987). Cross-cultural agreement in perceptions of babyfaced adults. *Journal of Cross-Cultural Psychology*, 18, 165–92.

McArthur, L. Z. and Baron, R. M. (1983). Toward an ecological theory of social perception. *Psychological Review*, 90, 215–47.

McArthur, L. Z. and Friedman, S. A. (1980). Illusory correlation in impression formation: Variations in the shared distinctiveness effect as a function of the distinctive person's age, race, and sex. *Journal of Personality and Social Psychology*, 39, 615–24.

McArthur, L. Z. and Ginsberg, E. (1981). Causal attribution to salient stimuli: An investigation of visual fixation mediators. *Personality and Social Psychology Bulletin*, 7, 547–53.

McArthur, L. Z. and Post, D. L. (1977). Figural emphasis and person perception. *Journal of Experimental Social Psychology*, 13, 520–35.

McArthur, L. Z. and Solomon, L. K. (1978). Perceptions of an aggressive encounter as a function of the victim's salience and the perceiver's arousal. *Journal of Personality and Social Psychology*, 36, 1278–90.

McCall, R. B. and Kennedy, C. B. (1980). Attention of 4-month infants to discrepancy and babyishness. *Journal of Experimental Child Psychology*, 29, 189–201.

McCluskey, K. W., Albas, D. C., Niemi, R. R., Cuevas, C. and Ferrer, C. A. (1975). Cross-cultural differences in the perception of the emotional content of speech: A study of the development of sensitivity in Canadian and Mexican children. *Developmental Psychology*, 11, 551–5.

Mehrabian, A. (1972). *Nonverbal communication*. Chicago: Aldine-Atherton.

Mehrabian, A. and Ferris, S. R. (1967). Inference of attitudes from non-verbal communication in two channels. *Journal of Consulting Psychology*, 31, 248–52.

Messick, D. M. and Reeder, G. D. (1974). Roles, occupations, behaviors, and attributions. *Journal of Experimental Social Psychology*, 10, 126–32.

Meyer, J. P. (1980). Causal attribution for success and failure: A multivariate investigation of dimensionality, formation, and consequences. *Journal of Personality and Social Psychology*, 38, 704–18.

Michotte, A. (1963). *The perception of causality*. New York: Basic Books.

Miller, D. T. and Ross, M. (1975). Self-serving biases in the attribution of causality. Fact or fiction? *Psychological Bulletin*, 82, 213–25.

Miller, F. D., Smith, E. R. and Uleman, J. (1981). Measurement and interpretation of dispositional and situational attributions. *Journal of Experimental Social Psychology*, 17, 80–95.

Miller, J. G. (1984). Culture and the development of everyday social explanation. *Journal of Personality and Social Psychology*, 46, 961–78.

Mischel, W. (1968). *Personality and Assessment*. New York: Wiley.

Mischel, W. and Peake, P. K. (1982). Beyond *déjà vu* in the search for cross-situational consistency. *Psychological Review*, 89, 730–55.

Monson, T. C. and Hesley, J. W. (1982). Causal attributions for behaviors consistent or inconsistent with an actor's personality traits: Differences between those offered by actors and observers. *Journal of Experimental Social Psychology*, 18, 416–32.

Monson, T. C. and Snyder, M. (1977). Actors, observers, and the attribution process: Toward a reconceptualization. *Journal of Experimental Social Psychology*, 13, 89–111.

Montepare, J. M., Goldstein, S. B. and Clausen, A. (1987). The identification of emotions from gait information. *Journal of Nonverbal Behavior*, 11, 33–42.

Montepare, J. M. and Zebrowitz-McArthur, L. (1988a). Perceptions of adults with childlike voices in two cultures. *Journal of Experimental Social Psychology*, 23, 331–49.

Montepare, J. M. and Zebrowitz-McArthur, L. (1988b). Impressions of people created by age-related qualities of their gaits. *Journal of Personality and Social Psychology*, 55, 547–56.

Montepare, J. M. and Zebrowitz-McArthur, L. (1989). Children's perceptions of baby faced adults. *Perceptual and Motor Skills*, 69, 467–72.

Montepare, J. M. and Zebrowitz, L. A. (1990). A cross-cultural comparison of impressions created by a youthful gait. Unpublished manuscript, Brandeis University.

Moreland, R. L. and Zajonc, R. B. (1979). Exposure effects may not depend on stimulus recognition. *Journal of Personality and Social Psychology*, 37, 1085–9.

Morency, N. L. and Krauss, R. M. (1982). Children's nonverbal encoding and decoding of affect. In R. S. Feldman (ed.), *Development of nonverbal behavior in children*. New York: Springer-Verlag, pp. 181–200.

Napolitan, D. A. and Goethals, G. R. (1979). The attribution of friendliness. *Journal of Experimental Social Psychology*, 15, 105–13.

Neisser, U. (1976). *Cognition and reality*. San Francisco: W. H. Freeman.

Nelson, C. A. (1987). The recognition of facial expressions in the first two years of life: Mechanisms of development. *Child Development*, 58, 889–909.

Neuberg, S. L. and Fiske, S. T. (1987). Motivational influences on impression formation: Outcome dependency, accuracy-driven attention, and individuating processes. *Journal of Personality and Social Psychology*, 53, 431–44.

Newtson, D. (1976). Foundations of attribution: The perception of ongoing behavior. In J. Harvey, W. J. Ickes and R. F. Kidd (eds), *New directions in attribution research*, vol. 1. Hillsdale, NJ: Erlbaum, pp. 223–48.

Nisbett, R. E. and Borgida, E. (1975). Attribution and the psychology of prediction. *Journal of Personality and Social Psychology*, 32, 932–43.

Nisbett, R. E., Caputo, C., Legant, P. and Maracek, J. (1973). Behavior as seen by the actor and as seen by the observer. *Journal of Personality and Social Psychology*, 27, 154–65.

Nisbett, R. E. and Ross, L. (1980). *Human inference: Strategies and shortcomings of social judgment*. Englewood Cliffs, NJ: Prentice-Hall.

Nisbett, R. E., Zukier, H. and Lemley, R. (1981). The dilution effect: nondiagnostic information weakens the implications of diagnostic information. *Cognitive Psychology*, 13, 248–77.

Norman, W. T. (1963). Toward an adequate taxonomy of personality attributes: Replicated factor structure in peer nomination personality ratings. *Journal of Abnormal and Social Psychology*, 66, 574–83.

Orvis, B. R., Cunningham, J. D. and Kelley, H. H. (1975). A closer examination of causal inference: The roles of consensus, distinctiveness, and consistency information. *Journal of Personality and Social Psychology*, 32, 605–16.

Orwell, G. (1949). Closing words, MS notebook, 17 April. Cited in *The Oxford dictionary of quotations*, 3rd edn (1989). Oxford: Oxford University Press, p. 365.

Osgood, C. E. (1966). Dimensionality of the semantic space for communication via facial expressions. *Scandinavian Journal of Psychology*, 7, 1–30.

Osgood, C. E., May, W. H. and Miron, M. S. (1975). *Cross-cultural universals of affective meaning*. Urbana: University of Illinois Press.

Osgood, C. E., Suci, G. J. and Tannenbaum, P. H. (1957). *The measurement of meaning*. Urbana: University of Illinois Press.

Ostrom, T. M. (1977). Between-theory and within-theory conflict in explaining context effects in impression formation. *Journal of Experimental Social Psychology*, 13, 492–503.

O'Sullivan, M., Ekman, P., Friesen, W. and Scherer, K. (1985). What you say and how you say it: The contribution of speech content and voice quality to judgments of others. *Journal of Personality and Social Psychology*, 48, 54–62.

Park, B. (1986). A method for studying the development of impressions of real people. *Journal of Personality and Social Psychology*, 51, 907–17.

Park, B. and Hahn, S. (1988). Sex-role identity and the perception of others. *Social Cognition*, 6, 61–87.

Park, B. and Judd, C. M. (1989). Agreement on initial impressions: Differences due to perceivers, trait dimensions, and target behaviors. *Journal of Personality and Social Psychology*, 56, 493–505.

Park, B. and Rothbart, M. (1982). Perception of out-group homogeneity and levels of social categorization: Memory for the subordinate attributes of in-group and out-group members. *Journal of Personality and Social Psychology*, 42, 1051–68.

Passini, F. T. and Norman, W. T. (1966). A universal conception of personality structure? *Journal of Personality and Social Psychology*, 4, 44–9.

Peabody, D. (1987). Selecting representative trait adjectives. *Journal of Personality and Social Psychology*, 52, 59–71.

Peevers, B. H. and Secord, P. F. (1973). Developmental changes in attribution of descriptive concepts to persons. *Journal of Personality and Social Psychology*, 27, 120–8.

Pepitone, A. (1949). Motivational effects in social perception. *Human Relations*, 3, 57–76.

Perlman, D. and Oskamp, S. (1971). The effects of picture content and exposure frequency on evaluations of negroes and whites. *Journal of Experimental Social Psychology*, 7, 503–14.

Pheterson, G. I., Kiesler, S. B. and Goldberg, P. A. (1971). Evaluation of the performance of women as a function of their sex, achievement, and personal history. *Journal of Personality and Social Psychology*, 19, 114–18.

Phillips, R. D., Wagner, S. H., Fells, C. A. and Lynch, M. (1988). Do infants recognize emotion in facial expressions?: Categorical and "metaphorical" evidence. Unpublished manuscript. University of Delaware.

Piaget, J. (1926). *The language and thought of the child*. New York: Harcourt Brace.

Pruitt, D. J. and Insko, C. A. (1980). Extension of the Kelley attribution model: The role of comparison-object consensus, target-object consensus, distinctiveness, and consistency. *Journal of Personality and Social Psychology*, 39, 39–58.

Quattrone, G. A. (1982). Overattribution and unit formation. When behavior engulfs the person. *Journal of Personality and Social Psychology*, 42, 593–607.

Read, S. J. (1987). Constructing causal scenarios: A knowledge structure approach to causal reasoning. *Journal of Personality and Social Psychology*, 52, 288–302.

Read, S. J. and Stephan, W. G. (1979). An integration of Kelley's attribution cube and Weiner's achievement attribution model. *Personality and Social Psychology Bulletin*, 5, 196–200.

Reeder, G. D. and Brewer, M. B. (1979). A schematic model of dispositional attribution in interpersonal perception. *Psychological Review*, 86, 61–79.

Reeder, G. D., Messick, D. M. and Van Avermaet, E. (1977). Dimensional asymmetry in attributional inference. *Journal of Experimental Social Psychology*, 13, 46–57.

Rees, L. (1968). Constitutional psychology. In D. L. Sills (ed.), *International encyclopedia of the social sciences*. New York: Macmillan, pp. 66–76.

Regan, D. T. and Totten, J. (1975). Empathy and attribution: Turning observers into actors. *Journal of Personality and Social Psychology*, 32, 850–6.

Riess, J. A. and Cunningham, J. G. (1988). The development of affect state understanding in two- and three-year-olds. Poster presented at the Conference on Human Development, Charleston, SC, March.

Roberts, J. V. and Herman, C. P. (1986). The psychology of height: An empirical review. In C. P. Herman, M. P. Zanna and E. T. Higgins (eds), *Physical appearance, stigma, and social behavior: The Ontario Symposium*, Vol. 3. Hillsdale, NJ: Erlbaum, pp. 113–40.

Robinson, J. and McArthur, L. Z. (1982). The impact of salient vocal qualities on causal attributions for a speaker's behavior. *Journal of Personality and Social Psychology*, 43, 236–47.

Rosch, E. (1978). Principles of categorization. In E. Rosch and B. B. Lloyd (eds), *Cognition and categorization*. Hillsdale, NJ: Erlbaum.

Rose, Y. J. and Tryon, W. W. (1979). Judgments of assertive behavior as a function of speech loudness, latency, content, gestures, inflection, and sex. *Behavior Modification*, 3, 112–23.

Rosenberg, S., Nelson, C. and Vivekananthan, P. S. (1968). A multidimensional approach to the structure of personality impressions. *Journal of Personality and Social Psychology*, 9, 283–94.

Rosenberg, S. and Sedlak, A. (1972). Structural representatives of perceived personality trait relationships. In A. K. Romney, R. N. Shepard and S. B. Nerlove (eds), *Multidimensional scaling: Theory and applications in the behavioral sciences*, Vol. 2. New York: Seminar Press, pp. 134–62.

Rosenfeld, H. M. (1982). Measurement of body motion and orientation. In K. R. Scherer and P. Ekman (eds), *Handbook of methods in nonverbal behavior research*. Cambridge: Cambridge University Press, pp. 199–286.

Rosenthal, R. and DePaulo, B. (1979). Sex differences in eavesdropping on nonverbal cues. *Journal of Personality and Social Psychology*, 37, 273–85.

Rosenthal, R., Hall, J. A., DiMatteo, M. R., Rogers, P. L. and Archer, D. (1979). *Sensitivity to nonverbal communication*. Baltimore, MD: Johns Hopkins University Press.

Ross, L. (1977). The intuitive psychologist and his shortcomings: Distortions in the attribution process. In L. Berkowitz (ed.), *Advances in experimental social psychology*, Vol. 10. New York: Academic Press, pp. 174–200.

Ross, L., Greene, D. and House, P. (1977). The "false consensus effect": An egocentric bias in social perception and attribution processes. *Journal of Experimental Social Psychology*, 13, 279–301.

Ross, M. (1981). Egocentric biases in attributions of responsibility: antecedents and consequences. In E. T. Higgins, C. P. Herman and M. P. Zanna (eds), *Social cognition: The Ontario Symposium*, Vol. 1. Hillsdale, NJ: Erlbaum, pp. 305–22.

Ross, M. and Fletcher, G. J. O. (1985). Attribution and social perception. In G. Lindzey and E. Aronson (eds), *The handbook of social psychology*, Vol. II, 3rd edn. New York: Random House, pp. 73–122.

Ross, M. and Sicoly, F. (1979). Egocentric biases in availability and attribution. *Journal of Personality and Social Psychology*, 37, 322–36.

Rubin, Z. (1980). *Children's friendships*, Cambridge, MA: Harvard University Press.

Ruble, D. N., Feldman, N. S., Higgins, E. T. and Karlovac, M. (1979). Locus of causality and the use of information in the development of causal attributions. *Journal of Personality*, 47, 595–614.

Runeson, S. and Frykholm, G. (1981). Visual perception of lifted weight. *Journal of Experimental Psychology: Human Perception and Performance*, 7, 733–40.

Russell, D. W., McAuley, E. and Tarico, V. (1987). Measuring causal attributions for success and failure: A comparison of methodologies for assessing causal dimensions. *Journal of Personality and Social Psychology*, 52, 1248–57.

Russell, J. A. (1980). A circumplex model of affect. *Journal of Personality and Social Psychology*, 39, 1161–78.

Russell, J. A. (1983). Pancultural aspects of the human conceptual organization of emotions. *Journal of Personality and Social Psychology*, 45, 1281–8.

Russell, J. A. and Ridgeway, D. (1983). Dimensions underlying children's emotion concepts. *Developmental Psychology*, 19, 795–804.

Sabatelli, R., Buck, R. and Dreyer, A. (1980). Communication via facial cues in intimate dyads. *Personality and Social Psychology Bulletin*, 6, 242–7.

Sabatelli, R., Buck, R. and Dreyer, A. (1982). Nonverbal communication accuracy in married couples: Relationships with marital complaints. *Journal of Personality and Social Psychology*, 43, 1088–97.

Sagar, H. A. and Schofield, J. W. (1980). Racial and behavioral cues in black and white children's perceptions of ambiguously aggressive acts. *Journal of Personality and Social Psychology*, 39, 590–8.

Sanbonmatsu, D. M., Sherman, S. J. and Hamilton, D. L. (1987). Illusory correlation in the perception of groups and individuals. *Social Cognition*, 5, 1–25.

Sande, G., Goethals, G. and Radloff, C. (1988). Perceiving one's own traits and others: The multifaceted self. *Journal of Personality and Social Psychology*, 54, 13–20.

Scarlett, H. H., Press, A. N. and Crockett, W. H. (1971). Children's descriptions of peers: A Wernerian developmental analysis, *Child Development*, 42, 439–53.

Scherer, K. R. (1979). Non linguistic vocal indicators of emotion and psychopathology. In C. E. Izard (ed.), *Emotions in Personality and Psychopathology*. New York: Plenum Press, pp. 493–529.

Scherer, K. R. (1986). Vocal affect expression: A review and a model for future research. *Psychological Bulletin*, 99, 143–65.

Scherer, K. R. and Giles, H. (eds) (1979). *Social markers in speech*. Cambridge: Cambridge University Press.

Scherer, K. R. and Scherer, U. (1981). Speech behavior and personality. In J. K. Darby, Jr (ed.), *Speech evaluation in psychiatry*. New York: Grune & Stratton.

Schiffenbauer, A. (1974). Effect of observer's emotional state on judgments of the emotional state of others. *Journal of Personality and Social Psychology*, 30, 31–5.

Schneider, D. J., Hastorf, A. H. and Ellsworth, P. C. (1979). *Person perception*. Reading, MA: Addison-Wesley.

Schwartz, G. M., Izard, C. E. and Ansul, S. E. (1985). The 5-month-old's ability to discriminate facial expressions of emotion. *Infant Behavior and Development*, 8, 65–77.

Schwartz, J. C. and Shaver, P. (1987). Emotions and emotion knowledge in interpersonal relations. In W. Jones and D. Perlman (eds), *Advances in personal relationships*, Vol. 1. Greenwich, CT: JAI Press, pp. 197–241.

Schwartz, N., Strack, F., Hilton, D. and Naderer, G. (1988). Base-rates, representativeness, and the logic of conversation. Zuma-Arbeitsbericht Nr. 87/10. Zentum fur Umfragen, Methoden und Analysen. Mannheim, W. Germany.

Sedlak, A. J. and Kurtz, S. T. (1981). A review of children's use of causal inference principles. *Child Development*, 52, 759–84.

Seligman, M. E. P. and Hager, J. L. (1972). *Biological boundaries of learning*. New York: Appleton-Century-Crofts.

Shaver, K. G. (1970). Defensive attribution: Effects of severity and relevance on the responsibility assigned for an accident. *Journal of Personality and Social Psychology*, 14, 101–13.

Shaver, P. Schwartz, J., Kerson, D. and O'Connor, G. (1987). Emotion knowledge: Further exploration of a prototype approach. *Journal of Personality and Social Psychology*, 52, 1061–86.

Shaw, R., Turvey, M. and Mace, W. (1982). Ecological psychology: The consequences of a commitment to realism. In W. Weimer and D. Palermo (eds), *Cognition and symbolic processes*, Vol. 2. Hillsdale, NJ: Erlbaum.

Sheldon, W. H. (1954). *Atlas of Men*. New York: Harper & Bros.

Shimoda, K., Argyle, M. and Ricci Bitti, P. (1978). The intercultural recognition of emotional expressions by three national racial groups: English, Italian, and Japanese. *European Journal of Social Psychology*, 8, 169–79.

Shoda, Y., Mischel, W. and Wright, J. (1989). Intuitive interactionism in person perception: Effects of situation-behavior relations on dispositional judgments. *Journal of Personality and Social Psychology*, 56, 41–53.

Shweder, R. A. and Bourne, E. J. (1982). Does the concept of the person vary cross-culturally? In A. J. Marsella and G. M. White (eds), *Cultural conceptions of mental health and therapy*. London: D. Reidel, pp. 97–137.

Shweder, R. A. and D'Andrade, R. G. (1980). The systematic distortion hypothesis. In R. A. Shweder (ed.), *New directions for methodology of behavioral science: Fallible judgment in behavioral research*. San Francisco: Jossey-Bass.

Sigall, M. and Ostrove, N. (1975). Beautiful but dangerous: Effects of offender attractiveness and nature of the crime on juridic judgment. *Journal of Personality and Social Psychology*, 31, 410–14.

Skov, R. B. and Sherman, S. J. (1986). Information gathering processes: Diagnosticity, hypotheses-confirmatory strategies, and perceived hypothesis confirmation. *Journal of Experimental Social Psychology*, 22, 93–121.

Skowronski, J. J. and Carlston, D. E. (1987). Social judgment and social memory: The role of cue diagnosticity in negativity, positivity, and extremity biases. *Journal of Personality and Social Psychology*, 52, 689–99.

Sleet, D. A. (1969). Physique and social image. *Perceptual and Motor Skills*, 28, 295–9.

Smith, C. A. and Ellsworth, P. C. (1985). Patterns of cognitive appraisal in emotion. *Journal of Personality and Social Psychology*, 48, 813–38.

Smith, M. C. (1975). Children's use of the multiple sufficient cause schema in social perception. *Journal of Personality and Social Psychology*, 32, 737–47.

Snodgrass, S. (1985). Women's intuition: The effect of subordinate role in interpersonal sensitivity. *Journal of Personality and Social Psychology*, 49, 140–55.

Snyder, M. (1981). Seek, and ye shall find: Testing hypotheses about other people. In E. T. Higgins, C. P. Herman and M. P. Zanna (eds), *Social cognition: The Ontario Symposium*, Vol. 1. Hillsdale, NJ: Erlbaum, pp. 277–304.

Snyder, M., Tanke, E. D. and Berscheid, E. (1977). Social perception and interpersonal behavior: On the self-fulfilling nature of social stereotypes. *Journal of Personality and Social Psychology*, 35, 656–66.

Sogon, S. and Izard, C. E. (1987). Sex differences in emotion recognition by observing body movements: A case of American students. *Japanese Psychological Research*, 29, 89–93.

Sorce, J. F., Emde, R. N., Campos, J. J. and Klennert, M. D. (1985). Maternal emotional signalling: Its effects on the visual cliff behavior of 1-year-olds. *Developmental Psychology*, 21, 195–200.

Soskin, W. F. and Kauffman, P. E. (1961). Judgment of emotions in word free voice samples. *Journal of Communication*, 11, 73–81.

Spears, R., van der Pligt, J. and Eiser, J. (1985). Illusory correlation in the perception of group attitudes. *Journal of Personality and Social Psychology*, 48, 863–75.

Spence, J. T., Helmreich, R. and Stapp, J. (1975). Ratings of self and peers on sex-role attributes and their relationship to self-esteem and conceptions of masculinity and femininity. *Journal of Personality and Social Psychology*, 32, 29–39.

Stephan, C. and Langlois, J. H. (1984). Baby beautiful: Adult attributions of infant competence as a function of infant attractiveness. *Child Development*, 55, 576–85.

Stephan, C. and Tully, J. C. (1977). The influence of physical attractiveness of a plaintiff on the decisions of simulated jurors. *Journal of Social Psychology*, 10, 348–61.

Stewart, J. E. (1980). Defendants' attractiveness as a factor in the outcome of criminal trials: An observational study. *Journal of Applied Social Psychology*, 10, 348–61.

Storms, M. D. (1973). Videotape and the attribution process: Reversing actors' and observers' points of view. *Journal of Personality and Social Psychology*, 27, 165–75.

Strack, F., Erber, R. and Wicklund, R. A. (1982). Effects of salience and time pressure on ratings of causality. *Journal of Experimental Social Psychology*, 18, 581–94.

Street, R. L., Jr and Brady, R. M. (1982). Speech rate acceptance ranges as a function of evaluative domain, listener speech rate, and communication context. *Communication Monographs*, 49, 290–308.

Swann, W. B., Jr (1984). Quest for accuracy in person perception: A matter of pragmatics. *Psychological Review*, 91, 457–77.

Swann, W. B., Jr and Ely, R. J. (1984). A battle of wills: Self-verification versus behavioral confirmation. *Journal of Personality and Social Psychology*, 46, 1287–1302.

Swann, W. B., Jr and Snyder, M. (1980). On translating beliefs into action: Theories of ability and their application in an instructional setting. *Journal of Personality and Social Psychology*, 38, 879–88.

Swann, W. B., Jr, Pelham, B. W., and Roberts, D. C. (1987). Causal chunking: Memory and inference in ongoing interaction. *Journal of Personality and Social Psychology*, 53, 858–65.

Swim, J., Borgida, E., Maruyama, G. and Myers, D. G. (1989). Joan McKay versus John McKay: Do gender stereotypes bias evaluations? *Psychological Bulletin*, **105**, 409–29.

Tajfel, H. (1970). Experiments in intergroup discrimination. *Scientific American*, **223**, 96–102.

Tajfel, H., Flament, C., Billig, M. and Bundy, R. P. (1971). Social categorization and ingroup behavior. *European Journal of Social Psychology*, **1**, 149–78.

Taylor, S. E. and Fiske, S. T. (1975). Point of view and perceptions of causality. *Journal of Personality and Social Psychology*, **32**, 439–45.

Taylor, S. E. and Fiske, S. T. (1978). Salience, attention, and attribution: Top of the head phenomena. In L. Berkowitz (ed.), *Advances in experimental social psychology*, Vol. 11. New York: Academic Press, pp. 250–89.

Taylor, S. E. and Thompson, S. C. (1982). Stalking the elusive "vividness" effect. *Psychological Review*, **89**, 155–81.

Tetlock, P. E. and Kim, J. I. (1987). Accountability and judgment processes in a personality prediction task. *Journal of Personality and Social Psychology*, **52**, 700–9.

Thakerar, J. N. and Iwawaki, S. (1979). Cross-cultural comparisons in interpersonal attraction of females toward males. *Journal of Social Psychology*, **108**, 121–2.

Thompson, D. F. and Meltzer, L. (1964). Communication of emotion intent by facial expression. *Journal of Abnormal and Social Psychology*, **68**, 129–35.

Thompson, S. C. and Kelley, H. H. (1981). Judgments of responsibility for activities in close relationships. *Journal of Personality and Social Psychology*, **41**, 469–77.

Toner, H. L. and Gates, G. R. (1985). Emotional traits and recognition of facial expression of emotion. *Journal of Nonverbal Behavior*, **9**, 48–66.

Trope, Y. (1986). Identification and inferential processes in dispositional attribution. *Psychological Review*, **93**, 239–57.

Trope, Y. and Bassok, M. (1982). Confirmatory and diagnosing strategies in social information gathering. *Journal of Personality and Social Psychology*, **43**, 22–34.

Trope, Y. and Bassok, M. (1983). Information gathering strategies in hypothesis-testing. *Journal of Experimental Social Psychology*, **19**, 560–76.

Trope, Y., Bassok, M. and Alon, E. (1984). The questions lay interviewers ask. *Journal of Personality*, **52**, 90–106.

Trope, Y., Cohen, O. and Maoz, Y. (1988). The perceptual and inferential effects of situational inducements on dispositional attribution. *Journal of Personality and Social Psychology*, **55**, 165–77.

Turner, J. C. (1978). Social categorization and social discrimination in the minimal group paradigm. In H. Tajfel (ed.), *Differentiation between social groups: Studies in the social psychology of intergroup relations*.

European Monographs in Social Psychology. London: Academic Press.

Tversky, A. and Kahneman, D. (1974). Judgment under uncertainty: Heuristics and biases. *Science*, **185**, 1124–31.

Vallone, R., Ross, L. and Lepper, M. (1985). The hostile media phenomenon: Biased perception and perceptions of media bias in coverage of the Beirut massacre. *Journal of Personality and Social Psychology*, **49**, 577–85.

Van Bezooijen, R., Otto, S. A. and Heenan, T. A. (1983). Recognition of vocal expressions of emotion. *Journal of Cross-Cultural Psychology*, **14**, 387–406.

van der Pligt, J. (1984). Attributions, false consensus, and valence. Two field studies. *Journal of Personality and Social Psychology*, **46**, 57–68.

Vinokur, A. and Ajzen, I. (1982). Relative importance of prior and immediate events: A causal primacy effect. *Journal of Personality and Social Psychology*, **42**, 820–9.

Wagner, M. L., MacDonald, J. and Manstead, A. S. R. (1986). Communication of individual emotions by spontaneous facial expressions. *Journal of Personality and Social Psychology*, **50**, 737–43.

Wallbott, H. G. (1988a). In and out of context: Influences of facial expression and context information on emotion attributions. *British Journal of Social Psychology*, **27**, 357–69.

Wallbott, H. G. (1988b). Facets in context: The relative importance of facial expression and context information in determining emotion attributions. In K. R. Scherer (ed.), *Faces of emotion*. Hillsdale, NJ: Erlbaum, pp. 139–60.

Wallbott, H. G. and Scherer, K. R. (1986a). How universal and specific is emotional experience? Evidence from 27 countries on five continents. *Social Science Information*, **25**, 763–95.

Wallbott, H. G. and Scherer, K. R. (1986b). Cues and channels in emotion recognition. *Journal of Personality and Social Psychology*, **51**, 690–9.

Walster, E. (1966). Assignment of responsibility for an accident. *Journal of Personality and Social Psychology*, **3**, 73–9.

Walster, E., Aronson, V., Abrahams, D. and Rothmann, L. (1966). Importance of physical attractiveness in dating behavior. *Journal of Personality and Social Psychology*, **4**, 508–16.

Watkins, D. and Astilla, E. (1984). The dimensionality, antecedents, and study method correlates of the causal attribution of Filipino children. *Journal of Social Psychology*, **124**, 191–9.

Watson, D. (1982). The actor and the observer: How are their perceptions of causality divergent? *Psychological Bulletin*, **92**, 682–700.

Weiner, B. (1983). Some methodological pitfalls in attributional research. *Journal of Educational Psychology*, **75**, 530–43.

Weiner, B. (1985). Spontaneous causal thinking. *Psychological Bulletin*, **97**, 74–84.

Weiner, B., Frieze, I. H., Kukla, A., Reed, L., Rest, S. and Rosenbaum, R. M.

(1972). Perceiving the causes of success and failure. In E. E. Jones, D. E. Kanouse, H. H. Kelley, R. E. Nisbett, S. Valins and B. Weiner (eds), *Attribution: Perceiving the causes of behavior*. Morristown, NJ: General Learning Press, pp. 95–120.

Weiss, D. S. and Mendelsohn, G. A. (1986). An empirical demonstration of the implausibility of the semantic similarity explanation of how trait ratings are made and what they mean. *Journal of Personality and Social Psychology*, 50, 595–601.

Weiten, W. and Upshaw, H. S. (1982). Attribution theory: A factor-analytic evaluation of internal–external and endogenous–exogenous partitions. *Personality and Social Psychology Bulletin*, 8, 699–705.

Wells, G. L. and Harvey, J. H. (1977). Do people use consensus information in making causal attributions? *Journal of Personality and Social Psychology*, 35, 279–93.

Wiggins, J. S. (1979). A psychological taxonomy of trait-descriptive terms: The interpersonal domain. *Journal of Personality and Social Psychology*, 37, 395–412.

Williams, J. E. and Best, D. L. (1982). *Measuring sex stereotypes: A thirty-nation study*. Beverly Hills, CA: Sage.

Wimer, S. and Kelley, H. H. (1982). An investigation of the dimensions of causal attribution. *Journal of Personality and Social Psychology*, 43, 1142–62.

Wishner, J. (1960). Reanalysis of "Impressions of personality", *Psychological Review*, 67, 96–112.

Wolfson, M. R. and Salancik, G. R. (1977). Observer orientation and actor–observer differences in attributions for failure. *Journal of Experimental Social Psychology*, 13, 441–51.

Woodworth, R. S. (1938). *Experimental Psychology*. New York: Henry Holt.

Word, C. H., Zanna, M. P. and Cooper, J. (1974). The nonverbal mediation of self-fulfilling prophecies in interracial interaction. *Journal of Experimental Social Psychology*, 10, 109–20.

Yang, K. and Bond, M. H. (1985). Dimensions of Chinese person perception: An emic approach. In C. Chiao (ed.), *Proceedings of the Conference on Chinese Modernization and Chinese Culture*. Hong Kong: Chinese University Press, pp. 309–25.

Yarrow, M. R. and Campbell, J. D. (1963). Person perception in children. *Merrill-Palmer Quarterly*, 9, 57–72.

Zajonc, R. B., Markus, H. and Wilson, W. R. (1974). Exposure effects and associative learning. *Journal of Experimental Social Psychology*, 10, 248–63.

Zanna, M. P. and Hamilton, D. L. (1977). Further evidence for meaning change in impression formation. *Journal of Experimental Social Psychology*, 13, 224–38.

Zebrowitz, L. A. and McDonald, S. (1990). The impact of litigant facial maturity on judicial judgments in small claims court. Unpublished manuscript. Brandeis University.

Zebrowitz, L. A. and Montepare J. M. (1990). Impressions of babyfaced and maturefaced individuals across the lifespan. Manuscript in preparation. Brandeis University.

Zebrowitz, L. A., Kendall-Tackett, K. and Fafel, J. (1990). The impact of children's facial maturity on parental expectations and punishments. Unpublished manuscript. Brandeis University.

Zebrowitz L. A., Tennenbaum, D. R. and Goldstein, L. H. (1990). The impact of job applicants' facial maturity, sex, and academic achievement on evaluations of hiring recommendations. Unpublished manuscript. Brandeis University.

Zillmann, D., Mody, B. and Cantor, J. R. (1974). Empathetic perception of emotional displays in films as a function of hedonic and excitatory state prior to exposure. *Journal of Research in Personality*, 8, 335–49.

Zuckerman, M., Hall, J. A., DeFrank, R. S. and Rosenthal, R. (1976). Encoding and decoding of spontaneous and posed facial expressions. *Journal of Personality and Social Psychology*, 34, 966–77.

Zuckerman, M. and Przewuzman, S. J. (1979). Decoding and encoding facial expressions in preschool-age children. *Environmental Psychology and Nonverbal Psychology*, 3, 147–63.

Zukier, H. (1982). The role of the correlation and the dispersion of predictor variables in the use of nondiagnostic information. *Journal of Personality and Social Psychology*, 43, 1163–75.

AUTHOR INDEX

SUBJECT INDEX